DUNKS, DOUBLES, DOPING

DUNKS, DOUBLES, DOPING

How Steroids Are Killing American Athletics

NATHAN JENDRICK

THE LYONS PRESS
Guilford, Connecticut
An imprint of The Globe Pequot Press

The Lyons Press is an imprint of The Globe Pequot Press.

10 9 8 7 6 5 4 3 2 1

Printed in the United States of America

ISBN-13: 978-1-59228-902-8
ISBN-10: 1-59228-902-9

Library of Congress Cataloging-in-Publication Data is available on file.

To help children make right choices, they need good examples. Athletics play such an important role in our society, but, unfortunately, some in professional sports are not setting much of an example. The use of performance-enhancing drugs like steroids in baseball, football, and other sports is dangerous, and it sends the wrong message—that there are shortcuts to accomplishment, and that performance is more important than character. So tonight I call on team owners, union representatives, coaches, and players to take the lead, to send the right signal, to get tough, and to get rid of steroids now.

—President George W. Bush,
State of the Union Address, 2004

Contents

Introduction

Men like muscles. The peak of a warm, pumped bicep is prized among so many other things in life for the average American male. The bigger the ball on the arm the better it looks. And big is never enough. Bigger, too, is never enough. There is always the thought, "It can be bigger." And to a point that's true, at least where lifting weights, eating, and growing naturally is concerned.

Some men shoot for the "V-Taper." A thick, wide, striated back that spawns like wings from the lats and leads down to a narrow waistline exemplifying the twenty-second letter of the alphabet.

This preoccupation, this obsession with the body, has been around since before trade magazines were covered with men showing off their rounded deltoids, tree-trunk-thick legs, and rippling abs. From the moment the first competition of strength between two men occurred, precisely at the same time a woman chose one man over another because of his lean mass, the thought that came about screamed, "My body did this for me." From that moment on, it was about striving for perfection, to be the biggest kid on the block.

For professional athletes this means furthering their livelihood. Stronger can mean a bigger paycheck. Faster can translate to twice the signing bonus. Tougher can be the difference between the minor leagues and the pro ranks.

In psychology, this fascination with oneself has a name: the Adonis Complex, named after Adonis, the character in Greek mythology who was loved by Aphrodite, the goddess of love and beauty, for his stunning good looks.

Some physicians and authors have labeled the men who subscribe to the Adonis Complex as depressed, despondent, and crestfallen. They blame the covers of *Muscle & Fitness* and *FLEX*, bodybuilding contests, and other forms of competition. But it isn't the fault of anyone. It's human nature to want to one-up a fellow man. It is natural to try and be bigger, stronger, better than the competition. Life is competition, Darwin's theory of evolution alludes to that—the survival of the fittest. And while the idea that only the strong survive is related to animals, insects, and invertebrates, men sometimes get the urge for primal competition. It is a built-in mechanism to want to be able to do something in a way that no one else can and to be recognized for it.

Obviously not everyone wants to be Mr. Universe, walking about on a theater stage in posing trunks that appear to be no bigger than the Olympic swimming racing suits of the 1980s, oiled up and covered with a liquid providing a fake tan. But the Adonis Complex isn't related only to the iron game of gaining muscle mass.

Computer programmers, lawyers, business executives, CEOs, CFOs, anyone who has any sort of occupation where paychecks are altered as a result of success or failure is liable to fall into the depths of the Adonis Complex. Here people do what it takes to be the best: lie, cheat, steal, cover up the wrong, and hide from the truth. It is, after all, survival of the fittest.

Enron, Tyco, and WorldCom are just three of the companies that have collapsed under the pressure of competition. Lying to stockholders about earnings seemed to be a good way to keep stock prices up, at least for a while. In the end, the lies that were essentially the braces of their empires buckled and crashed. It was bound to happen. And after a crash, it's a long road back up.

For those who compete on a field, a court, a track, or in a pool, the stakes are even higher. Fame drives people, and exceptional performances drive fans to appreciate an athlete. How can an athlete better his or her best? Get bigger muscles? Hit a longer home run? Run a faster forty? Many athletes in the modern era have chosen steroids. And as long as performances increase the digits on a paycheck, as they always will, the illegal industry will continue to thrive unless tighter regulations are put in place.

But are they really cheating? Many say no, that steroids are an advance in science, like moving from the horse carriage to the automobile. Others say yes, they're bad, they're wrong, inconceivable. They scream for punishments and enforcement of the rules. The late Dr. Mel Siff once said, "The widespread use of steroids and other chemical supplements is frequently an admission that one has run out of training ideas to produce further progress naturally."

Is Dr. Siff correct? Will fans stop coming out to the ballpark if home runs don't keep getting hit deeper into the stands? Will spectators quit shelling out for the increasing ticket prices of the NFL if a wide receiver doesn't cross the goal line one-tenth of a second faster than the season before? Common sense says no. But with steroids so available, apparently beneficial, and rules on their use in sports so lax that they become the material of Letterman jokes, there appears to be no reason to quit. If athletes don't quit though, and the battle to be better keeps raging, the floor will have to fall out at some point.

Cheating is doing something illegal, and steroids in the United States of America are illegal without a prescription. Their use constitutes cheating, negating anyone's particular emotions about them. But that won't stop widespread resolve to continue using them. Athletes have used whatever materials they could since the ancient Greek Olympics, and as long as they think they can get by, they always will.

During the ancient Olympics there were deterrents more severe than a two-game suspension. Heavy fines were imposed on those who cheated and some athletes were removed from the games and from any games they had the talent to compete in thereafter. Fines were also placed upon those who offered bribes, took bribes, and even on those who did not amount to what was expected of an Olympic athlete. History tells us that one athlete became so frightened of his competition, he fled the day before the festivals and matches were to begin. He was fined for cowardice. These monetary gains, not needed by the government, were used to set up statues of the god Zeus. Imagine the NFL using any of Terrell Owens's fine dollars for landscape improvements. Not likely.

But with those statues to honor their mythological god, the Greeks helped assist the continuance of cheating.

Zeus and the other gods of ancient Greece were not the only ones to have their image carved into stone and placed on the streets of Olympia for the entire world to marvel over. These works of art were left to remember and honor the legacies their real-life counterparts left behind. Athletes began competing not just for the olive wreath, but for their legacy, so that one day they may have their own statue.

Still, these athletes were willing to change their allegiances in the pursuit of further fame and monetary gain. Astylos, an Olympic champion in running and a hero in his city-state of Kroton (Italy), was paid to represent Syracuse instead. In retaliation his former home in Kroton was turned into a prison, and his statue was torn down. This, one may consider, is similar to the New York Yankees paying whatever amount is required to put together the strongest team money can buy. The dollars bring the athletes despite the backlash at home: think Ken Griffey Jr. leaving Seattle for Cincinnati, and Alex Rodriguez flying the coop for Texas and $252 million.

Unknown to most, the first recorded case of cheating in Olympic competition dates from 388 BC. A boxer, Eupolus of Thessaly, paid off three opponents who were instructed to fight carelessly at the beginning stages of the bout, and ultimately go down and lose. To no surprise, this method of fixing a fight has endured well into the present day.

Nero, the emperor of Rome, was so much obsessed with winning that he added the reading of poetry as a contested event. His influence was also so strong over the judges that he was declared the winner of the chariot race in 67 AD despite never having crossed the finish line. He fell out of his chariot and proceeded to the winners' stage. The more things change, the more they stay the same. At the 2002 Winter Olympics, a scandal overtook figure skating when judges confessed to accepting bribes and awarded the gold medal to a Russian pairs team despite obvious technical flaws.

To date, Jose Canseco, Jeremy Giambi, and Kelli White, among many notable others, have admitted to steroid use, while others have hinted about it, stopping short of fully confessing. Champion boxer Shane Mosely, along with Barry Bonds and White, was a client of Bay Area Laboratory Co-Operative (BALCO), which provided athletes with the performance-enhancing steroid tetrahydrogestrinone (THG). Mosely has never failed a drug test, but the boxing commission had never tested for THG prior to the BALCO scandal. Did he? Didn't he? These are the kinds of debates that start when steroids surface in sports. "Scandals," they are labeled, and they can scar the career of an innocent athlete. Naturally, at the same time, it can rightfully alter the career of a cheating athlete.

So the question simply becomes "Why?" Why cheat? Why risk disgracing yourself, your team, and even your country? It all falls back on the craving for fame and fortune. It might not be fair to only blame the athletes; it is after all human nature to want to improve personally. And for many who come from low-income homes and troubled families, the use of performance-enhancing drugs seems to be a potential way out. But pity aside, no one is forcing needles into the muscles of athletes' glutes or into the subcutaneous fat tissue of their abdomens. At least, that's the assumption. Prizes and pride were the catalysts for the East German doping scandal, which involved the systematic doping of the country's elite athletes in the 1980s, and it's the cause of cheating today.

One thing that is safe to assume is that as long as money is fueling desire, paychecks, and fame, for better or for worse athletes will continue to look for a secret edge. And as long as the governing bodies and powers that be stave off the implementation of any reasonable deterrents, no one can blame them.

In sports, dunks and doubles are as common on a crisp spring afternoon as sunshine, but as of late a third *D* is being added more and more to amateur and professional sporting events alike: doping. And the problem, unless serious actions are taken quickly, will kill professional athletics as we know them.

Dunks, Doubles, Doping is not an anti-steroid book. It is not a pro-steroid book. This book seeks only to fight against a bias that has put steroids at the forefront of the sporting world. The media say that steroids are bad, that steroids will kill users, but they cite no evidence. This book provides facts, clearing the air so that readers can walk away with a position they feel strongly about because they know the truth. As an example of how ridiculous the steroid controversy has become, the widely televised *World Series of Poker* on ESPN took a break during one telecast to show a card-throwing competition between players Chris Ferguson and Scotty Nguyen. The object was to throw the cards at bananas in such a way that the card would slice the banana. The announcer, trumping up the makeshift sport with attempts at sounding excited, said, "There will at some point in this history of this sport, be a steroid controversy." As sarcastic as the comment was, it also seems in line with the current hype over steroids. Bananas are probably safe from the juice, but other sports aren't so lucky.

Steroids are bad for the future of baseball, basketball, football, and other sports. Steroids and other performance-enhancing drugs are bad for most sports in general, except perhaps bodybuilding—which has taken what some have suggested should be a logical step for baseball and already created a "natural" (drug-free) division.

Many people condone steroid use. Many people don't. But even among those who use these drugs, the vast majority would never want to see their own children using them. With athletes turning professional earlier and earlier, and the bar in sports being raised so high, in part because of steroid and performance-enhancing drug use, how long will it be before preteen boys are scoping neighborhood gyms looking for a vial of steroids so they can try to be like their favorite baseball player? And after that, how long before it backfires? The list of side effects for children and adolescents who use steroids is long, but kids will always continue to dream of making it to the big leagues, to the pros. They dream of making it to the top, of taking their families out of their situations and locations and putting them somewhere nice, comfortable, into a new home. They want fancy cars and jewelry, they want to sign autographs and be on television, in magazines, on the big screen. And the longer steroids appear to be the avenue that helps get someone there, the more little kids are going to see it, want it, and go after it.

If the steroid mess in professional athletics isn't remedied in one way or another, the future of not just the Big Three sports, but all sports, looks very bleak. The only caveat is that one day, more likely sooner than later, steroids will be but an afterthought. A much larger and even more frightening nemesis is on the horizon.

DUNKS, DOUBLES, DOPING

1

The Other Gear in the Locker Room

To the average human, everything professional athletes do while competing in their sport is so far beyond comparison to anything, that trying to categorize it is an impossible endeavor. Many of their acts can be legitimately labeled "unbelievable" or even "ungodly."

Feats such as Major League Baseball's Adam Dunn, left fielder for the Cincinnati Reds, hitting a baseball 535 feet out of the Great American Ball Park. Powerlifting champion Gene Rychlak Jr. and his 1,005-pound bench press. Barry Bonds hitting 73 long balls in a single season. Michael Phelps winning an unprecedented six gold medals in swimming at the 2004 Athens Olympics. These are the things that make sports great, but with the ever increasing use, and discovery of past use, of anabolic steroids and other performance-enhancing supplements, fans are left to wonder if these athletes accomplished these things with their natural, God-given talent, or if they had some chemical help.

Olympic achievements are slightly more credentialed. Phelps, for example, was tested dozens of times before, during, and after Athens and passed every test. During that same time frame, Major League Baseball carried out no tests.

So our Olympic athletes are, apparently at least, covered. But the Big Three in the United States are hotbeds for cheating: baseball, basketball, football. Who knows anymore if a record set by an athlete in one of these sports is a scam? Bonds and his single-season home run record is already tarnished thanks to his involvement with the BALCO scandal and his admission that he used, although supposedly "unknowingly," several different types of steroids. But, thanks to his friend Bud Selig, commissioner of Major League Baseball, there will be no asterisk in the record book. It is players like Bonds and businessmen like Selig who prevent finding common ground in the steroids controversy. Prior to the 2005 season the MLB had no real hard and fast rules against steroids. But regardless, aren't anabolic and androgenic steroids illegal in the United States? If baseball wants players using steroids, they should lobby to legalize them. If they don't, and really want to get them out of the game, they should accept a zero-tolerance policy. Caught using steroids? Gone. Playing professional sports is a privilege, not a right. Making millions of dollars playing a game should be for the people who can play it by the rules. The conundrum this leads to is that fans want to see the ball hit further and records being broken. So what should MLB do? Decide what is more important, and stick with it.

With contracts growing larger, muscles are getting bigger. When muscles get bigger, pitches get faster, balls are hit farther, runners sprint faster, and linebackers hit harder. With the obvious risk of injury in competition aside, the real risk is the damage being done to American athletics as a whole. There are, thankfully, honest people out there who raise honest children, and these kids are smart to boot. They aren't all going to be willing to cheat to make it to the big leagues, and they aren't all going to look up to players who use baseball bats by day and syringes at night. When that happens, everyone loses. Stadiums empty and revenue is lost, but the most daunting problem of all is that little dreams are shattered. And for America, land of the free and home of the brave, the country that made the phrase "American Dream" so real for so many, it's a devastating blow.

Some adamant opponents of drug use argue that steroids are cancer-causing pills for cheaters. They're half wrong. No study has shown a direct correlation between anabolic steroids and cancer. But those who use steroids *are* cheaters because the drugs are illegal, at least in the United States. On the opposite end of the spectrum are those who think that injecting the right oil will give them the attributes of a Greek god. Countless people have found out in some pretty rough ways that that, too, is unfounded. Steroids allow for quicker recovery and the opportunity to take the body beyond a predisposed genetic limitation on muscle mass, but they don't do it with some sort of voodoo magic. It still takes hard work in the gym and on the field, and maybe, surprisingly, even more so in the kitchen.

Some athletes who use anabolic steroids know what they're doing, some don't. Some still have doctors watching over them, most don't. That's a problem in and of itself. A certain group of athletes in all disciplines—baseball, bodybuilding, wrestling—say steroids, when used correctly, are beneficial. If they mean in their profession and their passion for their sport, it appears they're right. If they mean regarding long-term health, that remains to be seen. Speculation is rampant that Arnold Schwarzenegger's heart problems are the result of many years of taking heavy doses, also called "cycles," of steroids. The media has no problem blaming the seven-time Mr. Olympia and current California governor for openly having used supplements such as testosterone and Primobolan. It's a shame politics are brought into this, as the Democrats tried to use this fact in the California governor's recall election, which ultimately put Schwarzenegger in office, because it terribly alters the truth.

While steroids are illegal now, it's important to remember they haven't always been controlled substances. In the days Schwarzenegger ruled bodybuilding, the drugs weren't looked down upon. Similarly, steroids were not even banned in Olympic competition until 1975. Bodybuilding is not, and has never been, an Olympic sport. Furthermore, steroids weren't illegal to sell in America until 1988, and were not illegal to possess until 1990. Schwarzenegger last competed in bodybuilding in 1980, winning the Mr. Olympia contest.

Fact: Schwarzenegger's heart problems have never once been medically proven to have anything to do with steroid use. His heart problems have, however, been diagnosed as congenital, which he had surgically corrected in 1997. His father passed away in 1974 because of a coronary attack.

But, despite these facts and others, when the media speaks, people listen, and all they are hearing is that steroids are bad. The irresponsible members of the press skew perceptions, running away from the truth as they try to unveil a scandal. These journalists and higher-ups of sports governing bodies are the cause of the doping stress in American athletics today. If everything was equal, if there was one true playing field for anabolic steroids—either everyone can use steroids or everyone is clean—the controversy would be a thing of the past.

Despite either side of the argument, steroid use in sports is climbing, maybe even higher than ever, although no one knows for sure. Beginning just recently and seemingly daily since, the public has watched as their now-former idols have turned to the truth, and turned on each other, to talk openly about steroids. It's current, it's fresh, it's a hot topic, and it won't go away. Anabolic steroids are killing American athletics, but it's not just the drugs themselves that are doing it, it's the athletes who try and cover up their use and lie to the public. When morals are sold for a paycheck, sports suffer.

Deciding whether steroids are truly hazardous when used in a way that the general public, with an understanding of anabolic steroids, would consider "responsible" is up for debate as much as anything else. As is customary in America, we are free to our own opinions. Instead of believing what the media says is a general consensus on the results of steroid use—guaranteed death, cancer, and womanly features in men—consider these commonly published side effects that are, in reality, possibly related to steroids:

- Acne
- Genital changes (atrophy)
- Water retention in tissue
- Jaundice
- Stunted growth
- Fetal damage
- Coronary artery disease
- Sterility
- Liver tumors and disease
- Euphoria
- Diarrhea
- Fatigue
- Fever
- Muscle cramps
- Headache
- Unexplained weight loss/gain
- Nausea and vomiting
- Vomiting blood
- Bone pains
- Depression
- Impotence
- Breast development (gynecomastia)
- Aggressive behavior
- Urination problems
- Sexual dysfunction
- High blood pressure
- Kidney disease

Now consider these health risks known to be related to everyday air pollution:

- Irritation to the eyes, nose, and throat
- Upper respiratory infections such as bronchitis and pneumonia
- Headaches
- Nausea
- Allergic reactions
- Chronic respiratory disease
- Lung cancer
- Heart disease
- Damage to the brain
- Nerve damage
- Liver stress
- Kidney strain
- Stunted growth of the lungs in children
- Potential to aggravate or further complicate medical conditions

In the London Smog Disaster in 1952, 12,000 are said to have died prematurely because of the high concentrations of pollution. Secondhand smoke, an explicit form of air pollution, kills over 40,000 people each year.

The London Smog Disaster killed more people than steroids ever have, and yet, people still live in Los Angeles, smoke, and drive vehicles.

Cars, too, may damage the health of more people who attend NASCAR events than steroids cause to users of anabolic drugs. Most people are unaware that the racing industry uses leaded fuels in its automobiles. Lead was removed from standard vehicle fuel in the United States in the 1970s and 1980s, but in 1990 Congress spared the aviation and racing industries from having to follow the same regulations. The Environmental Protection Agency says people in the area of a racetrack are being exposed to a "serious health risk."

Perhaps as proof that politicians don't always look out for the best interests of every citizen, according to the Environmental Protection Agency, lead causes damage to the kidneys, liver, brain, and nerves, among other organs. It is possible to blame the stock car industry for not solving this health-related issue, but it goes back to money. In this case, lead lubricates engine valves and helps the cars run smoother. Obviously if engines are continually replaced, the cost of maintenance skyrockets, meaning less overall revenue. And surely no industry would want to give up any of its hard-earned dollars to protect the health of its fans or employees. Studies of a tested NASCAR team have found lead levels in the blood of nearly half the crew that are far above average.

But the effects of steroids, unlike smoking and the emissions from leaded-fuel racing cars, are specific to the individual user. Secondhand smoke permeates restaurants, bowling alleys, hallways, and a large area surrounding the burning cigarette or pipe. All 250,000 fans each year at the Indianapolis Motor Speedway for the Indy 500 are exposed to toxic lead fumes. How dangerous this actually is has yet to be seen, but it provides a valid point of reference. People who use steroids also, generally, know the possible side effects of what they are choosing to put in their bodies. So do smokers. But the children and employees surrounding smokers aren't necessarily educated or have a choice; the same goes for fans of racing.

And while smokers may puff away for stress relief and NASCAR fans watch races for enjoyment, users of steroids expect many benefits of their own. And the benefit list of anabolic use rivals the list of potential hazards, but has far more science behind it than one might expect.

Steroid Myths and Steroid Truths

Few subjects in all of sports have been debated as much over the years as the lives of stars like Babe Ruth, Joe DiMaggio, or Joe Jackson; who is the best quarterback in history; or how great Michael Jordan was. But the most misconstrued and most often debated subject in gyms and, as of late, ballparks, stadiums, swimming pools, and other athletic outlets, is the truth about anabolic steroids.

For every different substance running through the veins of athletes, there are dozens of myths: how to use the gear best, how long it should be taken, what stacks best, how much to take, and so on. The list becomes especially long under "side effects," which is exactly where dangerous misinformation is spewed, most often from the media. It is not wrong to be against the use of anabolic steroids, just as it is not wrong to be for the use of anabolic steroids, but it is important to make sure that whatever your belief, it is founded on true, scientifically based information.

The following is a list of common myths surrounding steroids and other performance-enhancing supplements. Some are partially true, some are false, others are humorous, some are surprising, and some seem like they should just be common sense.

1. **Steroids permanently shrink your testicles.**
   Steroids do make your testicles shrink, but there is no documented evidence that it is permanent. When testosterone is administered from outside sources, the body realizes it has just been given more hormone in one shot than it makes on its own in weeks or months. With that, the body shuts down its own production of the hormone because it doesn't need to make its own to function. Because the testes produce the body's own source of testosterone, they naturally diminish in size when they aren't in use. When steroid use is discontinued, the body slowly returns to making its own hormone and, thus, the testes return to full size.

2. **Steroids make a male's penis shrink.**
   As stated, the body produces testosterone from the testes. The penis has nothing to do with male hormone production and, therefore, is not affected in any way by steroid use. This not only debunks the myth that the use of anabolics causes the penis to shrink, but also does away with the notion that hormones can cause the penis to increase in size, as advertised in the back of magazines. This myth is most popular in teenagers, a growing number of which are experimenting with steroids.

3. **Anyone could be as big as a pro bodybuilder by using steroids.**
   This is probably one of the less harmful but most ludicrous steroid myths in the world. The idea that steroid use alone makes muscles grow, let alone to the proportions of those of professional bodybuilders, is completely unsubstantiated and utterly false. The use of anabolic steroids actually places more importance on the athlete's diet and training regimen in order to achieve desired results. For the vast sizes professional bodybuilders reach, this has as much to do with genetic predisposition as anything. Muscle shape, for instance, can rarely be altered regardless of the amount of steroid administered. Synthol can unnaturally alter the shape of a muscle, but its use is obvious and provides unwanted lumps.

Another similar explanation of this myth is the common response from females looking to get fit or lose weight. They often ask how to achieve these goals and are often told to begin a weight training program. Their responses might include, "But I don't want to get bulky." As any bodybuilder can attest, it takes very hard training and a strict nutrition program to "get bulky." In the same sense, steroid use alone, even when coupled with a solid training schedule, does not in any way guarantee the proportions or aesthetics of a professional bodybuilder.

4. **Steroids cause "'roid rage."**

The topic of 'roid rage is seemingly enough to send many proponents of anabolic steroids into a fit of anger, but for it to truly be considered a disorder associated with steroid use is debatable. Studies have been conducted in which 'roid rage is discredited because the subjects encounter no bouts of rage at all. Other studies, on the contrary, show an increase in aggression with men using testosterone therapy. One can assume that 'roid rage is a myth substantiated by some and discarded by others. On the physical side effects, doctors disagree time and time again. An increase in aggression has been proven, but by definition alone, aggression and rage are largely different terms. Later in this book physicians and athletes discuss their beliefs and encounters with 'roid rage.

5. **Steroids will enlarge your heart and cause heart attacks.**

The idea that steroids cause an enlargement of the heart and other organs, thus causing cardiac irregularities, has been increasing in popularity because of the large midsections on many professional bodybuilders. These are athletes with extremely low body fat, but when not contracting their abdominals, they look as though they are overweight. This is caused by the excessive abuse of human growth hormone, which is not a steroid. HGH is the most common culprit of organ growth, although anabolic steroids have been shown to increase the size of the heart's left ventricle, though there is some evidence that this increase in size is not permanent after steroid use is discontinued.

6. **The more steroids the better.**

If 500 mg of testosterone helps an athlete add ten pounds of muscle over the course of one steroid cycle, some people would assume that two or three times that would result in two or three times the gain. This theory of "more is better" is completely, physiologically wrong and unsound. The body works hard to maintain homeostasis, and adapts as well as it can to changes. Small, slight alterations allow the body to work with the changes being made. When the body begins to work with amounts of hormone a few times larger than its normal amount, it can still move to produce muscle mass. But when the body finds it has far too much hormone circulating through it, it can only do so much and adapts to the larger amount. For future cycles, the user who started out too high will need to increase the doses even more, making that user susceptible to more side effects and decreased gains.

7. **Steroid users can't have children.**

For most steroid users this is only true if something in their life, unrelated to steroids, has rendered them infertile. For others, it is possible that after many years of high-dose usage, the body and its reproductive system are unable to return to normal. Many users must wait an extremely long period of time for full recovery before being able to conceive a child, but it is possible to become indefinitely infertile. In general though, the average, responsible steroid user experiences no problems.

8. **Steroids will cause infection.**

This is potentially true. The drugs themselves usually do not cause infection, but the use of dirty needles, unsanitary conditions, and improper production processes—something common with several Mexican steroid labs—can cause infections. Some of these can be very serious, others are mild.

9. **Steroids make your hair fall out.**

If an individual is genetically predisposed to what is commonly known as "male pattern baldness," then steroids can speed up this process. For men who are not, this usually isn't a worry. It is important to note that the receptive gene for baldness can be inherited from either parent, so it would be wise for a steroid user to examine both sides of the family tree.

10. **Steroids give men breasts.**

    Steroids don't give men breast tissue, estrogen does. The body keeps a natural balance between testosterone and estrogen in everyone. Obviously in men the balance is much higher on the testosterone side. When exogenous hormones are delivered, the body shuts down its natural production, but it still tries to keep itself balanced. The use of testosterone can cause the body to naturally raise its own estrogen levels, thus giving men breast tissue. The condition is called gynecomastia and cases range from small bumps under the nipples to very noticeable femalelike breasts appearing. Once the tissue has had sufficient time to form, the only usual recourse is surgery. Most bodybuilders use drugs made for women, such as clomiphene citrate, also known as Clomid, and tamoxifen citrate, known more commonly as Nolvadex, to keep estrogen down. Clomid is made for use in ovulation therapy, and Nolvadex is made for breast cancer treatment, but both have antiestrogen capabilities that have been known to control gynecomastia. It is important to note that Clomid has often been shown to have a negative result on eyesight, and Nolvadex is a carcinogen.

Benefits—Reasons, Expectations, and Realities

Some people hear the term "bodybuilder" and immediately think "steroids." Some people come to the same conclusion when they hear "Major League Baseball," "Barry Bonds," or "East German Olympic team." But the truth behind the use of steroids is that it isn't strictly limited to Olympic athletes, professionals in a Big Three sport, or the competitors of the Mr. Olympia stage in Las Vegas. The people who use steroids are as varied as the colors of the rainbow, from homosexuals to heterosexuals, from high school boys to, reportedly, even girls young enough to be in junior high school.

People of all races and creeds use anabolic steroids for different reasons, not all of which include creating a larger physique. Some use steroids and other drugs for their mass-creating capabilities while others use them for their fat-burning abilities, and still more use them for an increased red blood cell count. What is commonly misstated about steroids is that they are all bad, all of the time. The media won't tell you that steroids, including the infamously common testosterone, are used by physicians for hormone replacement therapy and gender transformation procedures. Steroids are used in medical procedures of many types, but their good is nearly always overshadowed by their misuse. And they face criticism from an even larger contingent of misinformed individuals. Anabolic steroids are illegal, which may be reason enough to be against them, but do the people who use them anyway in hopes of a slimmer waistline or bigger biceps really have to worry about an almost certain death? No, but even if that was the case, what needs to be understood is why people use these drugs, what they expect to get from them, and whether whatever risk they are facing could ever be considered worth it. To do this, we will take some examples of real people who used steroids, their reasons, and their results.

It is important to note that none of the following actions, dosages, or expectations are being condoned or are considered safe and any study or research completed before each cycle was done by and the sole responsibility of each user.

The High School Senior

NAME: Tom

AGE: 18

DRUG(S) USED: testosterone enanthate, 1,000 mg per week. Shots divided into 500 mg shot on Monday, followed by a second 500 mg shot on Thursday

LENGTH OF USE: 10 weeks

EXPECTATION(S): increase in lean muscle mass with the intent of improving interaction with women, and no expectation of side effects physically or mentally

RESULT(S): Tom's cycle of steroid use included a diet of lean proteins and low-GI (glycemic index) carbohydrates, ranging between 5,000 and 7,000 calories each day. His starting weight was 190 pounds on his six-foot-one-inch frame. His weight reportedly increased rapidly in terms of both body mass and body fat. He reported no shrinkage of his testicles, but reported rampant itching under his nipples. By the ninth week he reported unbearable discomfort in his chest and, after the formation of a hard lump under his left nipple (a sign of gynecomastia), Tom discontinued his cycle at a weight of 221 pounds. After one month off the drugs, Tom reported a body weight of 205 pounds.

The Aspiring Bodybuilder

NAME: Jamal

AGE: 26

DRUG(S) USED: during cycle, a combination of testosterone enanthate, 800 mg per week. Equipoise, 600 mg per week; and Dianabol, 40 mg per day. After cycle a "postcycle therapy" (PCT) of 60 mg of tamoxifen citrate daily for two weeks, 40 mg daily for another two weeks, followed by another 20 mg for a final two weeks

LENGTH OF USE: 16 weeks

EXPECTATION(S): increase in lean muscle mass for bodybuilding competition, acknowledged the possibility of breast tissue formation and shrinkage of the testes

RESULT(S): at five feet eight inches, 210 pounds, Jamal had previously run two separate cycles of anabolic steroids at ages 22 and

24. He says he keeps his cycles spread two years apart for adequate recovery time. In the past he reported no problems with gynecomastia, but often severe shrinkage of his testicles. On this 16-week course he admitted again to problems with maintaining testicle size. At the completion of his cycle Jamal weighed 233 pounds, in part he believed because of undisclosed measures to prevent water retention. One month later he reported his testicles being nearly completely normal again, but a very noticeable depreciation in his sex drive, which was reportedly at an "all-time high" on cycle. After one month his weight stood at 226 pounds.

The Collegiate Soccer Player

NAME: Javier
AGE: 23
DRUG(S) USED: stanozolol, also known as "Winstrol" at an oral-tablet dose of 50 mg each day, using the Ttokkyo-brand of 10 mg tablets
LENGTH OF USE: eight weeks
EXPECTATION(S): decreased body weight
RESULT(S): Javier admitted he found out about the use of Winstrol by reading up on Canadian sprinter Ben Johnson. He believed that if a drug was beneficial for a world-class sprinter, it could be for a soccer player wanting to decrease his body fat and increase his speed on the field. Javier reported a loss of 14 pounds over his eight-week cycle, but also described an onslaught of acne that he likened to "puberty all over again," a complete lack of libido, and severe lethargy. One month after discontinuing the drugs he said the acne and lethargy problems had remedied themselves, but his libido had still not returned. Note: Most educated steroid users strongly suggest never using steroids without a testosterone base.

The Accountant

NAME: Randy
AGE: 41
DRUG(S) USED: methandrostenolone, better known as Dianabol, in the form of the Russian brand Naposim
LENGTH OF USE: 10 weeks at 25 mg a day taken in one dose upon waking
EXPECTATION(S): increased muscle mass, slimmer waist
RESULT(S): Randy reported no change in muscle mass or waist size, reported no change in libido or mood. At five feet eleven inches, 240 pounds, Randy admitted he may have too much adipose tissue for the drug to offer many benefits at the dosage he was consuming.

The Waiter

NAME: Jared
AGE: 22
DRUG(S) USED: Sustanon at 500 mg a week, Dianabol at 25 mg a week
LENGTH OF USE: Sustanon for eight weeks, Dianabol for four weeks
EXPECTATION(S): increased self-esteem, muscular size and strength
RESULT(S): while experiencing a large degree of testicular atrophy, Jared took measures to counteract the problem and before the end of his cycle, his testicles returned to full size. Jared reported a great deal of size gain in his muscles as well as a large increase in self-esteem and confidence, even while off steroids. He experienced no crash in libido and plans on continuing to intelligently cycle anabolic steroids.

The PhD Chemistry Student

NAME: Danny
AGE: 22
DRUG(S) USED: testosterone enanthate at 600 mg a week, Equipoise at 600 mg a week, Dianabol at 25 mg a week
LENGTH OF USE: testosterone enanthate for 12 weeks, Equipoise for 11 weeks, Dianabol for 4 weeks
EXPECTATION(S): large increase in muscle mass
RESULT(S): Danny reported that his steroid use had an immediate affect on his sexual function. He reported a direct increase in his libido but a decrease in his ability to maintain an erection. After the introduction of HCG (human chorionic gonadotropin), also known as Pregnyl, he reported these symptoms began to subside. Afterward, his libido remained high and he experienced slight insomnia, which he remedied with a slight reduction in drug dosage. Danny admits to no reduction in testicle size, but a definite increase in acne, which remained until he added a prescription acne wash. While on cycle, Danny received a full panel of blood work from a physician who gave him a clean bill of health. During a six-week postcycle therapy of varying doses of Nolvadex, Danny reported a brief period of lost libido and joint pain. Overall, he was pleased with his results and plans to continue the use of steroids.

The Dad

NAME: Lou
AGE: 49
DRUG(S) USED: Deca-Durabolin at 200 mg a week
LENGTH OF USE: indefinitely

EXPECTATION(S): pain relief in joints
RESULT(S): Lou reports that several drugs prescribed by physicians gave him minimal relief with joint aches and pains and several caused him headaches. Lou said over-the-counter drugs like Advil, aspirin, and Tylenol had to be used in such high doses he felt pain in his kidneys after prolonged use. On the recommendation of a bodybuilding coworker of his, Lou began self-administering 200 mg doses of Deca-Durabolin and claims he has not seen a doctor since. He says since he started using Deca, he has remained pain-free.

An Interview with Dr. Roberto Olivardia

Roberto Olivardia, PhD, is a clinical instructor at Harvard Medical School. He is coauthor with Dr. Harrison Pope and Katharine A. Phillips of The Adonis Complex: The Secret Crisis of Male Body Obsession. *The book examined the compulsive desire to achieve physical perfection. Dr. Olivardia is an expert in the field of physical aesthetics and offers a professional look into the obsession of beauty.*

Q *You coauthored* The Adonis Complex, *which has to do with male body obsession. If you were to describe that to someone who hadn't read the book, how would you summarize it?*

A The Adonis Complex is a popular term we use to describe the various manifestations of body-image problems males are facing today. This includes general body dissatisfaction, eating disorders, body dysmorphic disorder, muscle dysmorphia, cosmetic surgery, and/or steroid use. We named it "Adonis" after the half-man, half-god, Greek mythological character who represented the ideal in masculine beauty.

Q *Though there are studies on the pros and cons, anabolic steroids are generally made out to be pretty dangerous substances. In your opinion, what is so important, particularly to adolescent males, that would make them risk potential side effects for aesthetics?*

A Adolescent boys are bombarded by images of muscular men in everything from action figures to video games to steroid-using athletes. They believe that it makes them more masculine and manly being bigger. They live in a culture that promotes an idea that the bigger and more muscular a man is, the more dominant, attractive, sexually virile, popular, and confident he is. Adolescents also have what's called "adolescent immortality," a belief that they will live forever regardless of their behavior. The societal ideal of muscularity combined with adolescent immortality makes for a bad combination when it comes to steroid use. On top of that, we have athletes that adolescents admire that stupidly promote the idea that steroids are okay if they are used "right."

Q *You mention that boys believe there are advantages to muscularity. How does this ideology differ from recent studies that show that people who are taller and male make more money than their shorter counterparts, especially shorter females?*

A There can be perks to having certain idealized appearances. The problem is the overvalued notion that having a "perfect" body makes one perfect. Many individuals who are obsessively preoccupied with their appearance feel that looking good will suddenly compensate for all of their weaknesses. Then when they realize it doesn't, they just seek to be bigger and bigger, rather than thinking that some traits are born internally. Those studies need to be examined more carefully. Are there other variables that could be responsible? Are men who are taller more assertive? If that is the case, is it the assertiveness or the height that is the real ideal?

Q *What other types of measures have you found men put themselves through because of this obsession with trying to improve their bodies?*

A Cosmetic surgery in men has dramatically risen. Hair transplants, liposuction, nose jobs, calf implants, pec implants, penile implants, face-lifts are all rising in men today. Men are also engaging in eating disordered behavior more and more, contrary to popular belief. These problems do not only affect women.

Q *How do you think athletic coaches and trainers contribute to the problems discussed in the book?*

A I have treated athletes who have wonderful coaches who support their treatment 100 percent. Some coaches are great role models and great supporters of healthy competition in sports. However, there are other coaches who can push an athlete to do their best at whatever cost, even if that price is their health.

Q *When it comes to steroids, what kind of psychological effects have you found on athletes?*

A Psychological effects of steroids include feelings of grandiosity, psychosis, mania, and depressive symptoms. One common effect is increased aggression.

Q *What types of studies have been done to confirm or deny the existence of what is commonly called "'roid rage?"*

A My colleague Dr. Harrison Pope Jr. has conducted the best studies to date documenting the existence of 'roid rage. He found that men who were taking doses of steroids much lower than what many athletes and bodybuilders take, become increasingly aggressive. This was subject to what is known as a placebo-controlled, double-blind study, the most stringent research design for a study like this.

Q *What steroids and at what dosages did Dr. Pope administer during his test that seemingly proves the existence of 'roid rage?*

A The study was not designed to test that 'roid rage exists; it showed a statistically significant increase in manic symptoms and aggressive responses on testosterone cypionate, 600 mg per week.

Q *What do you say to the critics who claim 'roid rage is actually a myth, and steroids can be harmless if used correctly?*

A If you believe that heroin is harmless if used correctly, then there is little that I can say that will change your mind. In other words, there is very little to say to total ignorance and stupidity. "If used correctly" means what? I have treated patients who thought they were "using it correctly" and ended up beating the hell out of their wives, or thought they were "using it correctly" and now have a heart condition at 38 years old. Many of these steroid users who think they are using it correctly will most likely not be around in 20 years to be proven wrong.

Q *In your opinion, to curb the problem of steroids in sports, what would be a better solution: harsher punishment or increasing the information available on the effects of steroids?*

A I think educating people about the dangers of steroids is more effective. If we begin to associate steroid use with cheating and lying and penalize athletes who use them rather than herald them, we would then erase the mystique around them. We need to be educated to look at steroid-induced bodies as the result of a pharmaceutical cocktail rather than a result of hard work. It is not hard work to stick a needle in your ass.

Q *With the negative side effects on one's mental state accompanying steroid use, which you claim have been found, have you ever found any beneficial side effects?*

A No. [Though] men who use steroids will say that the increased muscle mass is the beneficial side effect.

Let's Call it "Pin the Deaths on Steroids."

It's the game no one likes to play but everyone who has a voice and opinion on the topic does it: pin the deaths on steroids. There is no doubt that anabolic steroids can have adverse side effects if used improperly or abused. But there does remain a difference between *use* and *abuse*. It is generally accepted that most professional bodybuilders *abuse* steroids, whereas other athletes—baseball players, track athletes, and so on—are simply making *use* of the drugs, albeit illegally. But for this review, legality is not the topic, health is.

Below is a comparison of facts known about various causes of deaths, and how many lives are lost annually. Each number stated below is an average statistic of deaths caused between January 1 and December 31 of any year (statistics retrieved from various sources):

- Cardiovascular disease kills 720,000 Americans
- Small-plane crashes cause roughly 700 deaths
- 40,000 people die each year in automotive accidents in the United States alone, ranging on average between 45 and 252 daily
- Influenza kills 36,000
- On average, four people die each summer at amusement parks
- Over 20 children are listed as accidental deaths caused by pull cords on window blinds
- Secondhand smoke kills 3,000 people in the United States alone
- Tobacco products kill more than 400,000 people in America
- Cancer costs 500,000 lives
- Cerebrovascular disease kills 144,000 people
- Chronic obstructive pulmonary deaths account for 80,000 lives lost
- Pneumonia kills 40,000 people
- Diabetes kills 48,000 people
- AIDS kills 42,000 Americans
- Suicide takes 31,000 lives
- Chronic liver disease kills 26,000

- Hypothermia in Europe alone kills 30,000
- Pharmacy prescription errors kill 7,000
- Common household aspirin kills 10,000
- Strokes are the cause of death for over 17,000
- Alcohol is related to 100,000 deaths
- Prescription drugs cause 15,000 cardiac deaths in the United States and Europe
- Tornadoes kill 89 people
- In the state of Hawaii alone 27 people die walking through crosswalks. Between 1994 and 1999, one driver killed two people at crosswalks
- Diesel exhaust causes 200 early deaths in Connecticut
- Electrocution is the cause of 200 deaths
- In 2004, one man was seriously injured by an exploding outhouse

Of the 40,000 automotive deaths in the list above, the single most deadly day in 2004 was July 4, when 162 people lost their lives on American roads. This number of deaths, in a single twenty-four hour period, is 162 more deaths than those linked explicitly to steroids in the same year.

Official causes of deaths are, obviously, not the only measure of illness. Most orally administered steroids place great stress on the liver. Side effects of steroids have been listed as kidney and liver failure, and supposedly, steroids can cause cysts to grow in the liver. The important thing to remember with this theory is that while there have been studies using steroids to cause the cysts, there is no proof that the steroids are the actual cause. Liver problems, and potentially the cysts described in any study, are caused by stress placed on the organ. Oral steroids are designed to resist breakdown by the liver, and as such are all alpha-alkylated. Because the body is so resilient at doing what it's supposed to do with natural substances passing through the body, when foreign substances, especially those that resist breakdown enter the body, it causes the liver to work harder. Couple that fact with long-term exogenous administration, and steroids as drugs may or may not be the actual cause of liver problems.

Before blaming steroids unfairly, individuals should realize that Tylenol has this same nature and is the second leading cause of liver cirrhosis.

Often a societal problem that occurs is that steroids are blamed as the cause of death for any user—at least it seems true as far as celebrities go—who has ever tried steroids. Unfairly, steroids receive a bad name because the media and angry relatives go on the offensive against them, without looking deeper into the lives of the deceased.

Many perfect examples of deaths being unfairly blamed on steroids revolve around the world of professional wrestling. These athletes compete in a form of entertainment, albeit with predetermined results, that is largely oppressive of the body's natural ability to recover. Professional wrestlers are on the road the majority of the year, performing dangerous acrobatics day after day for weeks, months, and often years without proper rest to recover. It is true that many, perhaps more in the past, turn to steroids for assistance with recovery. But the hard lives these athletes lead in the ring are often mimicked outside of the arena as well. Sadly, it has cost more than a few well-respected athletes their lives. And, naturally, steroids were declared at fault.

Curt Henning, who competed under the pseudonym "Mr. Perfect," passed away at the age of 44. His father, also a former professional entertainer, said the cause of his son's death was a lethal combination of painkillers and anabolic steroids. But the cause of death was, as medical records show: acute cocaine intoxication.

Davey Boy Smith, aka "The British Bulldog," died in 2002 at age 39. A coroner said Smith had an enlarged heart and microscopic scar tissue that could have been a result of steroid use. But Smith was also using human growth hormone, which is not a steroid. If Smith's enlarged heart was in fact exogenous-drug related, HGH is more than likely the cause of his organs increasing in size. Growth hormone in large doses does not discriminate on what muscles it helps grow.

Louie "Spicolli" Mucciolo passed away at 27 from coronary disease in 1998, as reported in his autopsy. Reports suggest a vial of testosterone was found among his possessions, but also found were painkillers and anti-anxiety drugs. With the long history of pharmacy errors and the potential for these types of drugs to interact with preexisting cardiac conditions, steroids cannot be pinpointed as the cause of death and would have to be considered factually as the least likely to have caused Mucciolo's death.

Richard Rood, who competed in wrestling as "Ravishing" Rick Rude, passed away at age 40 in 1999. Steroids were blamed in the antidrug community, but his autopsy reports Rood died from an overdose of "mixed medications." He had testified half a decade earlier that he had, in the past, taken steroids.

Brian Pillman, known as "Flyin' Brian," was reportedly using painkillers as well as human growth hormone in 1997 when he passed away from heart disease at age 35. As expected, steroids were originally blamed for his passing, but growth hormone is not a steroid, and other than painkillers, no evidence was reported that Pillman was on a regimen of anabolic steroids.

Outside of wrestling, over the last decade as many as 80 professional cyclists have died from abuse of the drug erythropoietin, the blood-cell booster, which is more commonly known as EPO. EPO is not a steroid.

Also worth noting is the death of well-loved Strongman Johnny Perry. Perry passed away at 30, an age still very young for bodybuilders and powerlifters. He had ranked as high as fourth in the World's Strongest Man competition, stood six feet five inches, and weighed 390 pounds. Perry was a user of steroids and human growth hormone and did suffer from an enlarged heart, which may have been because he was either predisposed genetically or it was a result of drug use, or it was a combination of both. According to the report posted on StopCocaineAddiction.com, the average weight for the heart of someone Perry's size is between 365 and 460 grams. Strongman Perry's heart weighed 620 grams. But despite this, Perry was taken from his friends and family not because of steroids or growth hormone, but because of cocaine.

So the question remains, can steroids cause death?

Yes. Of course. Steroids are like anything else—aspirin, Tylenol, vitamins, even water—too much can kill you. But the media has tried to lead America to believe that steroids, miniscule amounts or the largest stacks taken by the biggest of abusers, all have terrible, adverse, irreversible side effects. Their message simply isn't true. The facts, and the truth, as compared to their bias remain:

- Steroids *can* kill. It is not guaranteed or even likely, but it is a possibility.

- Steroids *can* cause testicle shrinkage. It is almost never permanent.
- Steroids have *not* been clinically linked to depression.
- Steroids are *not* more likely to cause an individual to commit suicide.

And perhaps most important to be aware of:

- Steroids *are* illegal.

2

A Reality Check for Children

It's hard for members of the world's youth population to understand why they can't do something an adult can, but with anabolic steroid use, it's vitally important they learn to understand the consequences.

The physiological differences between a young boy and a grown adult male are blatantly obvious on the outside, but inside the disparities are even larger. Male youths are still developing vital organs, bones, joints, and physical characteristics. Adult men are already set in their ways, so to speak, as they are no longer growing.

The biggest risk to adolescents using anabolic steroids is the closing of growth plates. Side effects for Dad, at least the known short-term side effects, are reversible. Junior isn't so lucky.

In 2002 the National Institute on Drug Abuse (NIDA) conducted a study to find how many teens in high school had used steroids. The results said 2.5 percent of 8th graders had used steroids, 3.5 percent of 10th graders had, and 4 percent of 12th graders had. The numbers seem small, but there are a lot of high school students in America, and even 2.5 percent equals a fairly large number. With the increasing media attention over the last few years and the increasing number of professional athletes being found to have used steroids, as well as those who come forward and admit their use, those numbers are no doubt not declining. If anything, they're increasing. And for good reason.

The media focuses on who uses steroids, the hearings that follow, and the potential punishments. They also mention the side effects, often in horrific and vivid detail. But the average high school student is intelligent, at least with street smarts, and knows that the media isn't exactly the epitome of truth. Students know their government doesn't always give it to them straight, and when switching between news stations provides two different twists on the same story, they're aware that it's entirely possible the truth is being skewed. And they are right. Unfortunately, what many high school students—and even children younger than high school age—don't know is that while the laundry list of side effects the media spews are mostly faulty for grown men, they're often spot-on when it comes to side effects for teens. Naturally the news reports don't point this out, which leaves it up in the air for the discerning viewer to make a decision. That discerning viewer in this case could be a Little League pitcher dreaming of his team winning the World Series; a high school varsity quarterback already seeing headlines calling him the next Montana, Elway, or Manning; or a point guard who already envisions needing a golf cart to drive around his hundred-acre mansion outside Los Angeles on his off days playing for the Lakers. Ah, wishful thinking. And wishful thinking is what clouds the mind.

Athletes use steroids because they want to be the best. Olympic athletes often consider that representing their countries is an honor. Other professional athletes, while not representing their country, represent themselves and want simply to show the world they are the top athlete in their profession. Of course, with that comes big money, endorsement deals for products they don't always use, shoes named after them, and a slew of admirers. Not a bad deal, really. With the athletes' new-found windfall of cash and options comes a fleet of Escalades, Lamborghinis, maybe a new Porsche next to a BMW or Mercedes, and for the days they don't want to feel too fancy, a Jaguar. An S-Type, of course—nothing too crazy.

So there's the conundrum: steroids and potential side effects—which because of the inaccuracy of the media may or may not be true—or big-league fantasies? Most kids probably don't go to bed wondering what a cycle of Anadrol would do to them, but imagining what it would feel like to be a starting pitcher for the Yankees is as common as sunshine.

But what would that cycle of Anadrol do to Junior? How about some testosterone injections or Dianabol tablets? It comes back to fusing of the growth plates. And while height doesn't always equate to excelling in athletics, history shows that it doesn't hurt.

The average height of a 13-year-old, the age bracket in which about 2.5 percent of kids have used steroids, is 61 inches (five feet one inch). Compare that to the fact that the average height of an NBA player is six feet 7.2 inches. Sure, one five-foot-five-inch athlete won the slam-dunk contest, but the exceptions don't provide great comparisons.

For 15-year-olds, the "normal" height is 67 inches (five feet seven inches). Contrast that with the average NFL quarterback height of about six-feet-three inches, and the average elite male sprint swimmer height of six-feet-four, and it's easy to see that aspiring athletes have a lot of growing to do.

It seems sometimes like a catch-22: take drugs and try to get an advantage on the competition, but if this is started too young, the only advantage is definitely going *to* the competition. Granted, it's an athlete's and child's own fault if they choose to use anabolic steroids, fusing their growth plates too soon and thus potentially sealing them at a height much shorter than they should have been. It's also a child's own fault if he runs away from home and does something stupid, but parents somehow still catch the brunt of their child's actions. Debt too can be incurred by children, but Mom and Dad have to come forward when it's time to pay up. In this same sense, children are given the perception that what they do, at least until they're 18, isn't really their responsibility. Society lets children break down walls that were built for them, and when they do, the walls are rebuilt. In the case of fused growth plates, there is no turning back. Junior is on his own. Dad can't help

But is it worth it? Not every child dreams of becoming the next Michael Jordan. Not every child wants to be in the spotlight on an international level. Most kids, at least athletes, do what is accepted in school. And high school students often don't see outside the box. They can't see anything other than what will happen if they do or don't make the team, get the girl, look good at the beach. And sometimes the pressure to be what they aren't pushes them to do things they shouldn't.

For a child who doesn't want to make it to the NFL or NBA, or for one who wants to but accepts that he can't, the next best thing could be to make a name for himself while he can, while he is still in high school.

So Junior finds a local gym, makes friends with the biggest guys there, and eventually finds one who will get him some gear at a good price.

The first problem is that most steroid dealers don't give a damn what you do with the drugs. They don't care if you use them, if you throw them away, if you drink what's supposed to be injected. Doesn't make a bit of difference to them. This leaves Junior to inject his own goods, which is probably how he would prefer it anyway: fewer witnesses. But that leads to the interesting predicament that Junior has no idea how to properly give an intramuscular injection, let alone do it hygienically. Because steroids aren't inserted into veins there's no concern about pushing in an air bubble if a user aspirates, but if the needle is dirty or the area isn't properly cleaned, an abscess can form. Insert Supermom and Superdad to the rescue. That health problem can be fixed, but the mental damage of being ousted from one's team as a drug user and cheater could last a very long time.

Even if Junior does enough research and learns how to give himself a proper injection, what happens if he dopes up and still doesn't make the varsity team? Or, worse yet, even the junior varsity team? Does he up the dosage? Bigger is better, after all. Look at Barry Bonds, for example. His days playing for the Pirates left him as just another guy in the clubhouse. Put him in a Giants uniform with thirty pounds' more muscle and the guy looks like someone to be feared. And, he's hitting a whole lot more home runs. So the dosage is increased and the workouts get more intense. Next year is the year. What if Junior is a senior, and there is no next year? For kids, especially those going through puberty, steroids can cause an immense hormonal imbalance. Adults generally have stable hormone levels and can more easily deal with psychological changes. Children aren't always so lucky. It isn't even necessarily the steroids that cause the mental changes; it is often a misunderstanding of the drugs. A kid thinks because he took the steps and spent the money and time buying juice he should be the best. When he's not, it's worse than breaking up with his last girlfriend. The nerves get fried.

So take the best-case scenario. Junior juices, goes from a medium T-shirt, which is a loose fit, to filling out an extra large. He makes not only the football team as starting quarterback, but the baseball team in center, and the basketball team as a top guard. Then what? Well certainly he has to stay on the drugs. Remember, Junior isn't trying to just make the team, he's trying to leave a legacy. If it took a certain amount to make the team, it has to take more to be the best, right? There in itself is a broken rule of steroid use: never-ending cycles. Many adult steroid users report no side effects from relatively low doses of anabolic steroids used for eight to twelve weeks at a time, with sufficient time off to the let the body and its natural hormones rebound. Many have done this for decades and are, in themselves, long-term studies. They're happy and healthy and intelligent with their drug use.

Junior stays on for an entire school year, using steroids much like professional bodybuilders who stay on year-round, eventually coming off to take hormone replacement therapy (HRT) the rest of their lives. Was it worth it? Maybe Junior isn't afraid of needles, so the idea of injecting testosterone in his glutes the rest of his days doesn't bother him. But if he was juicing at 15, 16, or even 17 or 18, that's the least of his problems.

So Junior graduates, and for some reason doesn't grow an inch. Oh well, he was quarterback, and he was probably average height already anyway. He was, at one point, ahead of the game. After a little steroid use, he stopped his development right in the dead center of mediocrity. No big deal, millions of people are plenty happy that way. But what else is going on, or maybe better put, is *no longer* going on inside his body because of his steroid use? A main concern is fertility. Steroids can rarely cause a grown adult to become infertile, and when they do it is usually only temporary. In a teenager, whose body is still developing, they can adversely affect sperm production permanently. Sometimes this can be cured with advanced medical procedures, other times it can't. It's a risk.

And with risks come another problem, which pertains to keeping kids away from steroids. Scare tactics don't work. They never have and they never will. It's like knowing a neighbor whose father disciplines with the belt, but the kid still stays out too late, swears, breaks rules and laws, and repeats the process even after a good whipping. Kids shouldn't smoke, they know why, but they still do it. Why? For many it's because their parents do it, their friends do it. It's emulation. Underage individuals shouldn't drink, but they do. Why? Because their parents do it, their friends do it, maybe because their idols endorse the products. There's a myriad of reasons. Maybe they like the taste. It isn't always ignorance, but there's always a reason. Just like steroids, there's a reason people use them despite health risks.

Inaccurate reporting of the risks and those same talked-about scare tactics are only going to increase the problem. The Web site for adolescents called Kidzworld posted the following pertaining to steroids:

Kidzworld's Top Ten Reasons Not to Be a Juice Monkey

If you're using steroids or thinking about it, here's a pretty good list of reasons not to.

1. Gives you zits.
2. Gives you bad breath, which equals no kisses.
3. Makes you go bald sooner, which equals looking like your Dad when you're 16.
4. For Girls: it makes you grow a moustache—totally gross!
5. For Girls: it makes your boobies shrink.
6. For Guys: it makes your nuts shrink—do you really need another reason?
7. For Guys: it makes it hurt when you go to the bathroom—again, do you really need another reason?
8. For Guys: it makes you grow breasts—once again, see above.
9. Impotence: that means you can't get an erection.
10. Roid Rage: it makes you get all wacko and violent.

The lies and misinformation are abundant, and the rest is laughable. Steroids don't necessarily give you zits, and there's never been any proof at all that steroids cause halitosis. Steroids only increase the rate of male-pattern baldness *if* it runs in a user's family. The promotion of male features in women is probable, which is why steroids are definitely not recommended for women, but it's not the guarantee like this list makes it out to be. The "nuts shrink" comment is stated as if it were fact, which it isn't. And "hurt when you go to the bathroom" is too vague. Once again, the vast majority of male steroid users do not develop gynecomastia, do not develop impotence, and do not experience increased aggression. The misinformation could easily signal children that something isn't quite right with these warnings, so they may be even more inclined to try steroids. And yet, the scare tactics continue.

What makes it worse is that steroids, while potentially beneficial and safe for adults, are not beneficial and safe for adolescents—yet the more they're warned, the more it seems they want to try them. And it's those young people who are so enamored of wealth and fame. Sure, adults would love to be famous, but by the time many pick up their first steroid-filled syringe, they are well aware of being past the prime age to become a professional athlete. Instead, they're using steroids to feel better about themselves and reverse some side effects that come with aging. They don't need to go above and beyond the realm of logic, because they aren't trying to outclass anyone. When using steroids is a personal endeavor, for an adult they can be safely used. Any way you slice steroid use for children, it's bad. Mentally, physically, for their futures and the future of sports, it's bad.

The question is whether there is a way to successfully stem the problem. More and more kids are using steroids, that is something that is known and understood. But what can be done to keep it from getting worse? Telling them about the consequences won't work. If threatening legal action doesn't keep cartels from making millions of dollars dealing drugs internationally, over borders and through intricate workings of their own, it isn't going to keep a kid from dropping less than $100 on 10 weeks' worth of testosterone. And even if that is the chosen tactic, Juvenile Hall isn't something that frightens most street-tough kids anyway. Threatening to take away privileges at home probably isn't going to work either. With steroids, just like smoking and drinking, it ultimately comes down to each individual. If a kid wants to use steroids, he is going to use them. But they should know the consequences. If an aspiring quarterback reads in the media, "Adolescent steroid use will cause a male's penis to shrink," he's going to laugh and move on about his business. The message fails in a couple of ways. One, it doesn't tell him what he wants to hear: yes, anabolic steroids can potentially enhance athletic performance under the right conditions. Two, it is a blanket statement that, even the uneducated knows, may or may not be true. With the media, sometimes it's like a 50-50 shot at honesty. What would be better for the decision-making process is something like, "Anabolic steroid use, the root of many high-level athletic performances, has been linked in studies to cause a premature end to bone development." That instead does not come off as an attack; it's simply putting the information out there. Some people are going to be stupid no matter what, and no one can help those individuals, but it's a safe bet that if kids knew the real, studied side effects of steroid use, the majority wouldn't use them. Sometimes though, steroids seem to be the only way out for some kids. And for that, we can blame parents. At least, blame some of them.

Parents often try to fulfill their past dreams with their children's athletic performances. Parents live vicariously through their kids, and all the while the adults act like the babies. It's in the news regularly: a parent bashes a coach because he benched his kid. While it's not said in the news, it's obvious: if your kid was good enough, he would be in the game. Although some coaches carry immature vendettas against kids and parents, they still put in the best players. Their job is on the line if they don't. It's that simple.

And it's those same parents who boo Little League umpires; who step out onto their sixth-grader's court and throw a tantrum; who pressure their kids and belittle them when they miss a crucial free throw, don't juke one last linebacker, or when they don't hit the game-winning home run or swim a best time. These parents don't understand the concept of improvement, the ideology behind tapering in sports like swimming and track, and it's these parents who drive their kids to such measures as steroid use and abuse. Some people, even some teenagers, turn to alcohol when they get depressed. Some athletes, instead of turning to alcohol—which, most are aware, won't help their performances—turn to steroids, not knowing and/or not caring about the physical consequences. If it gets their parents off their back, there's nothing else that matters. And this behavior isn't limited to kids in high school sports. It starts before that, many years before college scouts even take notice.

The Weyerhaeuser King County Aquatic Center in Federal Way, Washington, is just like any other swimming pool in the United States where little kids learn to swim for safety and others chase the dream of Olympic glory. It's also, like anywhere else, the scene of repulsive behavior for some parents. The following, just one example, could happen anywhere (names have been changed):

> Two women sit in the front row of the stands, gazing occasionally down at the pool where their children were swimming in a club team practice. The women are casually dressed in sweaters, one in jeans the other in slacks, both with their hair done nicely, both knitting. They look like everyday, normal, sweet women. And then they speak. The younger of the two women said to the other, "I went ahead and told Ryan that he could forget about watching television. If he can go to swim practice for an entire month without missing a single day, and then not even go a best time at his next meet, he needs to spend more time training. I told him it was ridiculous for me to sit an entire weekend watching him swim if he wasn't even going to go faster than he did last time." The woman smiled. Her friend returned the grin and replied, "Oh I know it. I took away Michelle's phone and television privileges and I'm starting her on a weight-training program. It's just *stupid* that she isn't going faster." The first woman, apparently not wanting to feel outdone, added, "You know, I think I'll start making him do 100 push-ups before every meal, too. He must not be strong enough or something."

As a point of reference, this true story revolves around Ryan and Michelle, who at the time, were both nine years old.

For some children, the consequences are far worse. Some have abusive parents who will literally beat their children for not improving, making a needed shot, getting on base, or scoring a touchdown. Then they wonder why their bruised and battered children still aren't improving even after their abuse. It's a revolving circle. For a lot of kids, steroids and other performance-enhancing drugs are the way out. If they can satisfy Mom and Dad, they can live a relatively normal life. And for many, it gets even better. While mediocre performances induce pain and restrictions, excelling in a single game brings about gifts and respect, things that can easily be confused with love. Together, they are just more reasons for an adolescent to risk health by using anabolic steroids.

What's worse, it isn't just parents. It's coaches too. One infamous situation was printed in papers nationwide about a football coach contacting a doctor who had recently discovered how to increase muscle mass in mice via gene therapy. The coach asked what it would take to have this therapy for his kids. Not his children, his team. His entire high school football team. Some coaches promote the use of drugs because it helps them win, and some parents do the same. They don't see past a state championship.

The bottom line is that there needs to be a solution. And there are some, but they aren't going to be easily accepted. They violate privacy, but so do seat belt laws. The hypocrisy is evident (no seat belts on buses, but seat belts in your car) but also warranted. It's the government; the population has to deal with all sorts of strange rules. People fight and scream, and life goes on. It's not about issuing an open invitation to give away rights, but when something has to be done, it needs to be done at whatever cost. Saving the health of the nation's youth is important enough to suffer a little discomfort. How can teen steroid use be combated? Kill two birds with one stone: (1) put the cheating and condescending parents and coaches at bay, (2) drug test in high school sports. It's progression, and it's necessary.

The critics will say, "We've never had to do that before, we don't need to do that now." True, but in the United States for decades you didn't need a ticket, or even have to go through security checkpoints to get to airport gates. When dangers arise, measures are put in place to check them. Adolescent steroid use is a danger, and something needs to be done to solve it very, very soon.

3

Where Have All the Drugs Gone?

As long as steroids have been used to increase athletic performance, athletes have been trying to hide the fact that they use them. Even when anabolic steroids were legal and widely used, some athletes would claim to be all natural, just to rub other guys the wrong way when they beat them. The stories remain the same nearly 50 years later: athletes don't want to be viewed as steroid users.

Some professionals, generally bodybuilders, will admit and speak freely about their use of illegal drugs and other performance enhancers. They know that in their sport, the rules and standards have gotten so out of control that they have no choice but to use steroids if they want to compete. Think of it as a star-crossed love affair destined to be a risky venture. It isn't their fault they fell for benches instead of balls, iron over grass, posing trunks rather than jerseys. Many, when asked, will concede they don't like steroids or being as big as they are—because that much weight can be uncomfortable to bear—but they have to use steroids if they want to pursue their dreams.

But if drug testing ever hit the posing stage, how many bodybuilders would fail? Even of those who admit to injecting cocktails each and every week, how many would return a positive test? Maybe all, maybe some, possibly none.

How?

It goes back to the age-old quest to beat the test. Victor Conte, founder and president of BALCO, perhaps said it most famously, but dozens of other doctors, trainers, and athletes have all sent the same message: only the stupid athletes get caught. As disturbing as it sounds, it's a semiaccurate statement. "Stupid" probably isn't the best word, but if one were to say that only the unprepared athletes get caught, they could be spot-on.

Different federations test for different substances. What is banned in Olympic competition is, or used to be, legal in baseball, football, and/or basketball. This double standard makes for the saddest story of one man's life:

In 1998 the shot put gold medalist in the Atlanta Olympic Games, Randy Barnes, received a lifetime banishment from the sport when he tested positive for the hormone androstenediol, better known simply as "andro." But on what may as well have been the other side of the world, Mark McGwire was being praised for doing the unthinkable, hitting 70 home runs in a single season. The irony is that McGwire, who has since been accused of steroid use, admitted to using andro during his record-setting run of long balls. The same substance that took away one man's prize and athletic career, was earning another man millions of dollars, millions of fans, and a great deal of space in history books.

After the steroid blowout in American athletics, stories have circulated that McGwire simply used andro as an escape, a way to hide his anabolic steroid use. He has vehemently denied the accusation, but no one will ever know. McGwire was never tested for androstenediol, and even if he had been, his test would have come back clean. This type of double-edged sword is a loud and clear message that there needs to be either one standard for drug testing throughout all of sports, or none at all. One way or another, it needs to be fair for everyone.

But as long as there are banned substances that can help athletes excel, people will attempt to beat the testing procedures. In defense of testing, a record 24 athletes were caught doping at the Athens Olympics in 2004. But according to some, that was merely a fraction of the athletes who were actually cheating.

The following are methods that are currently used, were used at some point in history, or can supposedly be used to beat steroid tests in athletics. Some, perhaps many, of these methods have been put out to pasture by athletic federations. As always, it is simply a matter of time before good science catches up with bad science. By the same token, new methods of protecting athletes using performance-enhancing substances are most certainly being developed even faster.

The Strange

Fake This, Fake That

What happened to Minnesota Vikings running back Onterrio Smith in April 2004 is a perfect lead-in to a strange method of beating drug tests: urine replacement. It sounds simple, and the principle is, but getting it done can be just a little awkward. Just as it sounds, this involves exchanging an athlete's urine, which he knows is dirty, and replacing it with clean urine. The clean sample is often purchased from a teammate, a neighbor, even over the Internet. The kit Smith had, which was discovered at an airport, contained several vials of powder that he admitted was dried urine used to provide a clean drug test. The ready-to-use kit titled, affectionately, "The Original Whizzinator," was found along with some pills labeled "Cleansing Formula." Smith contends the kit was not for him, though he is no stranger to drug tests. In 2000 he was kicked out of college at Tennessee for testing positive for marijuana, the same substance that caused him to fail a 2004 drug test and to serve a four-game suspension handed to him by the NFL.

The Original Whizzinator is among several kits available for purchase online. They are simple and as cheap as $30 for a vial of urine and a holding bag, and can get up to over $100 for a full kit that includes two vials of a clean sample, a holding bag, temperature control measures, and, believe it or not, a five-inch, lifelike prosthetic penis. The kits are so advanced that the company offers the prosthetic organ in three colors: black, flesh, and Latino. Users contend that this advanced kit works so well because it looks authentic and, while tested athletes aren't alone when providing their sample, officials generally don't stare at genitalia close enough to notice the difference.

The Scientific

Epitestosterone

Steroids are derivatives of the male hormone testosterone, which provides an easy explanation why women suffer from much more intense side effects when using steroid compounds.

To provide an accurate screening for testosterone, drug control officials are forced to take into account that all men are not created equal. Because of this fact, which is unfortunate only because it complicates testing, natural levels are going to come back quite varied regardless of any exogenous testosterone administration. And because of this, testosterone is tested at a ratio of 6:1 (International Olympic Committee standards) to prevent any false positives. The ratio compares levels of testosterone to epitestosterone, an epimer that is naturally produced in the body opposite testosterone. The normal testosterone-epitestosterone ratio is 1:1, but because top athletes are often genetically advanced their ratios may differ compared to those of the average man.

The 6:1 ratio is for most a large variance in their natural levels. This leaves open the possibility for a certain amount of exogenous testosterone if one is careful enough to make sure the hormone stays within accepted limits. For other individuals already producing more hormone than their competition, or for those who want to use more than they can sneak in under the radar, epitestosterone is employed. When used, it increases the variable testosterone is compared to, thus allowing for increased amounts. As long as these levels are monitored, and the athletes who would be able to afford such substances would presumably have individuals available to do the monitoring, detection would be a very low risk.

Epitestosterone is not a steroid, nor is it illegal to own, distribute, or possess in the United States. It is available as a research chemical and those in the field of performance-enhancing substances, especially those who have a team working for them already, can easily obtain it.

Other tests for exogenously administered testosterone have been and are being developed, but have yet to work their way into the procedures of most testing labs. This method of beating drug tests is a popular way to stay ahead of the curve, and is a definite deterrent to those who are trying to eradicate drug use in competition.

Probenecid

Probenecid is a drug that has been around for over 50 years. It is used to treat gout (though it does not cure it). This drug alters other substances in the bloodstream and how the body passes those substances, and it changes blood composition.

Naturally most athletes don't suffer from gout. Instead, they use probenecid because it has been found to mask steroids in the blood and to drop levels of substances in the blood low enough so that they are not detected by standard testing fare. Most important, it's a renal blocking agent, which means it doesn't allow certain substances to be excreted in urine. For an athlete trying to beat the test this is fantastic news, but as was mentioned earlier, it is only a matter of time before drug testing procedures catch up to this sort of science. And they have. Because the drug can prevent a dirty athlete from testing positive, drug testers now test for probenecid. Therefore, this masking agent is of little to no use to athletes in the Big Three sports or Olympic competition, but it is used in high schools and some small college divisions that lack funding for more comprehensive testing.

Designer Steroids

The saying goes, "If you can't beat 'em, join 'em." In this game of cat and mouse that is steroid testing, one would assume that if an athlete can't get around the procedures he would just compete clean. But when millions of dollars are on the line that is just not so. No, instead of joining the clean athletes, certain individuals are turning back to the lab. By taking an old steroid that everyone is familiar with, and tweaking a few carbons and atoms and then playing with some trial and error, you have a new steroid that is undetectable. This is obviously cheating, but it's laughably unfair to the other cheats who can't afford the staff required for such a level of science. And, it's doubtful that anyone is going to share his or her newest creation.

The Natural

Herbs, minerals, and vitamins are just a few of the legal substances athletes use to try to hide the illegal ones. As one can imagine, these methods are some of the least effective. Science has the tendency to improve upon nature. And, for athletes who can't afford further help from the lab, they may have to rely on Father Time.

Diuretics and Perma Cleanse

Drugs in athletes can only be found if they are in the body and excreted through a blood or urine test. Urine tests are the cheapest and therefore most common method of testing. Athletes often take diuretics in an effort to cleanse their system before having to provide a sample. These can work tremendously well, and did for quite some time. But with the advent of unannounced testing in Olympic sports, diuretics became much more difficult to rely on. In sports where athletes are given a heads-up on impending testing, diuretics are still an effective means to prevent detection.

Many athletes still use diuretics prior to a competition where they are most likely to get tested, especially if they are not a big name and subject to consistent testing throughout the year. But because the use of diuretics had become so prominent, they were added to banned substances lists in the late 1980s. They too, though, have a half-life, the amount of time for half the drug to be eliminated from the system, and can still be used if given enough time to clear the body.

One mail-order system that is supposedly undetectable as a diuretic or in any lab test but uses the same means to evade a positive test—detoxification—is Perma Cleanse. According to the manufacturer, this product is not a masking agent and therefore leaves no trace. It is called all natural and does its job by speeding up the metabolism and therefore the excretion of pollutants in the bloodstream, and uses "controlled fluids" to clear the body. Special foods and liquids are then consumed to rid toxins from the user's body and in three to ten days, the product is said to ensure clean tests of urine, blood, or saliva. There have been no reports on whether this particular product does or does not work, but that has not kept the company from selling kits at prices ranging from $60 to $170.

Low Dose

As described in the section on epitestosterone, with many substances on the banned list a ceiling must be reached before a positive test is declared. To allow for natural genetic differences, the level is generally higher than most athletes produce naturally. For some, cheating "just a little" is enough to get performance benefits, and these athletes stay undetected by sticking to a low-dose administration of drugs that keeps them below the limits established by drug testing federations.

Fasting

The body likes to maintain homeostasis at all costs. For example, extreme dieters eventually find out that sometimes they have to eat more to lose weight, because the body will hoard everything it does get to fend off starvation if enough nutrients and food aren't passing through. When there is enough or an excess, the body can keep all its levels balanced and natural harmony ensues. When the body kicks into starvation mode, though, all the "rules" are essentially thrown out the window.

A classic method of evading positive drug tests is to couple the use of natural herb diuretics such as dandelion root, uva ursi, and caffeine with fasting. When the body begins to sense it is being deprived, it slows itself down. First, it slows the metabolism, which would seem like putting the body in a prime position for a positive test because it passes substances at a slower rate, but it's not. At the same time the metabolism is slowing to ensure the body doesn't burn vital fuel any faster than it has to, the body decreases its testosterone levels. The idea is that with this method, there are no diuretics to test for, and natural levels of hormones are dropped low enough that the exogenous drugs can be present without being found.

Timed Training

This is used mostly by athletes who are not subject to year-round and out-of-competition testing, either because their sport or federation does not conduct such testing or because they are not yet on a level to be subject to such measures. Timed training is not so much training as it is the systematic administration of drugs during a phase of training prior to competition. All drugs have a half-life and athletes who are aware of these half-lives can use steroids and other performance-enhancing drugs, gain the benefits from them during training—increased endurance, muscle growth, strength increase—and come off them in time for any testing they may eventually be subject to.

Administering steroids and ceasing in time to evade detection is another large thorn in the side of drug testers, because there are great benefits to cycling steroids during training. Drugs do not have to be in the system for a user to have gained in performance. A common misconception is that all the muscle and strength earned while on drugs is lost once the athlete stops the drug. The truth is that the only muscle lost, assuming proper training is continued for maintenance of muscle and/or strength, is what the athlete holds over his predisposed genetic limit. If a natural athlete is years away from his or her genetic muscle and/or strength threshold, but begins using steroids, this athlete could, with proper training, potentially reach that mark in a matter of months instead of years. Assuming that mark is met but not exceeded, that athlete can keep all of the muscle size and strength gained while on anabolic steroids, even without taking them ever again. At that point training excessively becomes more important than ever, but for individuals already dedicated to their sport, that does not present a problem.

Detection Times of Various Anabolic Steroids

Anadrol—2 months
Anavar—3 weeks
Clenbuterol—4–5 days
Deca-Durabolin—12–18 months
Dianabol (oral)—5–6 weeks
Equipoise—4–5 months
Halotestin (halo)—2 months
Nandrolone—12 months
Parabolan—4–5 weeks
Primobolan Depot—4–5 weeks
Proviron—5–6 weeks
Sustanon—3 months
Trenbolone (Fina)—4–5 months
Testosterone cypionate—3 months
Testosterone enanthate—3 months
Testosterone propionate—2 weeks
Winstrol (stanozolol) tablets—3 weeks
Winstrol (stanozolol) injection—2 months

Because of these various detection times and the inability of drug testers to keep up with athletes at all times, there is no doubt that countless athletes are able to abuse drugs for performance enhancement and face no consequences. And for testosterone, the wide range (6:1) before detection makes it extremely difficult, if not impossible, to catch an athlete with a team in place to keep track of blood levels.

International Olympic Committee 6:1

The best account of how ridiculous the IOC's 6:1 positive test result for testosterone comes from Werner Reiterer, an Australian Olympian, who wrote about his drug use in *Positive: An Australian Olympian Reveals the Inside Story of Drugs and Sport.* In it, he writes, "These extreme limits make it easy to use large amounts of *T* and have it remain undetected. What makes the situation even more ludicrous is the fact that certain ethnic groups have an inverted ratio. There's more epi-testosterone naturally prevalent in their bodies. These guys could take massive dosages of testosterone and easily stay within the rules."

Reiterer goes on to talk about the huge number of athletes he has come into contact with who have taken a large variety of drugs and never tested positive, and their methods used. He mentions that an entire group of selected Australian athletes were given over three times the amount of testosterone that the average male produces, and they still tested well within the acceptable limits. Generally, drug testing all comes back to the testosterone test because the hormone has such a profound impact on athletic performance. This failure by the IOC to properly test for this drug is the biggest disgrace of the drug-testing effort. "Over the twelve weeks of the steroid diet I'd taken something like 2,500 milligrams," Reiterer continued. "The peak weeks were at 400 milligrams, trailing down to 100 milligrams at the lowest." About his testing during this time, "Peterson tested me eighteen times—once a week for the twelve weeks of drug therapy, and once a week for the following six weeks when I was off all drugs. At no point did I get to 4:1. I was *miles* beneath the IOC limit. Even after engineering extreme circumstances (dehydration, stress, dietary experiments), I rarely went above 3:1. In other words, I could use as much testosterone as I needed, and I was assured a negative result. The million-dollar HRMS testing machines that will be used in the Sydney labs were completely redundant. There was no longer any need for protection or shadowy tactics. I could use all the drugs most effective for a track and field athlete, in whatever doses were needed, and be tested every day. And I'd remain 'natural'."

Interview with swimming superstar Gary Hall Jr. on balance in drug testing, what's right and wrong about it, and how to fix it for the future.

Brief biography of Gary Hall Jr.:

- Type-1 diabetic
- Three-time Olympian (Atlanta 1996, Sydney 2000, Athens 2004)
- Ten-time Olympic medalist (five gold, three silver, two bronze)

Q *Swimmers and other Olympic athletes are generally subject to more stringent testing than athletes making millions of dollars a year in a sport like baseball, and yet have far fewer positive drug tests. Do you ever feel underappreciated in the battle against drugs in sports?*

A I don't know if underappreciated is the right word. I think more testing is needed in other sports without question, but even in swimming there needs to be tighter control over athletes. There will always be athletes who try to slip through the cracks and cheat anyways. I think the severity of the punishment for a positive test really sets the standard for the sport, as to how many of those athletes will attempt to slip through the cracks, and how many are able.

Q *How many times would you say you get drug tested per year?*

A Between four and ten times.

Q *If punishments set the standard, what did you think about FINA reducing the standard four-year ban to a two-year ban?*

A I was against it. It was four years and I was a little disappointed they were persuaded to reduce that as compared to other sports that have blatantly failed at controlling drugs.

Q *If it were up to you, what would the rules be for a first positive test?*

A Without question a lifetime ban for any positive test with a performance-enhancing supplement.

Q *Do you take any special precautions to keep from testing positive?*

A I take a vitamin, but not even creatine, something which is allowed. And as for creatine, I don't believe that should be legal. I don't take anything, not so much out of fear for cross-contamination, as we're told to avoid those companies that produce banned substances, but because I don't believe in any type of substance to increase performance.

Q *The human growth hormone test results for Massimiliano Rossalino, 200 individual medley winner in Sydney, came back around 17 times higher than that of the average male. He kept his medal because there was no test. What goes through your mind when you know nothing will happen to him?*

A He gets absolutely no respect from me. And it's a shortcoming from our federation. And I think there should be retroactive justice. A perfect example is the East Germans, who we know were fueled on anything and everything imaginable. Now that we have hard evidence, we should be able to go back and award the clean athletes with something that is rightfully theirs.

Q *Do you think steroids and performance-enhancing supplements are a big worry in swimming?*

A I think less so than other sports without a doubt, swimming is as clean of a sport as you'll find today. But, there are going to be people who attempt to break the rules and we need to do anything we can to eliminate them, and the more strict we are with their punishments the cleaner we'll stay.

Q *With baseball and other sports under attack for steroids and substance abuse, do you think this is a good opportunity for swimming to come out from under their shadow and be promoted?*

A That's really up to the people marketing sports. There is an opportunity for the promoters to say, "We are a clean sport, these are good role models." There's a long history of athletes being endorsed by companies and it's really up to them to use that to our benefit. If a company were to sponsor Mark McGwire now, I think they would be sending the wrong message and it's really up to them to find clean athletes and have good athletes representing their products.

Q *Do you think it will actually come to that? That companies will use good, clean athletes to represent what they say is a good product?*

A It's a hope of mine and I think after the investigation of the NFL and MLB, people are recognizing that it's not OK for Lawrence Taylor to be smoking crack and then go pummeling quarterbacks and being more at risk to cause a lifelong injury or a career-ending injury. Traditionally those are the big sports with the biggest endorsements and they are the ones now bringing light to this issue.

Q *Money seems to be a big motivator for athletes to try steroids. Do you think if the Olympics reduced the amount of money and commercialization in the games, fewer athletes would take steroids?*

A MLB turning a blind eye to the rampant drug use has a lot more to do with the amount of drugs being taken than the money available to top athletes.

Q *So you don't think the money is a motivation for these athletes to use steroids?*

A It's speculating. But I really think that, for example, MLB knew for a long time that these players were taking drugs and it was [MLB's]

. . . lack of discipline that exacerbated the problem. You can say they're doing it for the money but I don't know that that is true, it's just one means to an end.

Q *Swimming and Olympic testing is much more strict than Big Three testing, which could mean that more people compete in your sport for the love of it rather than the celebrity. If swimming were to advance in market share of U.S. sports, do you think it would cause more people to seek chemical help?*

A I can speak very specifically for swimming and myself and say if there were hundreds of millions on the line for an Olympic gold medal, I still wouldn't take any performance-enhancing substances. I don't believe the majority of people would. I think it comes down to a person's ethics. Either you're a cheater or you're not, that's the bottom line. I think a person has and retains their pride and I think that alone is the biggest prevention of drug abuse in sport.

Q *With steroids being in the public eye, gene doping is on the horizon and really isn't that talked about at this point. Are you concerned with this for the future?*

A It's still sci-fi to me. I know it exists but until you see one of them have done it, we don't know what the results are, we don't know how much it will help. I've raced against people who have taken drugs and I've won, and I'm clean. I think the most encouraging thing is that, at least at this point in swimming, at least, a clean athlete can beat a dirty athlete.

Q *Have you ever known for a fact before a race that you would be competing against an athlete on drugs?*

A You look at a guy like Jose Canseco and a dirty athlete has a tendency to think all other athletes are dirty. I think a clean athlete then also has a tendency to think others are clean. Throughout the majority of my career I believe that everyone was clean, but there will always be rumors and things to cause suspicion. I'm just a little bit of an optimist.

Q *You've overcome amazing obstacles to continually be at the top of your sport. Because of that, has anyone accused you of using steroids or other performance-enhancing drugs?*

A Not to my face. I've heard secondhand, off-the-cuff comments and people making comments about my diabetes and the fact I take insulin and how that's supposedly helping me. It's just upsetting to me because I've always been so outspoken and pushing for a lifetime ban on a first offense. I've never ducked or dodged a drug test and it's something I'm proud of.

Marion Jones, for instance, and the Victor Conte deal—it came up at [the 2004 swimming] Olympic trials and I was very outspoken about my thoughts on it. To me the evidence was overwhelming and I think that punishment should follow. It wasn't a personal attack on Jones, but if there's proof, then that is the way it should be. While it is speculation, though, I think if she is guilty, then [four-time Olympic gold medalist] Amy van Dyken is guilty too because they're in the same situation. And, it's a shame, it really is. I'm not against any certain people, sports, or countries—I'm against cheaters.

Q *Baseball's punishments are so lax in comparison to that.*

A It's a joke that isn't funny. Baseball and athletes like McGwire are a joke.

Q *What would you like to see happen if they test positive?*

A I think if they test positive they should be kicked out for life.

Q *Steroids, though, are against federal law. Do you think federal law should step in as well and play a factor in the punishment for those who test positive?*

A Absolutely. Federal justice should be passed on as well. But you know, what they're doing, it's not just cheating, which is bad enough. It's theft. When you're talking about multimillion dollar contracts being signed by cheaters, it's theft. For every McGwire or Canseco or L. T. out there, there is a clean athlete who never made it to the big leagues. And, because of the way things are set up, to make it to the big leagues means money.

Q *So it's cheating and indirectly, it isn't even the worst crime being committed?*

A If I were to hold up a gas station, and steal a thousand dollars, I would go to jail. And yet, these athletes are stealing by way of opportunities from clean athletes and they're getting away with it. Then they finish their career, and are making more money writing books about it.

Q *And along with opportunities to make money, they're stealing dreams from kids who actually play for the love of the game.*

A It rolls off the tongue so easy, "dreams," but it's more than that, it's a lifetime of work. These athletes are reaching for their dreams and by doing so are putting in massive amounts of their time, effort, and money.

Q *How would you fix this type of theft?*

A Start with lifetime bans, first offense. Progressively toughen the rules, make punishments retroactive, so that when we find new drugs we can go back and make the wrong, right. Cheaters have to know they won't go unpunished. Using BALCO as an example, when substances are found, we need to go back and create justice, no matter how far past the test date, and the only way we can do this is bank blood samples for every finalist at the Olympics and World [Championships] and other major competitions. We need to make every effort possible to stay on top of the progress steroids are making.

Q *What about athletes who claim they test positive because of cross-contamination. Do you have any sympathy?*

A No, I don't. Cross-contamination is the cry of every cheater. Anything you take and put in your body is at your own risk.

An outspoken critic against drugs in sports, Megan Quann offers her point of view on drug testing and how testing is done in her sport. Quann is a two-time Olympic gold medalist, 27-time American and World record holder, and nine-time national champion in swimming.

In the short-lived ESPN television series *Playmakers*, the second episode of the show deals with drug testing. Suitably enough, the episode is titled "The Piss Man," a term of endearment for the league drug tester. Demetrius Harris, a fictional star athlete in the show, has a cocaine addiction. He uses steroids. Under normal circumstances, he would test positive after any test for any federation in any league. But it's football, and he doesn't test positive. He gets a whisper from a team official that he's on the list of players to get tested, and some arrangements are made. He gets a catheter inserted by a team doctor. The physician fills his bladder with a teammate's clean urine, and he heads off to get tested. In the show he's made to strip down naked in front of several officials and doctors, and fill a cup. He smiles, walks away, he passed another test.

Often, I get asked how drug testing works for swimmers. How many times a year I get tested, how the testing goes, if it bothers me, am I ever afraid I'll test positive, all sorts of questions. If someone mentions a testing procedure he saw on television, the first thing I can say for sure is that for Olympic athletes, it doesn't work that way.

The first contrast to the *Playmakers* scenario is that in real life there is no heads-up, no advance warning. Unlike the team in the show, people surrounding swimming—USA Swimming [the sport's national governing body], the USOC [United States Olympic Committee], the IOC—want to catch the cheaters. They want to clean up the sport. The only notice I get when I'm getting tested is the time it takes to walk from my front door, the pool deck, or the gym floor—wherever they found me—to the bathroom.

As a swimmer there isn't just one league or outsourced company that has jurisdiction to drug test. The Fédération Internationale Natation Amateur, the United States Olympic Committee, the International Olympic Committee, and the World Anti-Doping Agency can all send someone to test me. And they can choose the time and place, weekday or weekend, vacation or holiday. And they know where I am, every day of the year. I have to make sure of that by submitting a detailed schedule to USA Swimming, which distributes it, ensuring I'm tracked.

Depending on the year, I'm drug tested anywhere from 10 to 30 times. At some meets it's possible to get tested four times in a week, sometimes months pass without a test. Other times, much to the dismay of coaches, drug testers from two federations will show up two days in a row. It's just how it works, trying to keep up the element of surprise. In addition, unlike other sports, the same people don't continually test the same athletes. There are some drug testing officers I've seen half a dozen times, but generally they come from all over. Living in Washington I've had officers drive from Oregon; California; Idaho; Nevada; Victoria, BC; they've even flown in from Ontario and Toronto.

When they show up they go through the formalities, show the badge, say where they're from, why they are there. Then they follow me into the bathroom and watch while I provide a sample. If you don't have to go, they'll wait. And once they show up, the rules are that I can't leave their sight. If I go change, they follow and watch. If I shower, they watch. If I eat, they're watching. They're your best friend until your sample has been divided into two cups and all the proper paperwork signed.

Over the years I've had to cut dates and vacations short, cancel appointments and appearances, all in the name of drug testing. It doesn't bother me a bit. They show up at 4 A.M. or 11 P.M., at my house, the pool, or while I'm out at dinner.

Do I ever worry about testing positive? No. I do the best I can to make sure every supplement I take is clean. If I have the slightest doubt, I don't touch it. I don't take creatine because it has been reported as highly probable to be subject to cross-contamination. I only take supplements from one company, a nutraceuticals company to which I'm contracted. I believe in their products, and they believe in me. My contract states that they're responsible to keep their supplements clean and in line with the drug testing regulations to which I'm subject to. My career is invested in them, they're invested in me.

Do these strict rules bother me? No. What bothers me is that other countries don't test their athletes, or don't test them enough. Or, they cover up whatever they find and instead of working to clean up their sports, they work to cover their tracks.

In truth, I don't blame people who use steroids for their own reasons, in their own personal lives, outside of athletics. But rules are rules, and they need to be followed. If an athlete competes in a drug-tested sport, breaking that rule should be cause for immediate suspension. Athletes should support this, and one of the best ways is to fully cooperate with drug testing procedures. If I knew it was helping to keep the sport clean, I would submit to testing every single day of the year, no matter how inconvenient it is.

To me, sports means something. The Olympics mean something. For a lot of people the games are a means to an end, a path to fame. Maybe it's because I'm in a sport that tends to fade away from the public eye between each Olympiad, but I still smile when I hear the Olympic theme song, and I think about camaraderie, and national pride, not money and endorsements. For some time, USAToday.com has run a log of steroid-related stories on its Web site. And to look at it hurts, because it lists a disgustingly long list of steroid-related stories, positive test results, and confessions, right next to a picture of a very familiar Olympic gold medal: a gold medal from the Sydney games. I have two of those, and to think about them in the same context of steroids and other illegal performance-enhancing substances is disheartening. I'd like to think everyone who took one of those home was clean and achieved the top prize in his sport by his own merit, but I know it would be foolish to believe that.

At least when I get up on the blocks, I know I'm clean. When I hold my medals from Nationals, the World Championships, the Olympics, I can squeeze them and smile, because that was all me, hard work, and natural ability. And that makes winning so much sweeter.

4

Drugs: Who, What, and Why

So many different types of steroids and other performance-enhancing drugs are on the market today—both in pharmacies around the world and in makeshift labs in America—that it's impossible to test for them all. But there are still some drugs that just won't go away because of how they work and the benefits realized when they are used by an individual, no matter what the potential side effects are. In different sports there are different drugs of choice. Some can be modified for the right price to avoid detection, which was apparent with the BALCO scandal, and others are, at least as of yet, unable to be both effective and elusive. To better understand the situation of steroids and other drugs in sports, it's important to know what specific drugs are preferred in what sports and what type of activity. Naturally the expectation is that these drugs will increase performance—that's a given—but how? Why do some cyclists love EPO (not a steroid) and why do bodybuilders love testosterone? To understand it all, let's look at the form and function of different drugs and why it's improper and irresponsible for all drugs to be grouped under one banner.

DRUG: human growth hormone (HGH)

WHAT IT IS: HGH is not a steroid. Often in the media when an athlete is caught using or admits having used HGH, the "steroid" flag is falsely raised. HGH is a peptide hormone secreted and released from the anterior pituitary gland.

HISTORY: HGH has been around for decades and is available for use in antiaging programs. An engineered form called Serostim has been approved by the Food and Drug Administration for use by AIDS patients suffering from muscle wasting. Interestingly, this hormone used to only be available by extraction from the pituitary gland of cadavers, and thus was known to potentially infect an unsuspecting user with a disease.

COMMON USES: because of its tissue-growth benefits, it is often used to treat age-related issues. A study on the effects of human growth hormone in men over 60, "Effects of Human Growth Hormone in Men Over 60 Years Old," published in the *New England Journal of Medicine* in 1990 concluded, "Diminished secretion of growth hormone is responsible in part for the decrease of lean body mass, the expansion of adipose-tissue mass, and the thinning of the skin that occur in old age."

Because of these findings, HGH has been used to combat these deficiencies, but it has also been used by athletes ranging from competitive bodybuilders to hockey players to Olympic swimmers, but for many different reasons.

HGH has been shown to decrease adipose tissue, which is more commonly known as body fat. Bodybuilders can use the hormone to help improve their appearances quicker along with their limited diets. Endurance athletes have been known to use HGH because studies have proven the substance increases the number of oxygen-carrying red blood cells in the body.

SIDE EFFECTS: the downside of HGH therapy on individuals in need of the drug is limited to nonexistent. For healthy individuals taking HGH, several problems may occur. Edema, or water retention, is a more common, basic side effect. Acromegaly, the most serious, is unnatural growth of bone and thickening of the skin, which can cause physical features to become distorted. HGH can also cause organs to grow. There are also theories, though not strictly proven, that the use of exogenous growth hormone can speed the growth of cancers and tumors.

DRUG: testosterone

WHAT IT IS: various types of anabolic steroids deliver testosterone, the male hormone. The different esters of the drug release the substance over different ranges of time and provide various doses.

HISTORY: synthetic forms of testosterone have been used for decades to treat men who suffer from feminization because of high estrogen levels and for men whose bodies do not produce an adequate amount of the hormone.

COMMON USES: muscle building in recreational users and athletes. As of late, science has found that testosterone is also effective in treating depression, often better than other prescription drugs, some of which have been believed to cause suicidal thoughts. Testosterone has also been found to be very useful in increasing sex drive in patients with extremely low libido, with less side effects than drugs such as Viagra.

SIDE EFFECTS: testosterone use in some individuals at high doses can often lead to temporarily high levels of estrogen, which can lead to the formation of breast tissue in men. The drug also causes the body to shut down natural production, which may lead to shrinkage of the testicles. This side effect reverses itself as the body returns to its natural working order. Prolonged use of high doses can cause the body to naturally produce less testosterone when the user is off the drug. Hair loss can also be found in men prone to male pattern baldness, and prostate hypertrophy may occur.

DRUG: clenbuterol

WHAT IT IS: clenbuterol is often used to help clear blockage of the air pathways, much like ephedra. It is also used like ephedra for fat loss and as a stimulant by athletes and individual users. Clenbuterol is not a steroid.

COMMON USES: fat loss, energy stimulant. Often cycled with anabolic steroids because of catabolic effects.

SIDE EFFECTS: clenbuterol can severely raise blood pressure and internal body temperature, causing sweats and tremors for some users. While clenbuterol does increase the shedding of adipose tissue in the body, it also promotes a quicker breakdown and use of proteins, making it increase the rate of muscular catabolism. High doses of clenbuterol have also been shown to cause myocardial tissue damage in mice, though the same has not been proven to occur in humans.

DRUG: Cytomel (T3)

WHAT IT IS: a synthetic form of the thyroid hormone. T3 is not a steroid.

COMMON USES: doctors often prescribe Cytomel for individuals with thyroid irregularities. Because of the metabolic control the thyroid holds on the body, the drug is used by nonathletes, recreational athletes, and professionals alike to stimulate fat loss.

SIDE EFFECTS: hyperthyroidism, shutdown of natural thyroid hormone production, and lifetime reliance on Cytomel if used improperly. As with clenbuterol, T3 also increases the metabolism and can cause muscle breakdown with inadequate protein, and as such is used often in conjunction with anabolic steroids.

Steroids and other drugs are all very different compounds. While some are similar to others, their effects and potential side effects are different and should be treated appropriately. The media often portrays any illegal substance as a steroid; this isn't true. Society can't arrive at an honest perception of steroids, whether for or against, without the truth in hand.

But steroids, despite their intended benefits and, seemingly, their promises to increase performance, don't always do so. A main component in steroid use is the psychological effect, which is addressed by Dr. Charlie Maher in chapter 11. The following account serves as an example that, with steroids, better performance is not a guarantee.

Steroids: A Broken Promise

I won't say who I am because I still compete. What I can say is that I did use steroids, I was never caught, and I did go to the Olympics. While in Athens, supposedly at the biggest competition of my career, I was still taking drugs. The biggest problem wasn't beating drug tests, it was staying calm. I knew I was cheating, but it was an addiction. Not the drugs, but the rush. I was on a substance that I ran out of a week before my first competition, so I had a team assistant step out to a Greek pharmacy and look for it. She couldn't find it, and I was without something I thought I needed. I was suffering from severe anxiety at this point and almost wanted to withdraw. After telling a teammate, I found this person was on the same drug and had plenty to spare. I started to feel good again. I was training well, showing well, and it was time to compete. Basically I felt I already had a medal, and I was pretty sure it would be gold.

And then, even after being so confident, the eve of the competition came and I started to cry. I think this was the point I realized I hated myself for what I was doing. I was supposedly representing my country, my sport, myself, and I was cheating. Yeah, of course a lot of other people were doing the same thing, but I couldn't worry about them. It was me. I knew I was cheating, I knew I was lying. The needles didn't bother me, I didn't have any nasty, irreversible side effects, at least not physically. It was the mental side effects that were getting to me. I was on drugs, I was supposed to be better because of them. But in reality, since I started on the steroids I had only put together personal bests twice in 10 tries. I looked stronger, I felt stronger, but it didn't come together when I needed it. And it didn't at the Olympics, either. And I cried then, having not won a medal, having finished near the bottom of the final. And then I dried up and quit the tears. It came to pass that I was actually happy I didn't medal. If I would have, I would have never known if it was me or the drugs that won it. I'd be living a lie, living like a hero but knowing I was a cheater. I'm glad I don't have that on my heart. The only thing I regret is taking a spot on the Olympic team from someone who might have been clean. They deserved it, I didn't.

I'm drug free now and performing better than ever, better than I ever did when I was injecting myself and having other people inject me with drugs, most of which I couldn't even pronounce. If I make the next Olympic team, I'll do it clean, and I'll be proud.

A Clinical Look at the Psychology of Steroid Use
by Dr. Roland A. Carlstedt

THE CRITICAL MOMENTS AND ATHLETE'S PROFILE MODELS OF PEAK PERFORMANCE: PSYCHOLOGICAL FACTORS DRIVING STEROID USE

What motivates athletes to take steroids? What makes a player risk his health or reputation just to run faster, jump higher, or hit farther? What pyschosociological factors are at the heart of pharmacological cheating? Is it our success, money, and celebrity-oriented culture? Perhaps parents are to blame—you know, those pushy moms and dads who live vicariously through their children, in hopes their kids will achieve the athletic success they failed to attain. Or, is it more complex than that? Does it even matter knowing why an athlete cheats?

From a moralistic perspective the bottom line is clear-cut: athlete cheaters are fraudsters who should be punished. To the moralist, it doesn't really matter *why* people do things; the fact is, when rules and laws are violated, someone suffers—and someone must pay for the damage done to others.

From a clinical or psychological perspective, getting to the root of criminal or morally reprehensible behavior is a priority, since in order to induce, shape, or manipulate change in a positive direction, one needs to know what is driving a behavioral propensity or problem. When it comes to athlete drug use, clinicians and researchers need to know the root mediators of this taboo behavior before it can be addressed in the context of intervention or eradication programs. In contrast to the punitive-moralistic perspective—one that demands swift punishment—the psychological-clinical approach is to study a phenomenon, identify causal relationships among factors that induce or contribute to a problem, and eventually, to intervene on behalf of the perpetrator, who is viewed not as "amoral scum," but as a fallible human being who needs to be helped.

So what sort of an athlete dopes? What psychological traits or tendencies influence a player to risk it all for that elusive *zone* state? What mind-body processes underlie doping?

THE NEUROSCIENCE AND PSYCHOLOGY OF DOPING: AN EVIDENCE-BASED PERSPECTIVE

The frontal lobes of the brain are the seat of volition and analytic thinking. When an athlete decides to dope, to a certain extent, this brain region is involved in processing arguments for or against engaging in this behavior. We use the frontal lobes to plan, rationalize, envision our future, and even ponder our mortality. But, frontal lobes are not all the same. Especially in children and adolescents, this cortical structure is still evolving; it has not developed the mass and connection strengths that are associated with rational decision making and reduced impulsivity. In our youth the frontal lobes are very malleable and shaped by our experiences, culture, parents, siblings, and peers. It is a time when moral reasoning develops, a formative life-epoch that sets the stage for future behavior in adulthood. It is a life phase during which the environment and significant others can influence an individual, for better or worse.

Recent research has linked youth-perpetrated crime, violence, and antisocial behavior to underdeveloped frontal lobes (or frontal lobes in development). It appears that an underdeveloped or stunted individual's planning ability and awareness of the consequences of his behavior is overridden or dominated by base pleasure or reward-seeking impulses emanating from more primitive, deep-lying brain structures. In an individual lacking sufficient frontal lobe–based inhibitory and analytic abilities, the desire to achieve gratification is usually much stronger than one's ability to resist temptation (something that can and often does continue into adulthood).

Survival instincts also involve the frontal lobes—not only those used to avoid the proverbial saber-toothed tiger, but also, for example, those employed by an athlete who wishes to stave off being cut from a team. An athlete with frontal lobe dysfunction who is worried about being dropped from the team may not be able to appropriately distinguish stimuli—such as his team owner's or coach's feedback—as being either threatening or well intended. The frontal-lobe-challenged athlete who fears losing his contract and livelihood might easily misinterpret a coach's signal to mean they are in trouble, when all the coach wanted to do was give the player some advice. Because of a gross misinterpretation of a coach's body language or verbal inflection, a vulnerable athlete panics and tries to "instantly" improve, a dynamic that may lead to a decision to dope. Combine faulty frontal-lobe-generated irrational fears, an excessive desire to succeed and attain instant gratification, and the inability to inhibit survival or pleasure impulses and cope with adversity, and you have a recipe for substance abuse.

Essentially, abhorrent behavior (like doping and cheating) occurs when signals from primitive brain structures (that really don't give a damn about what anyone thinks) override the inhibitory and analytic function of certain areas of the frontal lobes in a quest for instant gratification or survival.

Individuals with dysfunctional frontal lobes (in the context of our societal norms and mores) have a diminished sense of behavioral consequences, and an inability to extrapolate the effects of their maladaptive behavior into the future. They are incapable of imagining how their behavior will negatively affect their future life, health, well-being, and social stature. Yet, paradoxically, they are very adept at envisioning the positive aspects of even socially unacceptable behavior; for example, believing that they will get away with doping and thereby reach fame and fortune. There is a tendency on the part of stunted "frontal-lobers" to live in the here and now, to seek out immediate rewards, and to avoid pain and effort—all in an attempt to find an easy way to riches and recognition. Add the stress associated with having to perform at the highest level, day in and day out, to the above equation, and a dysfunctional frontal lobe becomes even more erratic and chaotic, leading to instant decisions that one may regret for a lifetime—including the decision to dope.

EMERGING EVIDENCE:
FRONTAL LOBE SUBTYPES AND THE ATHLETE'S PROFILE

Evidence implicating frontal lobe involvement in addictive behavior and peak performance processes stems from various lines of research, including mine. Findings are converging to explain how shifts in brain hemispheric activation in the frontal lobes affect performance and drive addiction.

What has been found is that a significant number of athletes and dopers exhibit similar brain dynamics when it comes to certain moments of decision making, repetitive behaviors (training habits vs. drug-procurement habits), and the ability to benefit from interventions (e.g., psychotherapy, mental training, and abstinence).

Three key measures that have been localized in either the right or left frontal lobes have been shown to mediate how external or internal stimuli are processed and affect behavior. The first measure is *hypnotic susceptibility*. It can be viewed as the "focus" factor, in that people who are high in this trait have a heightened ability to intensely concentrate. Hypnotic susceptibility has been localized in the brain bilaterally. Depending upon whether one is involved in a verbal or a perceptual/imaginative task determines whether the left or right frontal lobes are more or less active in the context of the hypnotic state.

Obviously, intense concentration can be desirable if your focus is directed toward a task at hand, like hitting a ball, but disastrous if it is constantly and intensely directed inward and onto thoughts, especially negative ones, like "I hope I get a hit." Predominantly negative intrusive cognitions are a hallmark of *neuroticism*, the second measure in a troika of traits that are central to most behavior. High hypnotic susceptibility when combined with high neuroticism leads to problems, especially under conditions of increasing stress—similar to what an athlete faces during competition, or what an addict experiences when his next fix is due.

What occurs then is that neuroticism, which has been localized in the right frontal regions of the brain, activates in response to fight-or-flight signals emanating from the limbic region (amygdala) and infiltrates the left frontal lobe. The left frontal lobe is known as being the verbal, ruminative part of the brain. When negative thoughts are activated and overwhelm the verbal left half of the frontal lobes, people who are high in hypnotic susceptibility tend to intensely focus on these neuroticism-generated cognitions, instead of the task at hand (e.g., the flight of the ball). This undermines peak performance that is reflected in a seamless left-to-right shift in frontal brain activation prior to the initiation of a planned action, or doing something (e.g., starting to swing the bat).

During zone or peak performance states, one does not fixate on internal thoughts; instead, that "just do it" mode kicks in. By contrast, athletes who are dogged by constant neuroticism, in the presence of high hypnotic susceptibility, frequently experience turmoil that destroys motor performance. Negatively predisposed athletes often remain stuck in the ruminative left frontal brain hemisphere, especially come crunch time. They fixate on negative thoughts and emotions instead of pre-action strategic planning, which leads to performance breakdowns. These athletes end up "thinking it" instead of "just doing it." Athletes who are concurrently high in hypnotic susceptibility and neuroticism are at risk for a wide variety of problems, including health issues, addiction, and breakdowns in psychological performance.

The third factor in the performance and doping equation is *repressive* or *subliminal coping*. This factor is the "great facilitator" or "great protector," in that it has been shown to functionally inhibit or shut down the negative thought patterns associated with high neuroticism, thereby preventing them from entering the left frontal lobe to disrupt performance in athletes.

Dr. Denise Fortino's research in substance abusers and mine in athletes revealed that both of these populations exhibited similar shifts in brain activation and behaviors consistent with their levels of hypnotic susceptibility, neuroticism, and repressive coping.

The most protective profile of factors was found to be high or low hypnotic susceptibility, low neuroticism, and high repressive or subliminal coping. Athletes with this profile performed the best come crunch time, and addicts having this profile were most likely to recover. By contrast, athletes and addicts who were highest in hypnotic susceptibility, highest in neuroticism, and lowest in repressive coping were most likely to fail during critical moments, or fail to say no to a drug offer (a critical moment for an addict).

The *high hypnotic susceptibility/high neuroticism* combination is likely to be present in many dopers. Since athletes with this profile (in the absence of high repressive coping) are continually bombarded with disruptive negative thoughts, they are constantly under physical and mental stress. They are nervous, and desperately want to achieve a state of balance. Their high level of hypnotic susceptibility locks in on negative thoughts, and plots in a chaotic and irrational manner how to alleviate ongoing mind-body disharmony. Stress caused by unrealistic performance goals and the desire and hypermotivation to succeed in a grand manner can drive an athlete over the edge to cheat.

Athletes who are high in hypnotic susceptibility can convince themselves of just about anything (or be convinced of anything)—like they won't get caught if they dope, and will go on to become superstars if they do. They are also very good at rationalizing, and thereby quite capable of deluding themselves into believing that they are *not* cheating, or that since everyone is doing it, they are only leveling the playing field.

The high hypnotizable is also very prone to the placebo effect, and thus willing to believe that any medication or elixir will really work. Perhaps this explains why numerous suspected dopers who have come clean suddenly experience performance decrements that seem inexplicable. Jason Giambi, the admitted Yankees steroid user, is a case in point. It is likely he actually believed that chemicals were at the heart of his best successes, and since he appears to no longer be on dope, he probably feels vulnerable and a lesser athlete. Only now is he starting to come around. He is an important case study in that if he can return to his former form on the basis of hard work alone, his example will go a long way toward helping dispel doping performance-enhancement myths.

The *high hypnotic susceptibility/high neuroticism/low repressive coping profile* is one that should be red-flagged in all athletes. Not only are athletes with this profile more likely to choke during critical moments of competition, but also, because of the heightened pressure and internal chatter they continually experience, they are more apt to succumb to temptation and seek the easy way out of a performance hole or stress situation. They are more likely to dope than athletes who have a more neutral or psychological performance facilitative profile.

Fortunately, the high hypnotizable neurotic is usually very amenable to treatment or mental training. Consequently, coaches and teams should screen athletes using my protocol (Carlstedt Protocol) to establish an individual's *Athlete's Profile*. At-risk athletes can be assessed, monitored, and given psychological skills training to improve performance. This has been shown to work more effectively than giving in to doping, and merely hoping they will improve. Interventions also exist to directly exert a "corrective" effect on frontal lobe functioning (that can be objectively documented), using sophisticated brain imaging techniques. Neurofeedback, one of these techniques, can induce long-term positive change in the frontal lobe, or so-called executive functioning, to improve mental and physical health.

The evidence-based athlete assessment and mental training methods I use in my protocol have been shown to not only boost psychological performance, but also to have an impact on health and well-being by facilitating mind-body harmony both on and off the playing field. This cannot be said about doping. On the contrary, doping has not been found to unequivocally help the masses of athletes perform better. However, it has been associated with negative health consequences that need to—and can—be avoided.

DO STEROIDS REALLY ENHANCE PERFORMANCE? MYTH AND ANECDOTES

The suspects are known: the admitted and alleged consumers of steroids and other chemical substances that supposedly enhance athletic performance. In baseball there's Jason Giambi, a self-confessed injector of steroids whose admission of guilt has cast a shadow over his previous statistical accomplishments. Then there's

Barry Bonds, the ultimate superathlete, who, although not admitting to knowingly having taken steroids, nevertheless has emerged as the "überdoper" in the eyes of many baseball fans. Track and field also has a legacy of steroid abuse going back to Ben Johnson, who was virtually caught in the act of taking a "no-no" drug. More recently, Marion Jones has emerged as the Barry Bonds of sprinters, another vehement denier who has become stigmatized as a cheater. In tennis, two Argentinean French Open finalists, Guillermo Coria and Mariano Puerta, were caught taking steroid-based substances and were suspended from the ATP Tour for months. Even cycling great Lance Armstrong has not gone unscathed, with his incredible Tour de France performances being called into question.

I could go on and mention scores of other confirmed and suspected lesser-known dopers who have been outed in just about every sport, but nobodies are mostly average athletes who do not make the headlines. Their accomplishments are not stellar or record breaking. Pharma-cheaters could just as easily be your .220 hitter, 300th-ranked player, or last-finishing runner as your 60 home-run hitter or 2,000-yard rusher. Until they failed their drug tests, you probably never heard of Stefan Koubek, David Fuentes, or Alvin Harrison and other lowly athletes who have fallen into oblivion since being exposed. Other underachievers or just plain average athletes continue to dope without consequences, both in terms of being exposed and in failing to perform better. The same could be said of your superstar genre of dopers, some of whom think that the dope is the key to their success, when it most likely is not.

Ironically, many second-string dopers probably use the same concoctions, potions, and dosage levels as the hero-cheat colleagues they once dreamed of surpassing. Some of these tier-two druggies probably did not have a clue that certain superstars were taking drugs themselves. Others may have suspected or known such, and were seduced by the illusion that maybe their drugs were better than those of the star users, and that they would indeed achieve glory some day.

What were the superstar cheaters thinking? Did they believe that they would become even better athletes and performers, something they could not achieve without chemical help? Or did they have some of the same thoughts that plagued the athletes at their heels, namely, "If I want to stay ahead of the game, or excel even more, I'd better ingest or shoot up."

So why do athletes dope? Why do they take steroids and other illegal, so-called performance-enhancing drugs? The pervasive belief is that many, if not all, of the banned substances being ingested or injected by athletes do indeed enhance performance. Many argue that Barry Bonds's spate of 50-plus homer seasons can be traced to the onset of steroid use, since prior to that, at best he only had moderately elevated long-ball numbers. Similar speculation has dogged other baseball players, including Sammy Sosa and Mark McGwire, and, of course, Jose Canseco, who has openly attributed his improved performance to steroid use. Case studies of highly visible and successful athletes are often cited as proof that pharmacological intervention enhances performance dramatically. Performance gains are linked to well-known drug-mediated physiological and behavioral changes, including increased muscle mass, strength, and aggressiveness, as though an existing one-to-one or linear dose-response relationship between a drug and certain bodily processes (e.g., grip strength, oxygen uptake) automatically will improve an actual objective performance measure (e.g., increased home runs).

Sure, we can document increases in muscle mass and reduced body fat indexes, as well as "enhanced recovery" postinjury, or after grueling competition, along with other bodily effects. In sports like wrestling, weight lifting, and football, it's seemingly a no-brainer that "more muscle" equals "more strength" and the subsequent ability to overpower an opponent who does not match up physically. Although there may be something to these notions, and there is research attesting to the restorative and "physiologically enhancing" properties of numerous illegal potions and elixirs, there is much more to the performance equation than substance-driven bodily responses (e.g., strength increases because of steroids).

For example, there is not a one-to-one association between physical factors such as weight, height, muscle mass, and strength, and the ability to outblock, outwrestle, or outfight an opponent—or else the vastly undersized Denver Broncos' offensive line would not have been able to open the holes that allowed their rushing game to be one of the best in the NFL for the past several years. The technical acumen of their linesmen negated the hugeness of many of their defensive opponents. Although we don't know who, if anyone, on the Broncos' offensive line or other teams took steroids, the fact is that physical superiority, whether ill or legally gained, does not necessarily result in athletic success or dominance. Other David-versus-Goliath matchups—resulting in victories on the part of smaller and "weaker" athletes over "giants"—point to the complexity of the performance equation, a formula consisting of hundreds of predictor variables and numerous objective/quantifiable performance or outcome measures (e.g., Michael Chang's defeat of Ivan Lendl in the French Open in 1989).

The belief that drug-induced physiological changes—whether resulting in muscular genesis, greater oxygen-transporting red blood cells, or alterations in brain function (e.g., psychostimulant reduction in EEG theta activity to enhance focus, Ritalin)—will improve performance is fallacious when viewed in the context of sophisticated methodological and statistical approaches to the analysis of sport performance.

DOCUMENTING OR PREDICTING THE EFFECTS OF STEROID USE ON PERFORMANCE

In order to determine scientifically the effects of a given drug on performance, we need to operationalize the term "performance." To operationalize means to define empirically what a certain construct or measure means. Performance can mean many things. Consequently, we must establish, as precisely as possible, the statistical parameters or benchmarks of performance. One rudimentary statistical procedure to determine the effects of one variable on another is to use correlation or simple linear-regression techniques. In the context of examining the effects of, say, a steroid on performance, one could look at how this drug contributes toward influencing performance on an objective outcome measure—for example, batting average, or first-service percentage (tennis). We might observe a positive correlation between Barry Bonds's seasonal home run totals and use of steroids; that is, a linear dose-response relationship, with more home runs being associated with increasing levels or use of steroids.

On the other hand, we might find out that Jose Canseco, although hitting more home runs during a couple of seasons in which he took "more" steroids, actually had a lower batting average and even worse critical moments (e.g., men-on-base batting-average statistics), revealing a negative correlation between steroid use and batting average. However, single-case examples like the ones above can lead to premature and erroneous conclusions about relationships between specific drugs and performance outcome. The notion that because Bonds hit more home runs after taking steroids, steroid use leads to more home runs—and therefore all athletes should take steroids—has no scientific credibility. Yet, such logic is behind the decision of many athletes to take steroids.

In order to better study relationships between specific doping substances and outcome measures, we must achieve a level of statistical power that is acceptable for the purpose of establishing or predicting performance (e.g., steroid use and home run performance). This would require us to examine at least 25 baseball players who are known dopers to better illuminate the doping-performance link. Assuming these ballplayers all took the same doses at the same intervals, one would find that the drug has a canceling effect. That is, since all of these athletes took the same drug, it is doubtful that the key component or predictor variable in the performance equation would be the drug, especially since dosage and intervals were the same for each athlete.

One could argue, though, that not all athletes dope; and, of course, it would be very difficult to carry out a controlled study of athletes who do, since who among them would want to admit this, thereby exposing themselves to sanctions? If one grants that not all athletes dope, thus negating the canceling effect, one would still need to establish evidence that the effects of a drug supersede the influence of numerous other performance factors that have actually been shown to mediate a particular statistical outcome measure (e.g., the effects of visual acuity or reaction time on batting).

To illustrate, let's say Barry Bonds was a big-time doper, and Hank Aaron, as we know, was not; or, say Albert Pujols and three other members of the top-ten home run producers do not dope, and the remaining five do. If this was true, the question one would need to ask is, "To what extent can one attribute Bonds's home run prowess to doping, or Hank Aaron's, Pujols's, and clean top-ten colleagues' stats to nondoping or other factors?" Would doping still be the critical measure in the homer performance equation when comparing dopers versus nondopers who exhibit similar statistical output?

To answer the above empirical questions and address other performance issues associated with doping, we could do the following: we could test athletes who admit to doping at the same doses and intervals, and then are also controlled for weight, height, muscle mass, age, and other physical measures. We might be able to find these athletes in the sports of weight lifting, wrestling, boxing, rowing, and other strength sports. If given guaranteed anonymity, we might then be able to carry out a controlled experiment whereby athletes are tested relative to strength, quickness, and technical tasks, or are merely made to compete (e.g., powerlifting or wrestling). Since our subjects have all doped to the same extent and were perfectly matched on other physical measures, best performers or winners would emerge on the basis of mediating factors that have nothing to do with the taken drug. Thus, within this cohort of athletes, whether they were professionals or in high school, doping would not be a driving influence in establishing the best weight lifter or wrestler.

Of course, one could argue that irrespective of whether doping exerts a canceling effect, the fact is that most athletes in certain sports dope. In other words, in order to get to a high level in many sports, you have to dope, even though doping alone will not ensure that you will succeed once you get there. While it is suspected that most athletes must dope to reach the upper echelons of some sports, this must be unequivocally documented before one can reach an infallible conclusion about the need to dope to get to a certain level of skill. One would also need unequivocal evidence that nondopers in so-called doper sports cannot defeat dopers or perform at the highest levels before one can conclude with certainty that doping improves performance in a specific sport, or does so relative to a specific sport's important outcome measures (e.g., takedowns in wrestling).

Science defies or contests anecdotes and suppositions. It demands investigative rigor and hard evidence. Consequently, even in so-called known doper sports like weight lifting—where the utility of doping may be known (it'll get you to the top), because of its canceling effect—once you get there, the playing field becomes level. Success is then contingent on numerous other variables and their interactions, and not on the basis of doping per se.

Unfortunately, when it comes to many other sports, it's not that simple. There is no canceling effect—just suspected numbers of athletes who dope or do not dope. However, in sports that involve a plethora of personal, opponent, physical, technical, motor, psychological, and other factors, doping merely becomes one of many factors that differentially contribute to the performance equation, if at all. Using the Bonds/Aaron/Pujols example, it becomes clear that some great home run hitters were/are dopers, while others were/are clean. We know Aaron didn't dope, we suspect that Bonds did, and for the sake of argument, let us assume that some top-ten home run hitters dope and others do not. Obviously, in this scenario there is a quasi-canceling effect, with both dopers and nondopers being at the top when it comes to home run hitting. But let's also not forget about the scores of baseball players who—despite doping and having become bigger and stronger—still fail to hit many long balls.

Although Bonds's incredible records stand out, single-case studies or examples do not constitute the highest level of evidence. They lead to speculation and hypotheses, but must be viewed with caution. It is especially flawed to cite case studies selectively, choosing those that fit one's theory while ignoring others that don't. Remember, there have been *hundreds* of dopers, maybe even *thousands*, and yet only a handful of superstar and record-breaker dopers like Bonds have emerged. While the performance gains of some of these cheaters may appear dramatic, just think of the many dopers you have never heard of, or clean superstars who are contemporaries of known superstar dopers who achieve equally or even more superlative statistics (e.g., Ichiro Suzuki's hitting records). Spectacular performance gains are not necessarily attributable to illegal substances, and no drugs have been found that unequivocally enhance performance, especially during critical moments of competition.

Since the ability to exhibit optimal mind-body control when it counts the most is the ultimate benchmark of mental toughness, I would argue that doing drugs is the ultimate sign of mental weakness and the height of egotism. While drugs may have a placebo effect on *certain susceptible athletes* and appear upon superficial examination to help *some athletes* in specific sports during routine moments of competition, they have not been found to foster mental toughness, a complex ability developed over time that is not drug related. My research has demonstrated that mental toughness or weakness is driven by constellations or interactions of three crucial psychological factors and brain processes that are intimately linked to focus, intensity, and cognitive processing—key components of sport performance.

Research on the effects of common illegal drugs that athletes use can at best be described as global, and revealing only in terms of the drugs' ability to affect certain physiological changes. As previously mentioned, such changes, including more strength, do not equate with enhanced performance; that is an assumption, not a scientific finding. The effects of illegal drugs on microlevel mind-body processes (e.g., rate of neuron firing in the brain; motor-priming) and their ability to improve objective sport-specific performance measures (e.g., basketball field goal percentage in the last minute of a game) are to a large extent unknown.

Performance must also be looked at in the context of team performance. How many World Series has Bonds's team won? How do individual performance statistics of dopers contribute to a team's won-lost record? Importantly, what is the downside of drug use in the big picture? If we are going to speculate about the enhancing effects of drugs, it is justifiable to speculate about injuries, player downtime, illness, and even athlete deaths and their effects on teams.

Performance is a complex issue. I have coined the term *performance equation* to refer to all factors that might conceivably or demonstrably affect objective performance outcome measures. As you can imagine, there are hundreds of variables that predict or explain performance on objective statistical outcome measures. Predictor variables can be psychological or physical in nature, as well as technical and strategic. Doping could also be a predictor variable. What's more, these variables change in their ability to predict performance outcome as a function of critical moments, or at crunch time.

Predictor variables in the performance equation might include visual acuity, technical ability, foot speed, heart rate variability, heart rate deceleration, cognitive processing EEG markers, hypnotic susceptibility, subliminal attention, neuroticism, subliminal reactivity, repressive coping, subliminal coping, caffeine, and steroid dose (to name a few). If we were to analyze all of these measures relative to their effects on, say, the won-loss record of a tennis player, home runs hit or strikeouts pitched, or any number of other sport-specific objective statistical outcome measures, we would get to the heart of how much of an impact illegal substances or doping have on performance.

Complex multiple regression and other statistical modeling procedures would soon illuminate the contribution (or lack thereof), of, for example, steroids to a selected performance measure in a specific sport. Sure, if we were to analyze the effects of steroids on muscle mass or recovery time, or the extent to which blood doping increases oxygen uptake, we would find a high correspondence between doping (predictor measure) and physiological change (outcome measure), but one should not assume that physiological changes automatically lead to enhanced performance when objective statistical indicators are used as the benchmark of athletic proficiency. That has never been demonstrated.

However, what *has* been shown is that numerous predictor variables, including some of the ones mentioned above, do have a significant and potent mediating effect on performance. My research on critical moments during competition has implicated subliminal attention, subliminal reactivity, subliminal coping, and relative brain hemispheric activation as crucial factors in predicting crunch-time performance to a high degree of certainty. Data from my investigation of over 700 athletes from seven sports demonstrated that psychological factors and processes (brain-mind) supersede physical, technical, and motor (e.g., strength) in explaining or predicting performance during critical moments of competition. The measures that I have isolated can be considered Primary Higher Order (PHO) factors that influence virtually all processes associated with a sport-specific action or task—especially when peak performance is a must, or when the game is on the line (e.g., PHO psychological factors affect reaction time, speed, strength, etc.).

Come crunch time, steroid-obtained strength or more red blood cells won't help you hit a home run or get out of the blocks faster if your constellation of PHO factors disrupts the delicate mind-body balance that is required to respond in an efficient manner, free from subliminal, negative, intrusive thoughts.

Since drugs like steroids and psychostimulants, and procedures like blood doping, have not been found to enhance psychological performance, it is illusory to think that drugs hold the key to mental toughness and peak performance. Drugs that are intended to enhance muscle mass, strength, or increase cellular oxygenation will have minimal if any impact in regulating complex mind-body-motor interactions that research has identified as being crucial mediators of peak mental performance. In fact, they may disrupt the delicate mind-body balance so vital to zone states or flow, when it counts the most. Drugs are likely to be counterproductive at times when psychological control is crucial to clutch performance—such as when victory is not predicated on global undefined levels of speed or strength, but instead, on an athlete's ability to fend off intrusive cognitions so as to facilitate motor control.

Before athletes consider taking steroids or other substances, they should learn how to become critical thinkers and not allow myth or anecdotal suppositions to drive their performance-enhancement approaches, potentially ruining both their careers and their health. They should be aware that (1) not all dopers succeed, and in fact, the vast majority don't; (2) not all dopers who get bigger and stronger perform better; (3) scores, if not hundreds, of dopers we have never heard of do not reach the upper levels of their sport; (4) exceptions do not make the rule, so just because Bonds did it doesn't mean you will; (5) conversely, just because Bonds may have done it because of drugs does not mean that Rodriguez or Pujols won't or can't *without* drugs; (6) doping will not help you overcome negative psychological tendencies or make you mentally tough; (7) individual dopers have had little impact on a team's success; (8) hundreds of predictor variables have a greater impact in determining athletic success than do doping substances; and (9) I would predict that athletes who dope are more prone to choking during critical moments of competition.

STEROIDS VERSUS MENTAL TRAINING: LEGAL APPROACHES TO PEAK PERFORMANCE ENHANCEMENT

In contrast to the physical and technical game, which has an abundance of scientific information and data—along with huge volumes of actual objective performance statistics (especially in the sports of baseball, football, and basketball)—when it comes to the mental side of the game, there is a paucity of valid and reliable information about its dynamics. Consequently, potentially revealing measures, such as "zone," "focus," and "mental toughness," have *devolved*—instead of evolved—into potent constructs and sensitive measures of psychological performance. They have become misused and even abused terms that are thrown about carelessly. At face value, they mean nothing. Essentially, the assessment of psychological performance, mental training, and, ultimately, decision making regarding an athlete's mental game and predictions of future performance are often based on anecdotal notions instead of good science.

The sorry state of athlete assessment and interventions (mental training) is a contributing factor to the doping problem. Psychologically vulnerable athletes seeking guidance even at the highest levels of the game encounter anecdotal approaches to athlete evaluation and mental training. Most athletes—including dopers—although aware of the potential sport psychology holds, have not been shown potent data or methods that work. Yes, they have heard about and maybe tried visualization. They are told to set goals, do "self-talk," think positively, and breathe deeply. But in the end, do athletes really improve psychologically? There is little convincing data to support that these methods do much more than convey the *impression* that an athlete is doing something "mental." Athletes don't really buy in to methods that don't have any real or measurable immediate effects. And if they do, they are being fooled, just like dopers tricking themselves into believing they have found the royal road to peak performance.

By contrast, when a baseball player stays in the batting cage for two hours, or a golfer hits hundreds of balls on the driving range, they see an effect. They improve, their timing gets better, and their confidence rises. There's a big difference between hitting a home run out of the batting cage and getting a hit during a critical moment in a World Series game, but one thing is certain: physical and tactical practice have been unequivocally shown to improve performance. On the other hand, mental imagery and other methods (including doping) have not had a similar effect—despite what practitioners with a vested interest in the effectiveness of mental training may tell you. Research on mental training is full of holes, and to a large extent based on weak methodology.

Consequently, why should an athlete look to sport psychology to achieve an immediate gain in performance, when we know that psychological change is a long-term endeavor? Similarly, physical and technical training takes a lot of effort, and still might not erase discrepancies in talent among athletes. So, why not pop a few pills, shoot up, and presto, see an effect? Because an athlete *will* see an effect, and if so predisposed, is likely to associate increased muscle mass, perceived intensity, and focus with better performance. With these results, why wouldn't certain athletes dope? Drugs can exert an enormous placebo effect on athletes who are high in hypnotic susceptibility, more so than mental training, which seems much more nebulous in its effects than doping, and if not done "right," leaves an athlete wondering what did it do, if anything?

However, it's still all a matter of perception. You might believe that doping works—or that mental training does not (or even that it does)—but that does not mean improvement has been demonstrated, or that performance has been enhanced. In the end, the doper, like the devotee of visualization or positive thinking, really does not have a clue about whether that magic bullet really made him a better player—but many certainly think it did.

This "I hope" or "I know" or "I wish" mentality pervades the performance-enhancement arena, while scientific approaches to the mental and, ultimately, the physical-technical game are grossly lacking. This mentality exists despite the fact that potent scientific approaches to the psychological, physical-technical assessment, and mental training of athletes exist, and could be made available to all. Professional sport teams could lead the way by borrowing and adapting techniques from clinical psychology, behavioral medicine, and neuroscience to advance a more scientific approach to performance enhancement.

While knowledge about the physical and technical game is fairly advanced, and standardized methods to improve a player's skills exist in most sports, they have not adequately considered the psychological side of the performance equation. And as we know, the mental game can easily destroy a great physical game come crunch time.

The field of applied sport psychology to a large extent can be blamed for this dismal state. It remains mired in a paradigm that is based in part on weak data, nonvalidated interventions, and faulty assessment methods. It is thus no wonder that professional sports teams spend millions of dollars on the technical and physical development of athletes, yet allow unqualified persons to do "mental training" (usually stereotypical visualization or relaxation) exercises. Or, at best, they employ trained sport psychologists who are well intentioned but woefully unexposed to sophisticated methods and advanced knowledge, relegating sport psychology to the back of team priority lists.

It is also no wonder that many athletes dope, considering the inability of conventional approaches to performance enhancement to demonstrate their effectiveness.

Although it is widely accepted that the mental game is the most important aspect of peak performance, especially during critical moments of competition, sport psychology still has stepchild status when it comes to player-development funding by professional sports teams. Could that be, perhaps, because the field and its practitioners have very little to offer in terms of valid methods and hard data? Moreover, while teams recognize the importance of the mental side of the game, decision makers have received only minimal if any guidance regarding scientific approaches to mental peak performance from the field of sport psychology. Instead, general managers are sold outdated approaches that largely rely on visualization and relaxation techniques applied en masse, or worse yet, are seduced by charlatans peddling all sorts of mental snake oil as science (e.g., brain typing). Or worse, players and athletes seek help in the form of drugs and chemicals.

If the field of sport psychology is to make inroads into professional sports and provide all athletes the best possible service and methods—and an alternative for the many dopers seeking that edge at the expense of their health and reputation—a paradigm shift pertaining to athlete assessment and mental training needs to occur. It must be based on rigorous scientific approaches and methods, similar to those seen in the clinical realm, where major advances have been made in patient diagnosis and treatment. New approaches to athlete evaluation must produce meaningful and useful information—with a high degree of validity and reliability—regarding an athlete's psychological performance. Just as a professional scout or coach knows an athlete's vertical jumping ability, foot speed, performance average, technical propensities, body-fat index, and oxygen uptake, the time has come to develop individualized normative databases on psychological and neuropsychophysiological functioning in athletes for assessment/diagnostic, comparative, and intervention purposes.

Practitioners should know an athlete's "attention threshold," "brain processing speed and reaction time," "emotional reactivity," "critical moment psychological proficiency," "heart rate variability and deceleration response parameter," and "movement-related brain-macro potentials" among important performance responses if they are to effectively advise athletes, coaches, and teams. The era of telling athletes to "just relax" or "just imagine" or "shut out all negative thoughts" needs to evolve into a new era in which *just relax* means "generate more high-frequency heart rate variability" prior to critical moments, or engage in neurofeedback to achieve a higher attention threshold, or manipulate cortical activation to suppress intrusive thoughts. The current cliché-laden "just do it" approach needs to be replaced with methods that define the nebulous constructs so pervasive in sport psychology today.

We also need to be able to *precisely* tell an athlete what a drug is going to do to him physically, psychologically, and in terms of performance outcome.

It is no longer tenable for *any* practitioner delving into the arena of sport psychology to speak in imprecise terms, such as "he doesn't concentrate" or "she's a choker," or "he's not mentally tough," or for them to recommend interventions just because that's the in thing to do. Slogans employed to somehow involve a person in mental training—such as "You've got to visualize," or "Get your intensity up"—are insufficient. Athletes and coaches need to be provided with standardized measures and parameters of sport-relevant psychological and neuropsychophysiological functioning. The time has come for practitioners to use new language that is based on empirically derived data and operationalizations of psychological processes and their effects on performance. Advanced technology and methodologies are available to lift applied sport psychology to a new level of sophistication and credibility—they just have to be used.

When this occurs, doping can be eradicated, because we will be able to unequivocally show an athlete what doping does or does not do, and what more sophisticated, noninvasive psychological methods can do to *truly* enhance performance.

The following is an overview of an evidence-based approach to athlete assessment and mental training that I have developed. It is based on peer-reviewed, award-winning research, and has been field-tested on scores of athletes. It is the wave of the future, available now. Engaging these methods is critical to illuminating the athlete's psychophysiological status, performance, and the effects of any performance-enhancement efforts or substances, including doping.

THE CARLSTEDT PROTOCOL

1. Assessment of Primary Higher Order psychological factors using the Carlstedt Subliminal Attention, Reactivity, Coping Scale and related tests to measure an athlete's level of hypnotic susceptibility, neuroticism, and repressive coping.
2. Neurocognitive testing using the Brain Resource Internet-based test battery for assessing subliminal brain responses (www.americanboardofsportpsychology.org link to Test Center): reaction time measures at the level of the neuron; for example, in dopers versus non-dopers, or dopers with varying profiles of measures above (see 1).
3. In-the-laboratory psychophysiological stress testing with video stimulus/stress paradigm: checking for stress responding that could negate any benefit of mental training, and especially, doping.
4. Quantitative EEG (qEEG, brain mapping) using the Brain Resource Paradigm for assessing subliminal brain responding: a sophisticated testing methodology that could reveal long-term effects of chemicals on the brain, and determine whether doping myths relating to reaction time have any merit. Could also be used to see if doping has a positive effect on brain processes associated with peak performance.
5. On-the-playing-field assessment of brain responding using Bluetooth-based wireless EEG: measuring actual brain responses come crunch time; dopers could easily be exposed in terms of their critical-moment performance.
6. On-the-playing-field assessment of heart rate variability: heart rate variability is a powerful measure of reaction to stress;

HRV data can be used to predict the outcome of a tennis match, and probably other sport actions as well; could be used as a tool to expose dopers and/or the non-effects of doping.

7. Actual competition wireless monitoring of heart activity and post-competition heart rate deceleration analysis (see 6).
8. Critical moments analysis: an objective method to analyze how an athlete performs during critical moments. Another means of exposing a doper; after all, if a drug taker can't perform at peak levels during crucial situations, then what good is the dope?
9. In-the-field Technical and Focus Threshold analysis: used to analyze mind-body-motor control and ability to concentrate during practice and competition. Again, a means for testing doping effects on physical-technical, and indirectly, psychological performance.
10. Mental training as a function of Athlete's Profile of Primary Higher Order Factors, including:
    a. Heart Rate Variability and RSA biofeedback: used to regulate intensity and focus.
    b. Neurofeedback using Carlstedt Frontal Lobe Protocols: a means of directly shaping brain wave activity associated with peak performance components, such as attention/focus, motor control, and intensity. Used to manipulate key brain responses associated with zone states, responses that are much more vital to performance than supposed strength-related gains achieved through doping. If your subtle, subliminal brain responses are off, all the dope in the world won't help.
    c. On-the-field Glasses-Laterality manipulation training: teaches an athlete to induce immediate shifts in brain activation that have been found to underlie transition from strategic planning to perceptual pre-action preparation; left-to-right brain shift facilitation and relative shutdown or

idling of the frontal lobes, which can interfere with focus; keeping intrusive thoughts at bay.

d. Active-alert hypnosis: used with athletes who are high in hypnotic susceptibility to intensely focus and prime motor or technical responses while shutting out intrusive thoughts and external distractors.

e. Mental Imagery per Carlstedt Protocol: special mental imagery protocols customized to an athlete's profile and time demands of a sport.

f. Tactile Motor and Technical Learning: using motor learning principles to consolidate training and technique into long-term motor memory; used in athletes with most negative psychological profile to override mental influences; strength and confidence through dominating physical and technical ability.

g. Motor and Technical Control Threshold Training: using psychological learning principles to greatly increase mind-body control.

h. On-the-field Focus Threshold Training: same as (g), to enhance focusing ability.

i. Cognitive-behavioral methods per Carlstedt Protocol: so-called "talk therapy," to augment all other mental training methods.

11. Outcome or Efficacy Testing: investigation of effects of the above mental training methods. A critical component of the Carlstedt Protocol, designed to test whether assessment is accurate and an athlete is benefiting from mental training; it is rarely, if ever, used by the vast majority of practitioners, which is malpractice; vital to credible practice of sport psychology.

12. Comprehensive athlete database creation and management: documenting assessment and training measures over time. Databases are used for comparative purposes; for example, pre-slump versus post-slump; could be used to test doper pre- and post-doping, and effects on numerous performance measures.

13. Psychological performance statistics: statistics on the mental game that can be used to document psychological performance in real time, game to game; for example, with regular statistics, such as batting average.
14. Comprehensive report: the culmination of a complete analysis of a player's mind-body-motor performance.

The bottom line is that any athlete, coach, or team serious about the mental game and performance enhancement must use these methods and/or make sure that sport psychology practitioners are trained in these methods, or have access to my protocol. The Carlstedt Protocol is the most advanced approach to peak performance assessment and mental training to date.

Dopers, take note: The protocol is your salvation in that it will dispel myths that drive your drug use.

For more information on the Carlstedt Protocol, please visit the American Board of Sport Psychology Web site at www.americanboardofsportpsychology.org and click on Test Center. You can also E-mail Dr. Roland A. Carlstedt at RCarlstedt@americanboardofsportpsychology.org, or DrRCarlstedt@aol.com to learn more about the Carlstedt Protocol. You can also learn more about these methods and data by reading *Critical Moments during Competition: A Mind-Body Model of Sport Performance When It Counts the Most* (Psychology Press, 2004) and *The Carlstedt Protocol: Science-Based Sport Psychology* (DVD film, American Board of Sport Psychology, 2005).

Dr. Roland A. Carlstedt is a licensed clinical psychologist, board-certified sport psychologist, and chairman of the American Board of Sport Psychology. He is also the holder of an applied psychologist's license. Roland earned his PhD in psychology with honors from Saybrook Graduate School (with emphases in health and sport psychology and psychophysiology) in San Francisco, under the renowned personality psychologist and behavioral geneticist Dr. Auke Tellegen of the University of Minnesota.

He has completed postdoctoral continuing education in psychiatric neuroscience through Harvard Medical School, and received training in the joint Massachusetts General Hospital-Massachusetts

Institute of Technology-Harvard Medical School Athinoula A. Martinos Center for Biomedical Imaging Functional Magnetic Resonance Imagery (fMRI) Visiting Fellowship program. Roland is also a research fellow in applied neuroscience with the Brain Resource Company. He is also the clinical and research director of Integrative Psychological Services of New York City.

Roland's dissertation on neuropsychological, personality, and performance processes in highly skilled athletes (700) from seven sports (tennis, baseball, softball, basketball, golf, volleyball, and track and field) was honored with the seal of distinction. It was also the recipient of the American Psychological Association's Division 47 (Exercise and Sport Psychology) 2001 Award for Best Dissertation in Sport Psychology. His dissertation was also nominated for the Society of Neuroscience's Annual 2002 Lindsley Award for Best Dissertation in Behavioral Neuroscience.

5

Legal Logistics: A Look at Crime and Punishment Pertaining to Steroid Use

Gregg Valentino has never used crack, cocaine, heroin, methamphetamines, or any other drug classified by the federal government as a "recreational drug." In addition to never using any detrimental, lab-created nuisance, Valentino swears he has never even once, on any occasion, consumed alcohol.

But Valentino is full of experiences similar to those of a top dealer of any street drug. Valentino was arrested for his crimes and spent months in prison. After his arrest he was denied bail, and during his apprehension, the arresting officers confiscated from him one-quarter of a million dollars in cash and a $42,000 vehicle he had paid for in cash. Police also took from him weapons, which he later faced charges for, and in a step to build evidence against him, law enforcement agents entered his home and seized a spear gun Valentino had owned since he was 13, placing it as evidence of a weapon owned with deadly intent. Another pistol in the home, owned by Valentino's son, was nothing more than a pellet gun, but was also taken as evidence. If that wasn't enough, police seized a collection of movies, ranging from adult material to Ultimate Fighting Championship videos. Somehow, these supposedly had something to do with his crimes.

Valentino, upon appeal, was granted bail only on the condition that he relinquish ownership of the items taken from him. The police had to be able to keep everything. It was that or sit in jail, facing roughly a decade-long sentence. Had he taken that route, Valentino would have been in prison past his 50th birthday. His crimes, in fact, resulted from his involvement in a very well-planned and well-manipulated drug ring. Maybe a part of one of the biggest drug circles, Valentino was a very wealthy dealer on the East Coast of the United States. In the end, as far as the law is concerned, his punishment matched his crimes.

But should it have?

Valentino did deal drugs. He didn't deal crack, cocaine, heroin, methamphetamines, or, again, any other drug classified as a recreational drug. Gregg Valentino made his money differently, albeit illegally, by dealing anabolic steroids. In his own words Valentino defends his type of drug dealing by saying, "When I take or deal a performance-enhancing drug, I harm no one. If I were to take or deal a drug like crack, I can harm myself and everyone around me."

Quick to distinguish the difference, Valentino labels steroids and most other substances favored by athletes as "performance enhancers," and believes they deserve their own category instead of simply being entangled as a drug supposedly as bad as ecstasy, crack, and the like.

A convicted felon, Valentino is also an infamous celebrity. A writer for the muscle magazine *Muscular Development*, he is famous for one of the most unlikely reasons: having the world's largest arms. Valentino says that at their largest, his arms measured 27 inches ice cold. That means no warm-up, no "pump" that bodybuilders strive for, simply no excess blood in his muscles.

As opinionated in person as he is in his monthly magazine column, "The Ramblin' Freak," Valentino is eager to point out the "farce," as he calls it, that is Arnold Schwarzenegger, arguably bodybuilding's most prominent figure. But just as openly, Valentino is willing to do what nearly every other convicted drug dealer is not willing to do: talk about his crimes. On that same note, he openly speaks of performance enhancement use in sports and the intricacies involved in the world of muscle building.

For his own exploits, Valentino has faced things worse than prison. While horror stories abound about life behind bars, a steroid dealer faces potential consequences far direr than a negative judgment in a courtroom. One example Valentino vividly recalls is a deal gone wrong that almost put him in the clutches of certain death.

Generally, Valentino says, he dealt mostly to other dealers and to a select group. That group included professional athletes, including top bodybuilders still competing today. Among his other clients were police officers, firefighters, and other public servants. One individual Valentino had a dealing relationship with changed the terms of their dealings. Instead of the usual procedure, Valentino was set up with another person to complete an exchange. This individual changed the usual place and time, as well as his prices.

Having had a steady, proven business relationship with the original venture partner, Valentino hesitantly accepted the reassignment. Describing that evening, he easily recalls a gut feeling before the action really started that told him something was wrong. And for what it was worth, he was right.

Upon entering the apartment where the exchange was to take place, Valentino observed one Latino male sitting, motioning for him to come in. As he did, the butt of a shotgun collided with the back of his skull with a sickening thud.

With blood streaming from an open wound, Valentino was forced to his knees, execution style, waiting for death to envelop him. Stories like this would seem commonplace between low-end crack addicts, but because of their low profile, steroids are generally not mentioned in these types of drug-related news reports. To Valentino though, it was very real. And, he knew, it wasn't about the steroids. It wasn't the vials of testosterone these men wanted, it was the tens of thousands of dollars in cash he had in his pockets they were after. In the steroid world, like any other underground, it's always about the money, and people were willing to kill for it. Valentino was expecting to be just another statistic.

Until his late girlfriend, Julissa, whom he still fondly remembers—he has her image tattooed on his arm—entered the fray. Because the entire drug scene in the New Jersey/New York area revolved around the dealings of a prominent and powerful Latin street gang, many of those who were involved in the deals spoke only Spanish. Julissa would translate for Valentino. But, having felt uneasy about this transaction, he had insisted she wait outside in the car. They argued, but she stayed in the car; it was a life-saving decision.

Valentino kept a handgun in the glove box. Julissa heard a struggle inside the apartment and moved in with the gun in tow. She quickly put a bullet into the butt of the armed assailant who lost his grip on the shotgun. Valentino picked up the weapon and the situation quickly changed hands.

Julissa ordered the two men to take off their clothes, which she threw out the window to keep the men from chasing after them.

After leaving, Valentino reported the event to his original associate. He said the two Latin men who assaulted him were never heard from again. Asked if it was possible that they were disposed of by another person involved in the deal, he conceded it was likely, and that when it comes to money, people will do anything, whether it has to do with steroids or crack or anything else people will risk their lives to get.

So the question is, what does a story like this one of Gregg Valentino have to do with anabolic steroids, other than that he paid the price for selling them? What it does is bring up a bigger question of whether the law is currently in line with the crime. Valentino is a regular guy, like anyone else. He has a thick area accent from his hometown, a love for his work and his supporters (he won't use the word "fan"). He admits what he did was illegal and speaks of it with no remorse, but admits that things in the court of law don't add up. Whereas most criminals use the same defense, Valentino's might actually add up to something.

Sent to rehabilitation, Valentino said he was "stuck in rehab with crackheads. I was supposed to talk about how I had an addiction and how it ruined my life. But I couldn't relate, I didn't do the drugs this clinic was set up for, and I told them I enjoyed using steroids but they didn't run my life."

Whether that was true in a literal sense doesn't matter, but it's common knowledge that some people addicted to street drugs have been known to rob and steal to support their habits. For Valentino, he said, "I liked steroids, but it wasn't something I was strung out on. There was never a point for me as a steroid user, or anyone else I've ever known, where we would be like, 'Oh my God I'm going to go rob the next 7-Eleven I see so I can get a bottle of Equipoise.'"

Even alcoholics, Valentino points out, are known to do stupid things under the influence. He repeats that someone on steroids doesn't follow that same path and that he's never once consumed alcohol. "I'm fucked up on life," Valentino says, "I don't need drinks. I wish I could blame alcohol for the way I am."

So, in theory and in comparison, if street drugs cause people to act out violently and maliciously, and steroids do neither, why are they treated the same under the law? If alcohol, which statistically kills more people in one hour than steroids have ever killed, causes people to become abusive and incoherent—rendering them unable to do things properly such as operate a motor vehicle—why is it not controlled, while steroids, which again have no shared characteristics with alcohol, are put at the forefront of drug control?

Some people would say that steroids do actually make people lash out, which they call 'roid rage. This is highly debatable, as established professionals in psychology are equally divided on whether it does or does not exist. As expected, Valentino has an opinion on the subject: "Most bodybuilders are horrible human beings, bodybuilding breeds assholes." And when asked about a regular Joe using gear, he says: "'Roid rage doesn't exist. If you're an asshole before you use steroids, you'll be an asshole on them. It isn't a syndrome; it's idiots that cause it. If someone gets a few pounds of extra muscle, some of them think they're Superman and they try and act like it."

Whether the rage exists or not, the reality is that alcohol has a far more profound impact on an individual's psychology than bodybuilding-standard doses of steroids do. And yet, one is illegal to even have in your possession, and the other is a staple in many people's lives.

Despite accusations to the contrary, Valentino says he's completely clean these days. No steroids, no drugs, not even alcohol. He's a supporter of the intelligent use of anabolics and works a career surrounded by the sport that has, for better or for worse, assisted him in getting where he is today. "I'm just glad knowing the sun will come up tomorrow and it's another day I can play. That's all I need."

So Did the Punishment Fit the Crime?

In a truly fair judicial system, every prosecuted crime would have a fitting punishment. Unfortunately in the United States, it doesn't necessarily work that way. Often, drug dealers are sentenced to more prison time than murderers, rapists, and other sex offenders. But at the same time, jaywalkers aren't stripped of life as they know it just because they broke the law. Prosecuting someone for a miniscule crime would be an outrage. A system of law that made sense would, then, have sentences matching the infraction in severity.

How severe is drug dealing? That depends. First, it shouldn't be that simple. The use of methamphetamine is far more severe than the use of testosterone. The substances, while both drugs, are completely different. One causes well-documented and severe physical harm, and also costs local, state, and federal government agencies (and thus taxpayers) millions of dollars annually. Testosterone doesn't do that. In fact, for some men, their testosterone use is covered by insurance. No one's meth use is. Clearly, these drugs are vastly different and don't belong in the same category. But they are lumped together, exacting the same punishments as if they provided the same results. They don't, and they shouldn't be treated as such. Why can steroids be used to help someone change their sex, but not help a man become, in a sense, more of a man?

But, because professional athletes have hit the media lately amid various stages of steroid use, including lying under oath, it doesn't take much to question the legal status of steroids. On the nightly news there is mention of drug-testing policies from the commissioner of baseball and new rules for suspension, but never a mention that, despite what professional sporting leagues decide, anabolic steroids are illegal in the United States without a prescription. Somehow, this doesn't have the importance it should, even during congressional hearings on the subject. Drug dealers and recipients who aren't famous are liable to receive large prison sentences. Professional athletes aren't. The sense of this is more than questionable.

And, thanks to recent events, steroids and politics are like a one-two punch. Together they're like bread and butter, peanut butter and jelly: seemingly inseparable once mixed. But with this blend of legality and synthetic testosterone comes a disarray of quality information for the average human. It's like trying to explain to someone that 17 beta-hydroxy-1-methyl-5 alpha-androst-1-en-3-one is an illegal substance for an Olympic athlete but 1,3,7-trimethylxanthine or 3,7-dihydro-1,3,7-trimethyl-1H-purine-2,6-dione is perfectly fine, and in fact, might help his performance. To a few very educated people, it makes sense that way (it means Primobol is illegal, caffeine is not). But to most, in its original form, there's no meaning to it.

What the world needs are clear sources of information, especially when it comes to a subject as ravaged with disinformation as steroids and the law. This, though, is something the media and most mass-market news outlets have decided not to provide. So what does a congressional hearing cost? What about the prosecution of a father of two, a businessman—not an athlete—who wanted a little help in his search for a better body?

To get these and other answers, no one man knows more:

Attorney Rick Collins is the foremost authority on the legal aspects of anabolic steroids and performance-enhancing drugs. No one has been quoted more or turned to more often than Mr. Collins—not just by people caught up and involved in steroid prosecution, but by professional athletes, physicians, and even outfits of the law themselves. Mr. Collins is a certified personal trainer, a bodybuilder in his own right, and advisor to the International Society of Sports Nutrition and the International Federation of BodyBuilders. He is the author of Legal Muscle: Anabolics in America *(Legal Muscle Publishing, 2002), a columnist for the bodybuilding monthly magazine* Muscular Development*, and the founder of the steroid informational resource www.SteroidLaw.com. He has testified before the U.S. Sentencing Commission on steroid issues and in 2001 he received the President's Award of the Nassau County Bar Association. He is a partner of the New York law firm Collins, McDonald & Gann, P.C.*

Q *As the most well-known and respected lawyer on the subject of anabolic steroids, how do you feel the fight "against" them is going? Is it progressive, and is it in your opinion doing anything to curb the issues the law is going after?*

A Our nation takes a simplistic, militaristic approach to social problems. We declare "war" on poverty, crime, drug addiction, steroid use, and anything else we don't like. The effectiveness of this approach is open to debate. For example, since Congress criminalized the nonmedical use of anabolic steroids in 1990, teen use has increased, the black market has exploded, fewer users get medical advice or screening, the products are less sanitary, a culture of ignorance among physicians has flourished, and new instances of drug cheating in sports surface almost daily. The law has failed to solve these problems, and has actually contributed to many of them. A key focus of the 1990 law was to stop the use of steroids by "role models" in elite athletics. It was claimed that making nonmedical steroid use a federal crime would accomplish this. But over the last 15 years, I can't think of a single high-profile professional ballplayer who was ever arrested for possessing steroids. Can you? Rather, the people who've been dragged to court in steroid possession prosecutions are almost always adult personal users who do not compete in sports. Contrary to the media portrayal, most steroid users are cosmetic users, seeking improved appearance, not performance on a playing field.

Q *How much per year does it cost the system to prosecute steroid users/ distributors? Is this passed along to taxpayers? And, in your opinion, is the cost justified?*

A Most steroid prosecutions are brought in state and local courts, not federal courts. I doubt anybody knows how much it costs state and local authorities to prosecute these cases. While I'm sure it's a small statistical portion of the overall costs of the massive war on drugs, the taxpayers do foot the bill for every penny. I am in favor of laws that protect our children from drugs, including steroids. I'm also against cheating in sports. But I view the cosmetic use of steroid hormones by mature, informed adults outside the competitive sports realm as a matter of personal risk/benefit assessment, like breast augmentation surgery, Botox injections, or liposuction. Isolating physicians out of the equation—and taking a criminal justice approach to the issue—is misguided.

Q *For someone with your talent and resources, it could be assumed that the type of law you've taken up isn't the most rewarding in terms of payment. You could be using your skills for high-profile prosecutions/defense. Why steroids?*

A I'm a lawyer and a bodybuilder. Self-serving professional alarmists, sensationalistic media outlets, and poorly informed politicians have created a "Reefer Madness" atmosphere of misinformation and propaganda. Truth and justice can't survive in this climate. The situation has an unfair and improper effect on good people who are sucked into the criminal justice system for personal-use steroid offenses. I enjoy helping them. It's the reason I created steroidlaw.com, and why I feel great about what I do.

Q *On to steroids in sports; do you feel there is any good being done with Congress stepping in to question athletes and officials?*

A Predictably, the hearings have been less about finding the truth than about posturing for the national news networks. Time will tell whether all the exposure will actually reduce cheating in sports. There are ways to get around the doping tests, and genetic technology for performance enhancement is arriving. Steroids may be obsolete soon. When millions of dollars are at stake, those inclined to break the rules will find new ways to do so.

Q *To explain for the uninformed reader, because steroid use is against federal law, are there any legal repercussions for athletes who test positive for steroids? At the least, to your knowledge, is their address even flagged for deliveries?*

A Federal law criminalizes possession without a prescription, not use. Competitive athletes who fail drug tests face administrative sanctions, not criminal arrest and prosecution. Flagging a major leaguer's home address for the possible arrival of mailed steroid packages is probably a waste of time. Elite athletes have other sources.

Q *Because many Olympic-level athletes complain their daily supplements have been tainted, when it comes to the sport supplement industry, is there any legal pressure on companies that produce products that can be cross-contaminated.*

A I have urged members of the sports and fitness supplement industry to improve their quality control wherever possible. The alternative may be more and more regulation by the FDA, which has traditionally taken a dim view of supplements in general. I am now seeing lawsuits against supplement makers filed by competitive athletes who tested positive for banned substances and are claiming that contaminated products were the cause.

Q *Recently a judge ruled against the ban on ephedra. What does this mean for the supplement industry? Should companies be worried about legal issues if they can put this back out on the market?*

A Numerous companies have called me to ask about the recent decision on ephedra. The ruling is narrowly drawn, and may have very limited effect. Its impact remains to be seen. Those interested in the latest legal developments on ephedra and other dietary supplements should call my office. In any event, the Utah ruling does not permit the return of high-dose ephedra supplements to the market.

Q *If ephedra is able to return to the market, what type of position does that put prohormones and prosteroids in for a possible return? What about anabolic steroids?*

A Dietary supplements containing ephedra were taken off the market by the FDA. Prohormones and prosteroids were criminalized by an act of Congress. Congress didn't rule on safety risks or benefits as the FDA did, but rather added steroid precursors to the Controlled Substances Act because of their similarity to testosterone. I do not see the ephedra ruling as a springboard for Congress to revisit the new law, nor for a court to strike down the law.

Q *Since the ban on PH/PS, how many cases have you had to defend against prosecution for these types of substances?*

A None. While anyone who possesses the newly controlled products will be a drug criminal, for now the products are controlled only at the federal level (with very limited exceptions). This is important, since most steroid cases are brought in *state* courts, *not* federal courts. If the products aren't scheduled by state laws, state courts can't prosecute them as a controlled substance crime. Unless and until individual states pass legislation to make their laws consistent with the new federal law, which could take several months or even years, state authorities will have little incentive to go after prohormones. As far as federal prosecutions, although the federal government can prosecute possession of *any* amount of a controlled substance, the current system that guides federal criminal punishments apparently isn't harsh enough on steroids to make the DEA [Drug Enforcement Administration] want to pursue them on a grander scale. That could change if the guidelines are amended. Regardless, the people who have stocked up on prohormones have figured that the chances of getting caught are less once the item's safely in one's home. It's true, based on the hundreds of steroid possession cases I've seen in my practice, that the vast majority of people who've been arrested for steroid possession got caught during the process of *receiving* or importing the drugs, not after they had them hidden in their house. All things considered, I don't see an epidemic of prohormone arrests in the immediate future. But with prohormone prohibition, I see an impending rise in the black market of foreign veterinary steroids and resulting prosecutions for these products in state courts.

Q *Have you represented any professional athletes competing in the Big Three, football, basketball, and baseball? And if so, do they receive different types of treatment because of their profession, as compared to athletes in less profitable sports?*

A Big Three athletes don't seem to get arrested. That may qualify as a different type of treatment in and of itself. I'll let you speculate as to the reasons. Certainly, I've gotten calls from them seeking my help, but regarding positive doping violations, not criminal offenses.

Q *With the abundant amount of banned substances out there, most of which have side effects far overstated by the biased media, what is the most common steroid you find yourself defending?*

A Most steroid users take a variety of drugs—so-called polypharmacy. In criminal cases, the most common steroids are injectable esters of testosterone and nandrolone, although I also see many low-dose methandrostenolone cases.

Q *If the media were ever to wise up and read (your book, for example, or this one), and realize steroids aren't half as harmful as smoking, and the government one day reintroduced them for use to responsible adults, how do you think this would change sports?*

A Competitive sports bodies would continue to be free to make their own rules about performance enhancement, and athletes would have to follow them. That's always been the case. For example, for many years an athlete who drank too much caffeinated coffee would fail a doping test and be stripped of his medal. But mature adults outside of sports have been—and should be—free to drink as much damned coffee as they please. Outside of sports, individual freedom should be the paramount concern. But what's fair in life doesn't necessarily apply to sports.

Rick Collins's Testimony to the United States Sentencing Commission

April 12, 2005

Rick Collins, Esq.,

National Association of Criminal Defense Lawyers (NACDL)

As a life member of the National Association of Criminal Defense Lawyers and on the association's behalf, I wish to thank the Commission for the opportunity to offer my commentary. The subject of anabolic steroids has received massive media attention lately, as well as new attention from Congress. However, much of the attention has been extremely limited in focus. I would like to offer some observations of illicit steroid use outside of professional baseball. I believe that these observations are relevant to the determination of how to implement the directive to this Commission set forth in Section 3 of the Anabolic Steroid Control Act of 2004. In particular, I will focus on the equivalency of steroids to other Schedule III drugs, and to controlled substances in general.

My comments are offered on behalf of NACDL based upon my "in the trenches" experiences in dealing with anabolic steroid criminal matters. Following a five year stint as a state court prosecutor in the 1980s, I entered private practice focusing on the typical variety of criminal defense matters. Over the last five years, however, my practice has shifted toward a niche practice centering on civil and criminal matters involving steroids and sports supplement matters. I represent and advise several non-profit organizations in the field of bodybuilding, health and fitness, including one with 173 affiliated national federations. Hundreds of matters involving anabolic steroids and related issues have crossed my desk, affording me a unique and extensive view of the intersection of nonmedical steroid use and the criminal justice system in this country. I have attached a copy of my curriculum vitae for your reference. I hope that my practical experience in dealing with steroid cases of all types will be helpful to this Commission on the issue of drug equivalency.

ANABOLIC STEROIDS ARE DIFFERENT FROM OTHER CONTROLLED SUBSTANCES

At the outset, the Commission should consider that illicit steroid users are profoundly different from other illicit drug users, and a number of their differences bear upon the issue of equivalency. There is a stark contrast between the profiles, motivations, and patterns of possession and use of illicit steroid users and that of persons who use other drugs. Indeed, steroids themselves are different from other controlled substances.

Anabolic steroids are the only hormones in the entire Controlled Substances Act, and testosterone, the criminalized steroid by which all others are measured, is naturally present in the bodies of every American man, woman, and child. While the propriety of dealing with the societal problems associated with illicit steroid use via the mechanism of the Controlled Substances Act is not the primary focus of the Commission's interest at present, the Commission should understand that numerous legal reviewers have questioned or criticized the scheduling of steroids as controlled substances. I have attached a law journal article that analyzes the original Anabolic Steroid Control Act of 1990, which in turn references several other law review articles (by reviewers Black, Burge, and Hedges) that arrive at similar conclusions. These articles provide background information that bears on the appropriate equivalency between steroids and other controlled substances.

The profile of the typical steroid user has been misrepresented to the public, and to members of Congress. The "typical" steroid user has been presented as fitting one of two profiles: either the million dollar sports star, or the hapless teenager seeking to emulate him. Certainly, Jose Canseco was not the only steroid user in Major League Baseball. In fact, there are elite level athletes in a variety of professional and Olympic sports who are using or have used steroids to enhance athletic performance. A number of them use steroids in willful and unethical violation of the rules of fair play and may even deserve our scorn. But the Commission's concern cannot be about the regulation of athletic endeavors or the adulation deserved by athletes.

The star-struck adolescents who risk their health by emulating star athletes are deserving of our concern and protection and yet the Commission in amending the guidelines for anabolic steroids should first do no more harm to those young athletes as is likely to happen if penalties are increased without a thorough consideration and empirical analysis of the scientific and societal harms.

The steroid user who has been overlooked in the current focus of attention may be the most common user of steroids. Although I have met or corresponded with well over a thousand steroid users in the criminal justice context and have spoken with many of them expansively, it may come as a surprise that the majority of them were not teenagers, nor were they competitive athletes of any kind. The overwhelming majority were gainfully employed, health conscious adult males, between 25 and 45 years of age, using hormones not for athletic performance but to improve their appearance. These users typically are non-smokers who follow exercise routines including both strenuous weight training and cardio programs, and adhere to healthful diets. Do they put too high a premium on superficial appearances? In my opinion, absolutely. Are they overcompensating for underlying self-esteem issues? Perhaps, in many cases. Are they assuming risks that might potentially be harmful to them? Probably, yes, as do smokers, drinkers, and extreme sports enthusiasts. But however misguided we may judge nonmedical users of these hormones to be, I seriously question whether they are the sort of dangerous criminals deserving of extended prison terms. Their motivations are identical to the motives of women who seek surgical breast augmentation or to those of men who seek face-lifts, eye jobs, tummy tucks, and the like. Of course, while our laws permit cosmetic surgeons to anesthetize and cut their patients to cater purely to vanity, doctors are forbidden from using hormones for the same purpose.

In any event, the medical and scientific experts I have come to know in this field share my views on the analogy of cosmetic steroid use to plastic surgery. Sadly, though, this view rarely achieves mainstream public exposure, because the media and the recent congressional hearings seem to focus exclusively on the "hot" issues of steroids in pro sports and steroids as used by teenagers. Consequently, the public sees steroid use solely in the context of sports cheating, even though that is, in my experience, only a small part of the overall steroid pie, and only a minuscule fraction of the criminal justice steroid pie. The elite athletes whose steroid use draws public attention and congressional ire are virtually never prosecuted in the criminal justice context. In fact, I am unable to name a single professional athlete who has been arrested for steroid possession. On the other hand, I can show you file after file in my office of non-competing, mature adult males who have been prosecuted.

PATTERNS OF USE AND LONG-RANGE EFFECTS

Their motivation, whether labeled as vanity or an excessive quest for self improvement, is unlike the motivation that drives the use of every other controlled substance. However misguided steroid use without medical supervision may be, it is long-range, goal-oriented behavior. Steroid users are the virtual antithesis of the typical drug offender. Steroid users do not take these hormones for any immediate psychoactive effect, and these hormones do not have any immediate psychoactive effect. They are not stimulants, depressants, or hallucinogens. By contrast, the person who uses crack buys it, smokes it, and gets high from that dose. When he wants to get high again, he buys more.

The behavior is largely the same with marijuana, LSD, cocaine, and all other controlled substances, including all other Schedule III drugs. Not so with steroid users. Because they seek long-range effects, not an immediate high, their habits are very different from narcotics abusers. Most steroid users plan out—typically memorialized in writing—a cycle of use lasting weeks or months. The plan will typically involve the use of several different drugs in a sometimes elaborate system of methodically planned dosages. All of this long-range planning is reflected in the users' purchasing and possession habits. Steroid users never buy steroids daily or weekly. They typically purchase a quantity of steroids that will last for the full duration of at least one planned cycle. Many buy for several cycles. Steroid users are pack rats by nature. For example, those steroid users who use the oral steroid methandrostenolone will often buy it in a tub of one thousand five-milligram tablets, available for about $450 online from Thailand. Purchase and usage patterns must also be taken into account when examining the equivalency issue. One shot of heroin, one snort of cocaine, or one tablet of Ecstasy produces a desired psychoactive effect. It may even make sense to make one tablet of Oxycontin or Valium a dosage unit. One tablet of oxandrolone, oxymetholone, or any other steroid, however, does absolutely nothing. In fact, a number of medical experts have pointed out that a whole bottle of steroids most likely would have little adverse effect. Contrast that with the fact that were a person to ingest an entire bottle of aspirin, that person might die of an overdose. To designate a particular quantity as a "dosage unit," it must at a minimum have some effect. It must do something. Yet that is not the case with steroids.

Before amending the marijuana equivalency for steroids, the Commission ought to be able explain why it is selecting a particular number. It is unclear why the Commission set 50 tablets (the current equivalency) as the dosage unit for steroids, but it could have been a recognition that steroid users purchase and possess steroids in much more massive amounts than any other drug offenders. It may also be that there was some underlying uneasiness about Congress's decision—which was contrary to the testimony of the DEA, FDA, NIDA, and AMA, all of which sent representatives to testify against scheduling steroids—about forcing these hormones into the Controlled Substances Act. Regarding injectable steroids, to amend the guidelines to make half of one milliliter (0.5 milliliter) a steroid dosage unit would be a fiction, plain and simple. In all my experience with steroid users, I have never met or even heard of a person who regularly administered half of a milliliter at a time. The landmark 1996 *New England Journal of Medicine* study (that stunned many in the medical community when it found virtually no adverse effects when anabolic steroids were administered for 10 weeks) used a dosage of 600mg per week (about six times the natural replacement dose).

TARGETING TRAFFICKERS

The argument that increasing the penalties through a revised drug equivalency will target traffickers does not comport with the reality of these cases. In my experience, most people being arrested today for steroid offenses are not traffickers, but personal users. This is because the Internet has become the favored tool of international steroid commerce, with international mail order now a common method of delivery. The traffickers, whoever they are, are often far beyond the jurisdiction of American authorities. The defendant who gets arrested is most often the end user, caught in a "controlled delivery" of the package by undercover agents.

In state courts across America, where the current federal drug equivalency for steroids offers no protection, personal use steroid defendants are being arrested and prosecuted. All too often, they are charged with "intent to sell" offenses, based on the misperception by law enforcers as to the amounts consistent with personal use. I have seen firsthand countless cases of individuals erroneously charged with possession with intent. The "intent to sell" problem is particularly prevalent in cases involving low dosage oral tablets, such as Anabol (methandrostenolone) from Thailand. One of these little pink pentagons provides only 5mg of anabolic steroids, while it is common for users of oral steroids to take 50 to 100mg of oral steroids daily or even more. A man in New York was recently charged with intent to sell in state court for possessing less than four hundred 400 tablets in his car. In a California state case, prosecutors insisted that receiving a package of one thousand Anabol tablets by mail from Thailand proved an intent to sell, despite the reality that one thousand tabs is the *minimum* quantity that could be ordered from that overseas source. I have seen two car-stop state cases in New York where possessors of Anabol, in the amounts of 207 tablets and 280 tablets, were charged with possession with intent to sell without any other evidence of such intent. In one of the many cases generated by the Maryland State Police, a man was charged with possession with intent to distribute steroids when his mother accepted a controlled delivery package containing 100 Anadrol tablets, two bottles of testosterone cypionate, three bottles of nandrolone, and two bottles of stanozolol. The house search recovered an additional 400 steroid tablets, another steroid bottle, and some syringes. These are all typical examples of situations where the variety of substances combined with the total quantity was wrongly viewed by law enforcement as inconsistent with personal use.

To make each tablet a dosage unit, and every half a milliliter a dosage unit, would bring the injustices I have seen in state courts into federal courts, with heightened punishments not just for traffickers, but for the typical steroid possessors I have described to you. I suggest we should stop and consider whether that truly is beneficial to society. Personal users who are high profile cheating athletes should be dealt with through the administrative rules of their sports. If those rules are insufficient, let Congress continue to pressure the sports agencies. But as I said before, few if any sports heroes get arrested, and I have grave concerns that the ones who will suffer under a revised drug equivalency standard will be the gym rats. The only competitive athletes I predict will be targeted will be bodybuilders. I have known many former steroid users who have gone on to highly successful careers as lawyers and doctors. One of them went on to become the governor of the state of California.

I challenge the argument that the current drug equivalency for steroids must be increased in order to make their prosecution worth the effort by the Department of Justice. Enforcing laws should not be based upon the length of potential sentences. The position of the NACDL, and my personal position, is that the current drug equivalency reflects a balanced compromise of concerns and considerations that is better tailored to anabolic steroids than a "one size fits all" Schedule III equivalency standard. We do not support an amendment to the guidelines as to steroid equivalency, especially if it adopts the standard used with other Schedule III drugs.

I hope that my comments have provided some food for thought on this issue. Should the Commission be interested in further information, I would be happy to provide it.

6

An Inside Look at the World of Bodybuilding and Steroids

Because of his history, his open mind, and, essentially, his wide-open mouth on the topic of performance-enhancing drugs, Gregg Valentino offers an inside look at steroid dealing, use and dosage, hypocrisy, and the sport most associated with drug abuse: bodybuilding.

Note: Gregg Valentino's responses are derived from his own experiences and opinions, and are not to be mistaken for fact, correct or incorrect, or the opinion of any other individual.

Q *As a blanket statement, what comes to your mind when you think about professional bodybuilding?*

A It's a lot of bullshit. Bodybuilding is a disgusting world in a lot of ways. For one, bodybuilding breeds assholes. Most bodybuilders are horrible human beings, and it has nothing to do with steroids, they just are.

Q *There are still some bodybuilders who say they don't use steroids, or avoid the question so they don't have to admit what most people feel they know. You're around backstage at a lot of shows, and you've been around bodybuilding for years. Are there any natural professional bodybuilders out there?*

A Not a single one. No professional bodybuilder is natural, not one. You can't be natural and be that big, it's the nature of the sport. Every pro uses steroids, and every pro uses growth hormone. And people think they use the growth hormone to get big, they don't. A lot of them use it to get ripped for shows. But it makes their guts stick out and it's why a certain blond professional looks like Herman Munster when he competes. And at the shows, people want to see freaks, they don't care about anything else. Bodybuilding doesn't have a huge fan base as it is. It's small compared to other sports, and it would be smaller without the freaks. People pay to see things that aren't normal. And even then, the athletes get shafted, they don't make hardly any money from the shows.

Q *You mention bodybuilding being a small sport and athletes not making a lot, but a lot of the professionals look like they're leading fairly well-off lives. We'd like to think most professional athletes could make a living doing what they love if they've made it to be a professional. Where does the money come from?*

A I'll tell you one thing, not one professional bodybuilder hasn't sold steroids at one point. A lot of them use personal training as a front, but it's bullshit. Yeah, maybe they're personal trainers, but they're drug dealers too. And if they aren't now, they were. There's another thing too, called "Muscle Worship." I'll tell you what, bodybuilders are huge in the [gay] community. A lot of pros go to these parties and guest-pose, while there's a group of [gay] guys around them [pleasuring] themselves. They get a ton of money doing this. They don't have sex with them, but they use their muscles. And a lot of well-known guys do this stuff; Arnold did it, too. How else do you think he could run around Venice all day, lift weights, eat, and spend the rest of the time on the beach? His contract with Weider didn't pay for all that. There are even pros who have sections on their Web sites offering this stuff, offering clothes they've worn, all that.

Q *Before your arrest, when you were dealing steroids, who did you sell to?*

A Mostly other dealers, people I trusted. But I sold to a lot of professional bodybuilders and guys trying to come up. Cops, firefighters, a lot of different types of people.

Q *Did you ever sell to professional athletes outside of bodybuilding?*

A Oh yeah. And all professional athletes are the worst customers.

Q *Why?*

A They think they should get shit for free just because they're a professional. But it isn't like I can go fucking broadcast I sold steroids to a guy who competes in the Mr. Olympia, it isn't a mass-market business.

Q *And while you were dealing, you were a big user, too. What drugs did you use personally?*

A Increase the reps, increase the dosage, that's what I always said. But with my drug, I'm particular, rather, I was particular. For me, certain exercises, certain drugs. Other guys use an array of drugs. They use growth hormone and IGF [insulin-like growth factor]; I don't. I never used growth hormone. I'm a testosterone nut and I hate Deca.

Q *How much of each drug did you use?*

A I used test propionate and Equipoise regularly. I used probably a minimum of 3,000 mg of prop a week, and 2,000 to 2,500 mg of Equipoise a week.

Q *How much size did the steroids help you put on?*

A I had 21-inch arms naturally. I got to 27 inches cold after drugs. But understand, I trained 23 years without a single drug. When I finally used steroids, my body soaked it up. And I spot injected, not synthol like people claim, but I did inject steroids directly into my biceps. You know, people would eat dog shit if someone big said it would help them get huge, but it's about being smart and using the drugs right. I never used synthol, a lot of pros do. All it does is stretch the fascia with oil.

Q *And your massive arms are what made you famous. But there had to have been some downsides, weren't there?*

A I was a freak. I hated looking like that, but it made me money. It was hard to sleep, find clothes, and it looked retarded.

Q *What's your stance on steroids now, postlegal troubles?*

A I trained 23 years without touching anything, I didn't know what steroids were until the mid-'80s. I'm not anti-steroid or pro-steroid now, but I really feel that no kid, no one under 25, should be doing steroids. Yeah if you do you'll get huge, but the minute you come off, it's like "holy shit what happened to him?" They'll never get their dick hard when they're older if they screw up young. I swear if you wait until you're older, you won't have bitch tits or get ball shrinkage.

Q *Speaking of side effects, what did you experience when using steroids? Especially since your dosages were much higher than most average users are using today.*

A I started drugs when I started selling them, I felt I earned it. I figured, "Fuck it, I might as well take advantage of it." And I saw it as an advantage. I trained over 20 years natural, and I was fine then and I'm fine now. Never had any ball shrinkage, and I never had bitch tits. The problem with my arm was using a dirty needle, it wasn't the steroids.

Q *When you started selling steroids, how did you get involved, where did the drugs come from?*

A For your life and mine, don't print names. But I'll tell you what, it wasn't hard. [A certain doctor] from the Dominican Republic came over here to the United States and set up shop. The drugs came from him and revolved around [a Latin street gang]. It was a big operation and it brought in a lot of money. Most people think that the drugs people in gangs deal are only crack and heroin and that stuff, but it's not. It's whatever would make a lot of money. The doctor dealt with male impotence, so it was very easy for him to get a lot of drugs. He started with a clinic in the Dominican Republic and after he came over here, he ordered testosterone for the clinic by the truckload. Supposedly he was treating hundreds of men, so no one thought twice about it. Eventually his partner died, though, in a plane crash, and that was the end of his involvement.

Q *How much did you make selling steroids?*

A Over a million.

Q *Are drugs the biggest problem in bodybuilding?*

A There's a shitload of problems in bodybuilding. Pompous, arrogant pricks like Lee Priest; hypocrites like Arnold Schwarzenegger; the drugs, there's a lot of problems.

Q *What's your opinion on Governor Arnold Schwarzenegger now and his involvement not just in bodybuilding, but in the entire supplement industry surrounding sports?*

A Listen, Arnold is the biggest farce there is. He says steroids were legal when he used them, they weren't. You still had to have a prescription and he never had a need for drugs. He deserves some of the shit he gets about his steroid use. He has his name on the Arnold Classic contest and calls for tougher standards on steroids, but he used them and that's how he got famous, and his own contest isn't even drug tested. He should come out and change things; he has the power to do it. If he told the truth he could help the bodybuilders today and bring bodybuilding to the next level, make it a much more advanced sport.

Q *What do you think would happen to bodybuilding if a comprehensive drug testing policy was put into place?*

A It would probably kill the sport. But that's why steroids need a different category of classification, get them away from drugs like crack and cocaine. It isn't so much the drugs in bodybuilding, it's what the judges are rewarding. I mean, Ronnie Coleman is a good guy, but with everyone getting bigger and heavier, they're going to be killing themselves. There's a difference between use and abuse. And people need to know that you can be 300 pounds, huge and shredded and ripped, and still never make it as a pro. It's about structure and how it looks, how the muscle is shaped. Guys think they just need to keep getting bigger so they just keep taking more and more. Bodybuilding should strive to reward guys who looked like the pros did back when Arnold was winning the Mr. Olympia. Already guys are close to dying, we got guys so heavy they're winded walking up a fucking flight of stairs because they can't carry that weight. They start breathing hard when they're picking their nose.

Q *Having been on the receiving end of steroid punishment, do you feel that the current regulations in the United States are appropriate?*

A We need regulation, not incarceration. Nobody is carjacking cars or robbing houses to support their steroid habit. I loved using steroids, but I never stole from anyone to get them. There are a lot better things the government can be spending time and money on than steroids. It's ridiculous that I had to go through rehab with crack-heads because I used steroids. They didn't control my life, yeah I used them and I liked them, but I never hurt anyone by injecting myself with steroids. Athletes use performance enhancers, junkies use party drugs. They aren't the same thing, they shouldn't be in the same classification. Back to Arnold, he's a politician now, he should come out and defend steroids, not say they should be illegal or legal in bodybuilding, but to get them in their own class like they should be. People need to realize the difference between drugs, the ones that hurt other people and the ones that don't.

Q *What about 'roid rage, and its supposed existence?*

A It's a myth. If you're a little asshole, steroids will make you a bigger asshole. That's all.

Q *So do you think steroids should just be legal?*

A Let me ask you this instead, why is it OK for a woman to have an abortion, but not for a man to use a steroid? Why does a woman have the right to kill something that has a separate heart, a separate everything, just because it's in her body? She had to work to put that baby there, so why can't I put a steroid in me?

7

Excuses, Excuses

Cross-contamination is the cry of every cheater.

—Gary Hall Jr., three-time U.S. Olympian, ten-time Olympic medalist

Naturally, innocent people proclaim their innocence in the face of accusations. Especially when those accusations insinuate illegal drug use. But, as society would have it, it isn't just the innocent crying foul. Nearly every athlete who has tested positive for a banned substance has said that he was innocent, that the test was faulty, that he was being targeted. Few eventually tell the truth, even fewer face their punishments without complaint.

After Major League Baseball started its crackdown on steroid use and a push for stricter testing, a fight from players ensued. As testing revealed more and more athletes failing the standards, new excuses came forth. By May of 2005, more than half the players suspended for positive tests in both the major and minor leagues were born in Spanish-speaking countries. Cries went out that those athletes didn't understand the rules. Unfortunately, that line of defense is full of holes.

While it is acceptable for professional athletes competing in America to not speak English, they are generally always associated with someone who can translate for them. If not, how would they order a hamburger at McDonald's? Negotiate multimillion-dollar contracts? Ask where the bathroom is? L.A. Dodgers third baseman Jose Valentin was quoted as saying, "I think it's just a lack of communication. [They] don't understand the language. They probably don't know what's going on and they're not into it, in terms of meetings and stuff like that. . . . you get some papers in your locker during spring training and during the season, and they're in English." The papers, assumedly, cover all of the intricate details to ensure passing drug tests. But to those who don't speak English, and can't read those papers, Valentin went on to say, "They don't even read it. They just throw it away."

And that is their fault, and they open themselves up to failing drug tests with no room to complain. Their translator, whoever that is, could inform them of the rules. The translator could read it to them while they stretch before practice, while they eat dinner, anytime before the season starts would suffice, really. But the athletes aren't the only ones to blame. Their coaches, agents, and everyone who has a vested interest, specifically a financial interest, should take every measure possible to ensure that their athlete, and their reason for a paycheck, is updated with complete knowledge of every rule. This type of knowledge should be instilled when the athlete is still young, as a preventative measure at the very least. In countries where *buscones*, or street agents, are scouting young talent, they should pass the message on.

But still, common sense has to come into play. Anyone of any nationality or of any language should be fully aware that being injected with a needle isn't par for the course. They should take the initiative on their own to ask questions, stand up, and say no. And granted, hundreds of banned substances come in pill form, but then too one can only wonder why someone would swallow a pill he knew nothing about.

But is this excuse even valid?

In a May 2005 hearing with political leaders, Bud Selig, commissioner of baseball, was asked by Representative Bobby Rush (D-Illinois) why the majority of players testing positive had been Latino and African American. Don Fehr, executive director of the Major League Baseball Players Association, made the point that perhaps the language barrier was the cause. Selig, at odds with that, responded, "They have been told, and really have been told time and time again." Selig explained that over the course of the off-season and during spring training, at both the league and club levels, materials and warnings were being produced for all athletes. Pamphlets and videos were being used and were available in both English and Spanish—thus making it the players' responsibility to listen, because they could clearly understand it should they have paid attention.

8

Caught Cheating, and the Careers After

Pain heals, chicks dig scars, glory lasts forever.

—*Keanu Reeves, as quarterback Falco in the movie* The Replacements

To put steroids into the context of the above quote, pain heals faster with a little juice, and scars may come more gallantly. But what about glory? Is it the same when the accomplishments are achieved by an athlete using performance-enhancing drugs?

The following is a summary of just a couple of athletes who have been caught using or who have admitted to using steroids and other drugs to improve their game, their run, their ride, or whatever it is they do for, supposedly, the love of the game. What happened to them, what the fans thought, and how the public in general reacted, varies by sport. Should it? As always there as so many questions, and so few answers.

Barry Bonds

First implicated in the BALCO mess, Barry Bonds denied any and all allegations regarding steroid use. When he hit 73 home runs, the public thought very little about potential steroid use. When this came to light, it became a very plausible explanation. Eventually,

Bonds admitted he used two steroid compounds better known as "the clear" and "the cream," but did so without knowing their true composition. To his knowledge, he said, he was being provided flaxseed oil and a cream for arthritis. In 2000, prior to using these supplements, he hit 49 balls out of various parks. One year later and a little addition to his daily regimen, and he added 24 more.

In 2005 Bonds sat out most of the season trying to heal a knee injury and undergoing several surgeries. It is widely speculated that his lack of recovery, something seen as impeccable in previous seasons, was the result of his no longer using anabolic steroids or, no longer using the same doses. Steroids and human growth hormone are known widely for their benefits in rapid recovery to muscle trauma. Certain steroids, such as Deca-Durabolin, are very beneficial to joint health.

Hulk Hogan

In a very Barry Bonds way, but years before the slugger did it more famously, Hulk Hogan (Terry Bollea), denied using steroids several times before finally admitting he used various substances in 1993 during the World Wrestling Federation Steroid Trial. Hogan estimated in his testimony that as many as 80 percent of professional wrestlers were using some sort of steroid.

Hogan's career never faltered, even after his admission to the use of steroids. He has since made successful stints with World Championship Wrestling and in the reincarnation of the World Wrestling Federation, the WWE (World Wrestling Entertainment). Hogan has starred in movies as well as in the VH1 hit television show "Hogan Knows Best."

Marion Jones

Some people just have bad luck. Others make their own bed and just refuse to lie in it. Whichever scenario a person feels fits track athlete Marion Jones, knowing the company she keeps may be the tie-breaker. Her ex-husband, C. J. Hunter, was banned from athletics for repeated failed drug tests. Her boyfriend and father of her child is Tim Montgomery, also suspended on the grounds of illegal performance enhancement. Her former associate Victor Conte of BALCO infamy said publicly he has watched Jones get injections of illegal drugs. And yet, she defends herself by pointing to the fact that she has never failed a drug test. But what must be remembered is that not all cheaters fail drug tests. Jones went from a five-medal haul in the Sydney Olympics with BALCO, to a lackluster showing in Athens just four years later without BALCO.

And whether she is guilty of doping or not, many track officials in 2005 didn't want her to even appear at their events. Independent Online (IOL), a South African online news source, quoted Svein Arne Hansen, director of a meet in Oslo, Norway, as saying about Jones, "We will not invite her, or any other athlete under investigation, until the BALCO situation is cleared." Also stated in the article: "Several meet organisers interviewed said Jones commanded appearance fees of between $75,000 and $150,000 (about R500,000 and R1-million) after winning three gold medals at the 2000 Olympics in Sydney. The fee is now about $5,000–$10,000 (about R30,000–R60,000), if she gets any at all."

Was it the drug controversy, her demands, or her performance? Maybe it was a mixture of all three. Her first meet of 2005 produced a time she bested as a high school athlete, certainly not showing the form of an Olympic gold medalist. Either way, whether Jones used drugs, she has since slowed to midlevel performances and, worse, attracts negative publicity whenever, and wherever, she does compete. Another reason she is not wanted could have something to do with her enjoyment of lawsuits. Prior to the 2004 Athens Olympics she threatened to sue USADA if it attempted to keep her from competing in the games, and she filed a defamation lawsuit against BALCO's Victor Conte for $25 million.

Mark McGwire

Mark McGwire had never hit more than 52 home runs in his career before driving out 70 in 1998 to break the coveted single-season record previously held by Roger Maris. To combat steroid suspicion, McGwire admitted he was using a prohormone known as androstenediol, or "andro." Later, when Jose Canseco wrote his tell-all book, McGwire's andro use was claimed to be a decoy to cover his actual use of anabolic steroids. Until he testified, very unconvincingly, in front of Congress, simply repeating he had no comment, fans were generally forgiving. This fact, and perhaps what causes the most suspicion, is that andro converts to estrogen as well as to testosterone. Between 1997 and 1998, McGwire's stroke when he swung the bat looked identical, signaling little to no change in his technique. But his home run total skyrocketed, leading everyone to believe there had to be an increase in strength. Because of andro's chemical properties, an increase in strength simply can't be the sole reason for the more than 30 percent increase in long balls.

McGwire also further conceded his guilt without admission by offering a little more than useless, tearful testimony during congressional hearings. McGwire would not answer questions about his alleged steroid use with Jose Canseco, and said he was looking only to speak of the future and announce he believed steroids were "bad." In a poll of sportswriters after the hearings, McGwire was scored as far less likely to be admitted to the Hall of Fame.

Nina Kraft

After winning the Hawaiian Ironman Triathlon in 2004, 35-year-old Nina Kraft shocked the world when she tested positive for recombinant erythropoietin, commonly known as EPO, which is used to boost an athlete's red blood cell count. After her test, and subsequent admission to using the drug, Natascha Badmann was named champion.

Kraft, like some athletes and unlike many others, admitted her guilt. What made her confession unique was that the federation that tested her requires a positive result returned from both the A and B samples taken after competition. She publicly acknowledged and confirmed her positive test after only the A sample came back tainted. She claimed to have taken EPO for three weeks leading up to the biggest Ironman contest of the year. Afterward, Kraft is quoted as saying, "I never really rejoiced over the victory in Hawaii. I was ashamed the entire time, especially in front of my family. I cheated." Her cheating was so successful that she ended up winning the Hawaiian event by an amazing 17 minutes.

Kraft, like Kelli White, admits she was ashamed of her drug use. So then, why do it? It's amazing what revelations come about after athletes get caught. Supposedly, they feel guilty, but they don't admit it until after they're confronted with a dirty sample. Apparently, the guilt wasn't too intense. At least, not until everyone knew about it and Kraft's title was stripped from her.

Kraft's positive test proved very bad for her career, especially at home in Germany. Her win matched the win of fellow German Normann Stadler. The German double win brought pride to the country and a surge of interest in the sport. Her fellow Ironman distance-event winner and Germany native Nicole Leder is quoted as saying, "The German double win at Hawaii was so big, so good for the sport in Germany. Now this tears it all down. . . . It is bad for her. It is bad for the sport. It is bad for all of the German triathletes and the sponsors." And that's a lot of bad for a lot of people.

Jason Giambi

Both Jason Giambi and his brother, Jeremy, have admitted to using steroids. But, they did so in different manners. Jeremy was quoted by *USA Today* as saying, "It's something I did. I apologize. I made a mistake. I moved on. I kind of want it in the past." And apologizing is all his brother, Jason, seemed to do.

Originally Jason took the road many athletes take, he denied ever using steroids or other performance-enhancing drugs. And then a report was released that he confessed to a grand jury that he did in fact use steroids. Publicly, he tearfully apologized for what he had done, even though he didn't specifically mention steroids. Presumably without steroids, Giambi's performance fell off and it was thought very likely that he would lose his massive $120 million contract with the New York Yankees. As fate would have it, the Yankees kept Giambi and the 2005 season eventually shaped up so well for him that Giambi was awarded Comeback Player of the Year. The notable part? The award was a result of fan voting.

So This Means . . . What?

Judging by the careers of most professional athletes who have been caught using steroids, and judging by the careers of athletes who admitted wrongdoing, it would seem the public, at least in America, is very forgiving. For Giambi, he found his stride again after a hard off-season plagued by rumors and investigations and ultimately, admission of guilt. The fans were back on his side. Even Bonds, while saying he didn't know he was using steroids but still admitted to using the drugs, is still a fan favorite. It seems that those individuals who continually deny their steroid use even in the face of large amounts of evidence—in the cases of Jones and McGwire, who supposedly had eyewitnesses—suffer the largest consequences. If nothing else, this should serve notice that athletes who have done wrong should salvage whatever they can of their careers and admit to what they did and move on.

9

Steroids and Money—They Make Each Other

There are reasons people cheat. A lot of reasons. Usually, they come on four shiny wheels, in gated communities, in skimpy bikinis, and in the form of magazine covers. Somehow, it seems like performance-enhancing drugs and money have a lot in common.

Baseball has seen its share of slumps, bounced back, and has always seemed to remain the pride and joy of America, the favorite pastime in the United States. But after the 1994 players' strike, it was becoming very difficult to fill the seats of stadiums around the country. People were having trouble spending their money for tickets to watch players who make millions a year, and yet still complain for more. In an incident unrelated to the strike but memorable for its precedent, Mike Piazza, in negotiations with the Dodgers, complained he was only receiving $81 million from the Dodgers and not his preferred number of $88 million.

In 1985 there had been a two-day strike in Major League Baseball. It dealt, naturally, with revenue distribution. In 1990 a lockout during spring training lasted just over a month; again it had to do with money. Not to change the pace, in August 1994 players, fearing a new distribution deal over television revenue would prevent them from cashing in on every possible dollar, went on strike. The following month, the declaration announcing the cancellation of the World Series was made official. It was the first time the World Series would not be contested in 90 years.

Overall, 920 games were cancelled during the more than 230-day strike. Nineteen ninety-four marked the first year since 1869 that no team was labeled as baseball's best. The 1994 strike also marked the eighth time in baseball history that players refused to play, but it was the third time in just the last 23 years.

When players returned in 1995 to play a revamped, shortened schedule of 144 games, fans felt little incentive to go support childlike greed. It was one of the smallest opening crowds ever for most teams, including the Yankees. While the NFL and the NBA were taking in extra fans, and revenue, thanks to the self-inflicted wounds of Major League Baseball, baseball officials knew they had to do something to get people back in the seats. The first step was lavish celebrations and promotions of anything they could get their hands on: records, home runs, big plays, cheap gifts to the first 10,000 fans, anything they could do. Cal Ripken Jr., playing his 2,131st game, breaking Lou Gehrig's consecutive game streak, was the first high-profile moment since the strike. Ripken, who stayed with the Baltimore Orioles despite options elsewhere, was always seen as a true "good guy" in the sport and as such was the perfect candidate to show a lighter side of baseball. Fans, though, still wanted more. They wanted to see home runs. In 1998, fans were treated to plenty.

The battle for home run supremacy between Mark McGwire and Sammy Sosa raged throughout the entire season before McGwire ended the fight with 70 home runs, smashing the previous record of 61. The season brought back fans and millions of dollars, both for the league and for collectors of autographs, baseballs, and other types of memorabilia. In 2001, Barry Bonds eclipsed McGwire's still fresh record, inducing another year full of hype. Cash poured in, fans were happy, and as fate would have it, allegations a few years later would thrust both McGwire and Bonds into the midst of a cheating controversy. Steroid allegations hit McGwire most powerfully from Jose Canseco who says he himself injected McGwire, and by Bonds who admitted using steroids, but said he did so unknowingly. Fans, again, felt dejected.

That players would cheat to win is nothing new—it has been happening since the ancient Greek Olympics through modern times. The only thing that has changed are the reasons why. It used to be for pride, for winning at all costs. Olympic champions of ancient times won acclaim, a lifetime of servants, homes, power. Now, it's money, and as the old cliché goes, money is power.

Before 1996, sponsorships for Olympic athletes were fairly rare. By 2004 Olympic athletes were in high demand. In 2005, reports of swimming star Michael Phelps signing a deal with a Japanese MP3 player company for up to $4 million made some people do a double take. It was huge. But for players of a Big Three sport, that's pocket change. Let no one forget Latrell Sprewell, the recipient of $17 million a year, famously saying of his need for a large contract, "I need to feed my family."

So what do players do to ensure that fans keep filling seats? When there are sellout crowds, there's big money to be made, and thus more and more to be demanded and more families able to be fed (no doubt the finest of foods at every meal, every day).

The problem lies with players continually feeling the need to raise the bar. No fan wants to sit through an entire baseball game with the possibility of only a home run or two, especially if the entire season looks the same. If football players can hit harder, there's more money. If basketball players can jump higher, there's more money. If baseball players can hit the ball farther, there's more money. If a track star can run faster, there's more money. In professional sports it's about records. In the Olympics it's about records. Records mean money. Money means . . . everything?

Here is a look at the top salaries in baseball during pivotal periods of the game:

Note: all salaries from *USA Today Web* site.

1993—One year prior to baseball's biggest strike

Top 10 players and their salaries:

1.	Bonilla, Bobby	$6,200,000	New York Mets
2.	Sandberg, Ryne	$5,975,000	Chicago Cubs
3.	Gooden, Dwight	$5,916,667	New York Mets
4.	Larkin, Barry	$5,700,000	Cincinnati Reds
5.	Carter, Joe	$5,500,000	Toronto Blue Jays

6.	Maddux, Greg	$5,500,000	Atlanta Braves
7.	Morris, Jack	$5,425,000	Toronto Blue Jays
8.	Finley, Chuck	$5,375,000	Los Angeles Angels
9.	Puckett, Kirby	$5,200,000	Minnesota Twins
10.	Ripken Jr., Cal	$5,100,000	Baltimore Orioles

1995—One year after baseball's biggest strike

1.	Fielder, Cecil	$9,237,500	Detroit Tigers
2.	Bonds, Barry	$8,000,183	San Francisco Giants
3.	Cone, David	$8,000,000	Toronto Blue Jays
4.	Carter, Joe	$7,500,000	Toronto Blue Jays
5.	Griffey Jr., Ken	$7,500,000	Seattle Mariners
6.	Thomas, Frank	$7,150,000	Chicago White Sox
7.	McGwire, Mark	$6,900,000	Oakland Athletics
8.	Bagwell, Jeff	$6,875,000	Houston Astros
9.	Ripken Jr., Cal	$6,600,000	Baltimore Orioles
10.	Dykstra, Lenny	$6,200,000	Philadelphia Phillies

1998—Year of McGwire/Sosa home run race

1.	Belle, Albert	$10,000,000	Chicago White Sox
2.	Sheffield, Gary	$10,000,000	Florida Marlins
3.	Maddux, Greg	$9,600,000	Atlanta Braves
4.	Bonds, Barry	$8,916,667	San Francisco Giants
5.	McGwire, Mark	$8,333,333	St. Louis Cardinals
6.	Clemens, Roger	$8,250,000	Toronto Blue Jays
7.	Williams, Bernie	$8,250,000	New York Yankees
8.	Griffey Jr., Ken	$8,010,532	Seattle Mariners
9.	Galarraga, Andres	$8,000,000	Atlanta Braves
9.	Piazza, Mike	$8,000,000	Los Angeles Dodgers
9.	Sosa, Sammy	$8,000,000	Chicago Cubs

1999—Year following the breaking of Roger Maris's 61-home run record

1.	Belle, Albert	$11,949,794	Baltimore Orioles
2.	Martinez, Pedro	$11,100,000	Boston Red Sox
3.	Brown, Kevin	$10,714,286	Los Angeles Dodgers
4.	Maddux, Greg	$10,600,000	Atlanta Braves
5.	Sheffield, Gary	$9,956,667	Los Angeles Dodgers
6.	Williams, Bernie	$9,857,143	New York Yankees
7.	Johnson, Randy	$9,700,000	Arizona Diamondbacks
8.	Cone, David	$9,500,000	New York Yankees
9.	Bonds, Barry	$9,381,057	San Francisco Giants
10.	McGwire, Mark	$9,358,667	St. Louis Cardinals

2001—Year Barry Bonds breaks Mark McGwire's home run record

1.	Rodriguez, Alex	$22,000,000	Texas Rangers
2.	Brown, Kevin	$15,714,286	Los Angeles Dodgers
3.	Delgado, Carlos	$13,650,000	Toronto Blue Jays
4.	Piazza, Mike	$13,571,429	New York Mets
5.	Johnson, Randy	$13,350,000	Arizona Diamondbacks
6.	Vaughn, Mo	$13,166,668	Los Angeles Angels
7.	Ramirez, Manny	$13,050,000	Boston Red Sox
8.	Martinez, Pedro	$13,000,000	Boston Red Sox
9.	Jeter, Derek	$12,600,000	New York Yankees
10.	Griffey Jr., Ken	$12,500,000	Cincinnati Reds
11.	Maddux, Greg	$12,500,000	Atlanta Braves
12.	Sosa, Sammy	$12,500,000	Chicago Cubs
13.	McGwire, Mark	$11,000,000	St. Louis Cardinals
14.	Bonds, Barry	$10,300,000	San Francisco Giants

2002—Year after Bonds broke McGwire's home run record

1.	Rodriguez, Alex	$22,000,000	Texas Rangers
2.	Delgado, Carlos	$19,400,000	Toronto Blue Jays
3.	Brown, Kevin	$15,714,286	Los Angeles Dodgers
4.	Ramirez, Manny	$15,462,727	Boston Red Sox
5.	Bonds, Barry	$15,000,000	San Francisco Giants
6.	Sosa, Sammy	$15,000,000	Chicago Cubs
7.	Jeter, Derek	$14,600,000	New York Yankees
8.	Martinez, Pedro	$14,000,000	Boston Red Sox
9.	Green, Shawn	$13,416,667	Los Angeles Dodgers
10.	Johnson, Randy	$13,350,000	Arizona Diamondbacks

The year 2002 was the first time that the top 25 highest paid players in baseball made at minimum $10 million per season.

2004—Year of the breaking BALCO scandal

1.	Ramirez, Manny	$22,500,000	Boston Red Sox
2.	Rodriguez, Alex	$22,000,000	New York Yankees
3.	Delgado, Carlos	$19,700,000	Toronto Blue Jays
4.	Jeter, Derek	$18,600,000	New York Yankees
5.	Bonds, Barry	$18,000,000	San Francisco Giants
6.	Martinez, Pedro	$17,500,000	Boston Red Sox
7.	Vaughn, Mo	$17,166,667	New York Mets
8.	Green, Shawn	$16,666,667	Los Angeles Dodgers
9.	Piazza, Mike	$16,071,429	New York Mets
10.	Bagwell, Jeff	$16,000,000	Houston Astros
10.	Sosa, Sammy	$16,000,000	Chicago Cubs

2005—Year of continued BALCO and other steroid allegations

1.	Rodriguez, Alex	$26,000,000	New York Yankees
2.	Bonds, Barry	$22,000,000	San Francisco Giants
3.	Ramirez, Manny	$22,000,000	Boston Red Sox
4.	Jeter, Derek	$19,600,000	New York Yankees
5.	Mussina, Mike	$19,000,000	New York Yankees
6.	Bagwell, Jeff	$18,000,000	Houston Astros
7.	Clemens, Roger	$18,000,000	Houston Astros
8.	Sosa, Sammy	$17,000,000	Baltimore Orioles
9.	Piazza, Mike	$16,071,429	New York Mets
10.	Jones, Chipper	$16,061,802	Atlanta Braves

In 12 years the top salary in baseball increased by almost $20 million. For Barry Bonds, he went from making $4.4 million in 1993, his first year with the Giants, which was a slight pay cut from what he made with the Pittsburgh Pirates in 1992, to $22 million twelve years later. He's hitting more home runs and making almost $18 million more for it. No doubt the pay increase was part of his ability to put fans in seats, and not just his stats.

With the average American household income hovering just above $40,000 a year and the average Canadian income in U.S. currency just under $52,000 annually, there's a lot of temptation for anyone, in any walk of life, to find a way to excel. Many athletes would rather fail to reach the pinnacle of their sport than cheat, others will do anything to try. This isn't to say that every baseball player, or even most players who make big dollars cheat, but the correlation between big numbers and big dollars is a lot for some, especially impressionable children, to handle. The draw to make the big salaries, however, isn't just related to baseball, basketball, and football. The Olympics and their continued commercialization has plenty to do with it as well.

The Olympic Flame—Fueling the Drug Fire

The modern Olympics were created for the love of sport, for the competition. Pierre de Coubertin brought back the Olympic Games in 1896 to trump human inequality, country strife, and all else that was wrong with mankind. The Olympics were to encourage people, athletes, to dig deep within themselves and reach for more, want the best, give everything they have to become champion. Unfortunately, over the past several decades, giving everything one has is more than physical effort—for a lot of people, that means money for drugs, and perhaps their pride for the gold.

Cheating in the Olympics is nothing new. It has no doubt been occurring since the first Olympics in ancient Greece, but the causes and effects were different than they are today. Decades ago the Olympics stopped pretending to be simply a collaboration of the world's best amateurs, and perhaps the last bit of innocence the games possessed was taken away as sponsorship dollars started pouring in. According to a Russian proverb, "When money speaks, the truth keeps silent."

Before getting into the discussion of money inducing cheating, it is important to note that the biggest casualties of this trend are the clean athletes who are being ousted from their rightful places atop podiums. No, not every gold medal winner in the Olympics is using illegal performance-enhancing drugs, but history has told us many have, and the glory of individuals and countries are being tarnished, the former rightfully so and the latter as guilt by association. Long gone is the goal of competing for one's country, much of it now has shifted to competing for the glory of oneself. The Olympics take place every four years, and an athlete who isn't capable of making the big leagues in baseball, basketball, or football usually has but one opportunity to really capture the attention of the world. Kids, teenagers, adults, so many dream of becoming a professional athlete, a star, that some are willing to do anything. Health consequences aside, good or bad, breaking the rules is despicable, and the use of performance-enhancing drugs and gene therapy is illegal.

Most Olympic athletes are upstanding individuals. Even those who choose to try to beat the system are generally law-abiding citizens, many probably attend a place of worship, assist in their community, are their parents' pride and joy. But even good people can slowly tilt to a path of corruption, even if it's just in one facet of their life. Benjamin Franklin once said, "He that is of the opinion money will do everything may well be suspected of doing everything for money." When money is the ultimate goal, the path to that goal is often a path of doing whatever it takes to possess it.

The Olympic flame still stands to many as a symbol of national pride and joy, accomplishment, and the culmination of years, sometimes decades of hard work. For corporations, it's bigger than the Super Bowl. It's the biggest worldwide opportunity to put their name out there in front of billions of viewers. NBC, for example, paid over $600 million for the rights to broadcast the 2006 Winter Olympics in the United States and almost $900 million for the 2008 Summer Olympics in Beijing. At the same time, the companies that are advertising with NBC want to capitalize on their Olympic lockdown, and are offering big contracts to athletes to endorse everything from fast food to credit cards. And these companies want gold medalists, they don't want silver or bronze or athletes who "almost medaled." It's a simple, understandable part of promotion—buy what sells. Winners sell. Winners of the Olympics then, can make a whole lot of money.

The United States is one of several countries that pay their athletes for their performance in the Olympics. Whereas once it was enough for an athlete to earn a free trip to the Olympics, compete for his flag, and the right to have his national anthem played, now the USOC is finding it necessary to pay the best of the best. While the reasoning behind the prize money is that it assists the athlete to continue to train for a high level of competition, some governing bodies, such as USA Swimming, pay their national team members monthly stipends to assist with the training and living expenses of their elite, a method no doubt much more efficient than paying only medal winners large sums of money. When you must be the best of the best to get endorsements, or to even get paid, many unscrupulous athletes will attempt to do whatever it takes to get there. And on paper, being at the top is a very lucrative place to be.

Since 1984 the USOC has given $25,000 to gold medalists, $15,000 to silver medalists, and $10,000 to bronze medalists. To a lot of people, that's not a great deal of money, but to a lot of people, it is, it's an extraordinary sum. Perhaps to a kid growing up in poverty, with a substantial gift of running fast or lifting heavy things, that's a way out. And if Barry Bonds and Mark McGwire can use steroids and get better and be rich, why can't any other kid? Better yet, why shouldn't he? Try explaining national pride to a kid who just wants to have enough money to buy a place where his mother can sleep somewhere besides the living room floor. It's possible to instill national pride, but someone has to be there to do it, to point out all of the possibilities, the rules, the consequences. Tunnel vision isn't inescapable, but it's prevalent among kids who look at their heroes doing one thing while politicians and other suits tell them it's wrong.

And it isn't just the medal money, either. It's the potential sponsorships afterward. American swimmer Michael Phelps was offered $1 million by his swimwear endorser, Speedo, if he tied or broke Mark Spitz's record of seven Olympic gold medals. A lot of people may not have had Phelps's fortitude and some may have tried to cheat the system for a better shot at the seven-figure bonus, not considering the future. One gold shy of the seven, Phelps later signed an endorsement deal that was reportedly worth up to $4 million.

The money is provocation no doubt, and it's always more enticing in large sums. The governing bodies that give money to their athletes and developmental programs are doing much for their sport, maybe without even thinking about it, as far as keeping it drug free. Many athletes who have been caught cheating claim it was their first time trying the drug, or they say it was only to rehabilitate this injury or that, or they make some reference about how it was only to be used for a certain period of time. Maybe they say it was because they know the longer they use an illegal drug, the more chance they have to get caught. But if it's the Olympic money they're after, and it comes in one lump sum, the time period to test the system is short. By dividing up the money and promoting a system that rewards continual high-level performance, not just gold medal performances in every Olympiad, athletes are more likely to consider the long-term effects both mentally and physically, and also the risks of getting caught. One would assume they can only push their luck so long. And, maybe, the extra time to think will make athletes realize that despite anyone's stance on drugs, winning within the rules is much more rewarding. That, combined with other methods of controlling drugs and testing procedures could clean up the sporting world. Until then, we have words like the following from Werner Reiterer, an athlete who has seen the Olympics in their glory and in their darkest hours and as they became submerged in pitch black:

> Despite the flashing cameras, tears, hugs and kisses in the arena and farewells from athletes whose paths may cross again in four years' times, or ever at all, and despite the roar of the crowd bedazzled by what a few million dollars can do for an Olympic closing ceremony, [I] knew that somewhere along the line, it had all gone terribly wrong. Sport was so horribly mutilated it no longer had a value, ethic or thread of truth to cling on to. With the extinguishing of the Olympic flame in Seoul, the last vestige of anything human in sport seemed to disappear from the face of the earth. I watched as the living flame instantly became darkness. To me, sport—in that instant—also died. It was as if the clean, natural athlete, who represented the Olympic sporting ideal, whom we could point our children to as a role model, had never even existed. There were those, of course, who knew they never had.

10

Drug Letting

It isn't hard to criticize various sports governing bodies on the lengths they are willing to go to combat drug use in sports. Baseball, for example, had no real drug testing policy until the BALCO investigations began and then fought with Congress over the proper way to go about policing its players. The NBA on the other hand has a solid drug policy, and seems to find the most frequent offenders failing drug tests for marijuana, not steroids. The NFL is also strong on paper, having a tiered suspension policy for positive steroid tests: four games for a first offense, six games for a second, one year for a third positive test. Six players from each team are drug tested each week, but rumors of corruption in the policy aren't new, though they are unsubstantiated.

Even surfing is enforcing a drug policy, with the Association of Surfing Professionals' first-ever positive test returned in 2005, which resulted in the athlete's 12-month suspension.

Olympic sports are governed under several organizations for drug testing. For example, elite swimmers on an international level can be drug tested by the U.S. Anti-Doping Agency, the World Anti-Doping Agency, and FINA, the sport's actual governing body.

And yet, using BALCO as evidence, some athletes are slipping through the cracks and doping, using drugs that are undetectable. The rift seems like it's only growing wider between the cheats and the testers, and with the reluctance of some sports to enact a solid policy, and the refusal of others to support the policy they already have, it seems like it may never close.

The biggest mirage of a drug testing policy in the entire world of sports is that of professional bodybuilding. This opinion is shared by physicians and even many athletes in the sport, most of whom are unable to publicly voice their opposition because of the judging tactics during competitions. Bodybuilding is often viewed as a very political sport, where certain faces—often those who endorse major sponsors' products—are rewarded with victories, despite not having the best physique of the day. Because of this, the sport is funneled into the "do or die" category, with athletes forced to play the size game. The sport is supposed to be judged based on aesthetics and symmetry as well as size, but over the last decade it seems that size remains king.

The July 2004 issue of *FHM* magazine offered an insight to the general public (those who don't follow bodybuilding regularly) on what life is like for a professional bodybuilder. The magazine did a piece on Jay Cutler, three-time Arnold Schwarzenegger Classic winner. They quoted Cutler as saying, "I know I'm a freak, but that's the state I need to achieve to win." Even his father agreed. Also quoted in the piece, his dad said, "I'm impressed with what Jay does, but the sport doesn't impress me. The judging is subjective . . . your body's only created to do so much and Jay's making his do more than it's supposed to." Near the end of the article Cutler admits, "I look at myself in the mirror and it's not my ideal to look the way I do, but that's what it takes to win."

Cutler is stating nothing but fact. Each Mr. Olympia is bigger than his predecessor. It goes with the territory. Bigger is better. Bodybuilders often get called freaks, but to those same people they could often turn around and say, "And you're fat, so what?" Everyone has his place.

Naturally it is up to each bodybuilder to decide how far he wants to pursue the sport, but it's an unwritten rule that if you want to be a professional bodybuilder, you must use steroids. It's almost a punishment for falling in love with the sport. The human body just can't reach the size needed to compete on the professional level of the sport without drugs. In the International Federation of BodyBuilders (IFBB), the recognized leading body of the sport, there isn't one natural (drug-free) athlete. That's not to say there aren't athletes who may be able to pass drug tests, as it has been proven drug tests don't catch every individual who uses steroids, but in the IFBB, drug testing is a joke.

The IFBB Anti-Doping program states in its 47-page manual that "The IFBB shall conduct doping control at all international Championships held under its direct jurisdiction and sanction." It continues on to specifically point out the World Championships, but neglects any mention of the sport's two biggest shows, the Mr. Olympia contest and the Arnold Classic. The program also reserves the right to randomly test any athlete at any time—this doesn't happen. It goes further to say that it is a signatory of the World Anti-Doping Agency. All bodybuilders would fail if the WADA tested them. Because there's no news of that happening, it's apparent they simply don't get tested. Finally, in what may be the biggest slap in the face to anyone, the IFBB Anti-Doping program says, under a heading that reads "Article 14—Responsibilities of the IFBB":

14.1 The IFBB shall:

1. Fully support the ideals of the Olympic Movement as demonstrated by the International Olympic Committee (IOC).
2. Fully support the World Anti-Doping Agency (WADA) and the WADA Code.
3. Ban the use of prohibited and restricted substances and prohibited methods.
4. Implement doping control programs throughout the IFBB, to include all affiliated National Federations.
5. Promulgate rules, regulations, guidelines, and directives for doping control.
6. Maintain and update, as required, the IFBB *Anti-Doping Program* manual.
7. Control and supervise doping control at IFBB-sanctioned international competition.
8. Determine the number of athletes selected for doping control, for both competition and out-of-competition testing.
9. Assist the National Federations in establishing their own doping control programs.

10. Receive the laboratory Certificate of Analysis and issue letters of notification of doping control results.
11. Apply and enforce sanctions on athlete-members and National Federations who are found guilty of having committed an anti-doping rule violation.
12. Establish appeal procedures for athlete-members and National Federations who wish to appeal doping control results or sanctions.
13. Provide educational material on the use and abuse of performance enhancing substances and on healthy alternatives.

For a certain period, bodybuilders were drug tested for diuretics. Oddly enough, while some athletes have failed these tests, their placing and prize money was never revoked.

It's tough, though, to blame bodybuilding for its sins. Bodybuilding has always been a niche sport, a small cult following keeps it alive and thriving in its own little world. A breakthrough to the mainstream is desired by some, shunned by others. In either case, professional bodybuilders are popular because of their size. No one wants to pay money to watch a pay-per-view event such as the Mr. Olympia and see guys on stage as big as the guys they see in their gym every single day. Yes, the competitors would be very happy if they didn't have to take drugs to compete at a high level, but then where does the notoriety go? Arnold was famous for his muscles. Zeus and Hercules wouldn't be nearly as daunting on the big screen at 180 pounds. It's unfortunate for the sport that the big competitors keep it afloat, but it's a fact. Drug testing would kill bodybuilding as a money-making endeavor, but would almost certainly open it up to more people wanting to give it a shot.

And while the bodybuilding community accepts its relation to drugs, there are other sports, mostly in the Olympics, that are trying with all their might to rid their fields, pools, and courts of the drugs. And it's hard to tell whether or not their efforts are effective. More athletes are being caught, but is that because the athletes are getting sloppy or the drug testing is getting better?

Funding is a big problem for testing organizations. Drug manufacturers and underground labs have more free cash than drug testers. The money they have can be used to continually research new drugs. Testers, on the other hand, have to keep paying to test samples and not just endorse research and development of new tests. Because drug testing is mostly a grant-funded operation, meaning that collecting urine and blood samples generates no revenue, it's always going to be lagging. The USADA for example had a 2005 budget of just $11.89 million, the vast majority of it from a government-funded grant, and the rest from the U.S. Olympic Committee. With a slightly smaller budget the year before, the USADA was able to perform just 7,630 tests. With the number of contests and the number of athletes competing in sports under its jurisdiction, that number isn't nearly as big as it may seem.

To a lot of people, drug testing just doesn't enhance the sport. It isn't something you watch or cheer for while it happens. As entertaining as athletes providing a urine sample might be, it won't fill 50,000-seat stadiums to watch them walk in and out of a restroom, drug tester in tow. While the majority of people want a clean sport, others just want home runs. It doesn't matter how. Another group of people want both: better facilities and entertainment structures as well as clean sports. The odds of the two ever being on equal playing fields are slim to none. As an example, the $11.89 million budget of the USADA is a drop in the bucket compared to the costs of things like new stadiums, which have a tendency as of late to keep popping up. The new Yankee Stadium is expected to cost as much as $1 billion, with $800 million coming from the Yankees themselves. The plush furnishings in the private boxes will no doubt cost more than $11.89 million. The Washington Nationals, building their new stadium, were originally given $440 million, a much more modest amount, but enough to build a 41,000-capacity stadium.

It all comes down to business. New stadiums bring in more fans. Better teams bring in more money. Goliath-like bodybuilders draw attention and sell nutritional supplements. The same owners and players who condemn performance-enhancing drug use aren't helping. If each professional team in the United States gave even 1 percent of its operating budget to drug testing, a whole stock of new tests would come out and it's a certainty that more cheaters would be drawn out. Even the idea of a properly funded drug testing organization could cause countless drug users to quit in fear of being ousted; they know they're only getting away with it because they're ahead of science. Science is money, and it's a game of catch-up.

Professional athletes too could support the antidoping efforts. With the number of athletes making over $1 million, let alone over $10 million and $100 million, a donation of 1 percent or even ½ percent would boost drug testing capabilities beyond the scope of current efforts. Is it ludicrous to consider athletes funding their own drug testing? Not in the least bit. For a lot of athletes, it could end up meaning more money in their own pockets, even after a small donation to testing efforts. If the cheaters are gone, that is less competition. A small few of the best athletes in sports have admitted using drugs; imagine if their salaries had been divided among others. The program would more than pay for itself.

But even if a plan like that was considered, would it be accepted? It seems, at least on the Olympic level, it would have to be an official procedure. Some top athletes in sports outside the Big Three don't support drug testing. In an article in *VeloNews*, American skier Bode Miller and Belgian cycling legend Eddy Merckx both spoke out to some degree in promotion of drug use in sports. Miller expressed disapproval of the ban on EPO and Merckx said he would never support a zero-tolerance policy. Miller believes EPO would make his sport safer because of its ability to increase the transportation of oxygen in the body, which he believes would assist in the decision-making process of downhill skiing. On the other hand, EPO can also thicken the blood with too many red blood cells, causing increased stress on the heart and other organs. This has been the cause of numerous athletes' deaths. Under physicians' supervision, though, the risks could be reduced.

Merckx, who won the Tour de France five times, said he supports drug testing but a zero-tolerance policy was not an option.

Neither Miller nor Merckx have ever failed a drug test.

And if teams, groups, and individuals are unwilling to make a tax-deductible donation to fight doping, the next best thing may be to follow the role of one small country and impose jail sentences for cheaters. After all, what people tend to forget is that steroids remain, despite evidence proving any benefits or side effects, illegal in America. And for this reason, it makes one wonder why the government allows for such negotiation with sports federations regarding penalties on violations. Since when did people who break the law get to negotiate their sentences?

Italy—The Final Frontier?

The Italian government has, since 2004, developed one of the strictest policies against steroid and other performance-enhancing drug use in the world. And it's working. At least, for the intended purpose. Instead of putting the use of drugs in sports on the back burner, the Italian government has made it a prime target.

In the United States and most other countries, it is illegal to possess and distribute anabolic steroids and various other related agents. It is not illegal, in a technical sense, to have used them or have them in your bloodstream. A positive test for steroids in America comes with its own consequences in the form of discipline by the workplace or, in the case of elite athletes, the revocation of medals, placing, prize money, and so on. There are, naturally, many cases in which nothing more than a warning is passed along. It depends on the basis of the drug test, who carried it out, the validity of the test, and the sport. Major League Baseball, for example, carried out an entire year of anonymous drug testing simply to see how many positive tests came out of it. No suspensions were passed out at all. MLB moved the following year to introduce a policy of punishment to doped-up athletes. In any case, testing positive for anabolic or androgenic steroids in nearly any country in the world does not pose the threat of any life-altering punishments other than those related to the sport. In Italy, it's completely different. In Italy, testing positive for steroids or other performance-enhancing drugs means not only banishment from athletics, but jail time as well.

As host of the 2006 Winter Olympics in Torino, the Italian government was poised to produce one of the cleanest drug-free games, at least as clean as an the Olympic Games can get. And then, in a show of weakness and stupefying curiousness, the IOC and its president, Jacques Rogge, asked Italian officials to provide a 60-day moratorium on the law that would jail cheaters found during the games.

Why?

The IOC said it would work to remove cheaters from sports and strip them of their medals, but not jail them. Its reasoning for that remained unclear. The Olympics is continually described by its leaders as an event of honor, dignity, respect, and the like. Morals could sum it up nicely. Athletes who cheat by way of using anabolic steroids and other drugs to gain the edge over competition are certainly not competing with morals.

When Italy was given the Olympics its steroid laws were lax. As the years passed and the Olympics grew nearer, Italy's laws became tougher and tougher, which was seen as a huge boost for a potentially clean winter. In 2004 Italian officials carried out more than 10,000 drug tests. The U.S. Anti-Doping Agency carried out under 8,000. Italy has a population of just over 58 million, with the United States home to over 300 million. With those tests and because of them, Italian officials seized 10,000 units of drugs in 2003 while arresting 20 people, and over 900,000 in 2004 while arresting 115 individuals. And unlike the United States, where some high-profile athletes have been accused of getting a free pass by having their positive test results hidden or destroyed, Italy makes no such alterations. It prosecutes small names and big names alike, including Riccardo Agricola, the Juventus soccer club doctor; cyclist Marco Pantani; and even Libyan leader Muammar Gadhafi's son. Prosecution for steroids under Italian laws means an almost certain end for cheats. Agricola, who was jailed for providing his team with various performance-enhancing substances, was sentenced to 22 months in prison. Pantani, the 1998 Tour de France winner, went into a serious depressed state after his doping results came to light, and eventually overdosed on drugs, which ultimately killed him.

Italian laws are strict, and perhaps to some too strict, but they are effective. They not only remove drugs from circulation among athletes, but from around the world. In 2005 Italian police ended a five-month investigation that resulted in arrests that ended a ring that supplied various countries with anabolic steroids, including American soldiers in Iraq and Afghanistan.

For the Olympics, the worry prior to the Opening Ceremonies was potential raids on the athletes' village. So long as the competitors weren't sleeping at the time, this shouldn't have even been a concern. It should have only been viewed as a positive law that provides much opportunity to catch cheaters. Any clean athlete would applaud the measure. Italy's law should have been rewarded, cheered for, and supported, not fought against. The message Rogge and the rest of the IOC is sending is along the lines of "We're against the use of performance-enhancing drugs. Kind of."

The truth is the IOC is not supporting its supposed zero-tolerance policy on doping, and the lead-up to Torino proved it beyond any doubt whatsoever. Even members of Italy's sporting government were trying to follow IOC wishes instead of their own laws. Mario Pescante, supervisor of the 2006 Winter Games, was quoted in an Italian newspaper as saying, "You think American professional hockey players, paid in the millions, will risk being put in handcuffs to come play in Turin? Come on, let's be realistic."

Yes, let's be realistic. If American or Canadian or Russian or any hockey player for that matter was on drugs and knew he would be arrested if caught, he probably wouldn't go play. But that's not a bad thing. That's the best thing that could happen to the Olympics and to the clean athletes competing. That's exactly what the world of sports needs if the consensus is to rid the games of drug use.

Pescante also said, "I expected a strong reaction to my proposal, but now I'm being treated as a lobbyist for dopers." Which, ultimately leading into the Olympics, he was.

Did the IOC push for a law change because it's afraid of cleanliness in sports? It has reason to be. Without drugs, world records aren't going to be broken nearly as often. That's fact. Humans develop, or evolve, slowly when it's natural. A lot of fans watch only to see records broken. What happens when fans think there won't be any records broken? They sometimes tune out. And then, the Olympic cash cow starts feeling as if its pockets had been robbed.

Bottom line: if the IOC doesn't want a zero-tolerance policy on drug use, it shouldn't pretend to support one.

Italian Foreign Minister Gianfranco Fini hit the antidoping note right on the head when he said, "I believe that one of the principles of sports is fairness. An athlete who uses banned substances comes under this principle, and therefore I would not support measures to render our legislation—which is one of the most just and severe in the world—weaker for people who use [illegal] substances."

Apparently there are two groups of people against drug use in sports: the IOC, and everyone else.

11

For Every Problem, a Solution

The following are three potential solutions to the epidemic of steroid use that is enveloping American athletics. If money is at the heart of the problem, it can be solved in one way or another.

A Solution, and Its Problems—The Most Controversial Approach

The Answer?

Legalize anabolic steroids.

Why Do Such a Thing?

When a substance or product is legal and in full view of the public, as compared to being dealt behind closed doors, a lot more information is available. The stigma that steroids are bad and users of steroids suffer horrible, intolerable side effects, is beyond hyperbole. The facts prove that. But the majority of media reports against steroids is essentially yellow journalism in the new age.

Tetrahydrogestrinone, also known as THG, essentially spurred the entire BALCO investigation and subsequent grand jury testimonies by many of the top athletes in the nation. This steroid, known as a "designer drug," was only discovered after being sent in by a track and field team manager.

Had these types of substances been legal, once THG was created, the government and governing bodies of sports would have known about it, known its chemical composition, and been able to test it from its inception. There is little information, at least reliable data, on when THG was really created. As far as anyone knows, multiple Olympic and World Championships medals have been won by athletes using THG. The question about how many other designer steroids are out there can never be answered as long as these substances are kept on the black market. The people who make them have no desire to get caught, and the people who buy them have no desire to be known, either.

Would It Be Healthier?

Potentially. Legalizing anabolic steroids would be much healthier than keeping them banned, at least for the people who would use them regardless of their legal status. For the most obvious reasons, legalizing steroids would be much healthier for the using population because usage by athletes could be monitored. Liver, kidney, and blood values could be checked regularly and any potential side effects could be handled immediately by trained professionals. Steroids have been illegal since 1991, and the majority of steroid-related health problems, which have been reported in the last decade, compared to the health risks of smoking or drinking alcohol, are relatively few. Legalization's largest opponent is the theory that more people would use these substances, but still not be monitored or use them "as suggested."

How Would This Change Sports?

When someone or a group, in this case we'll use the World Anti-Doping Agency (WADA) as an example, knows what it's fighting against, it can do a better job. Legalizing steroids for use by the general public would not constitute legal use by sporting associations. On the contrary, it would allow tighter restrictions on substances.

The USOC, for example, still has restrictions on aspirin, and prior to the banning of ephedra, had restrictions on its competition use as well.

Caffeine, 3,7-dihydro-1,3,7-trimethyl-1H-purine-2,6,-dione or 1,3,7-trimethylxanthine, was also banned at doses over 12 micrograms until 2004. Several athletes, including 1988 Olympian in the modern pentathlon, Alex

Watson, have tested positive and been banned from future competition for caffeine-positive tests.

A Solution, and Its Problems—The Most Unlikely Approach

The Answer?

Withdraw prize money from the Olympic Games and reduce their commercial appeal.

Why Do Such a Thing?

Major League Baseball has drawn much attention with its rampant steroid and other performance-enhancement use, but the majority of the problems is still prevalent in Olympic competition. And as long as there is money and notoriety in winning a gold, silver, or bronze medal, it seems there will always be those willing to cheat their way forward. Long ago the Olympics stood for something other than fame, and to many it still does. But there are now those who want to use the five rings as a means to an end; that end being money and big endorsement deals.

The U.S. Olympic Committee pays athletes the following bonuses according to their medal color:

Gold: $25,000
Silver: $15,000
Bronze: $10,000

Is USOC supporting the habit of cheating? Obviously that wouldn't be the intent, but it may be the truth. If these bonuses were removed and a tighter limit placed on the sponsorships going into the games, there would be less incentive to use steroids.

Would It Be Healthier?

Health would be a minor factor in a solution such as this. Potentially fewer athletes would be doping, but it doesn't necessarily mean that those who still choose to use performance-enhancing drugs will do it under any safer conditions. Steroids have been proven to be both harmless (at least short term) and harmful (again, at least short term), all depending on the amounts used and the type of administration. What may not be healthier is that many athletes still compete for the love of the sport and their country, and the withdrawal of prize money and endorsement opportunities may prevent them from purchasing proper training equipment or household necessities while they train.

How Would This Change Sports?

It would return the emphasis to the athletic events themselves rather than showcasing the individual athlete as a corporate icon. It isn't a likely solution, it isn't even highly feasible, but it's possible.

A Solution, and Its Problems—The Most Likely Approach

The Answer?

Pass one set of rules to supersede all sports. Beginning with the BALCO investigation, the U.S. Congress has since decided it wants to be involved in the fight against steroids. Rather than questioning athletes and allowing them to hide behind their lawyers, forego the time, effort, and chance to spend money on pointless question and answer sessions. A federal law has been in place since 1991 that declares anabolic steroids a Class III illegal substance, which makes them a felony to possess and/or distribute. Since 2005, steroid precursors known as "prohormones" have been declared illegal also. A user of methylated 1-testosterone (M1T), a popular prosteroid until its ban in January 2005, is as much a felon as a user of cocaine.

If baseball players were using cocaine or heroin, the powers that be would threaten to shut down the league. But steroids? They have yet to make any major changes. Revisions beginning with the 2005 season have increased the number of players being suspended, but suspensions are a paltry punishment compared to the sentences handed down to individual steroid users, those who aren't rich or famous, who are caught in possession. Illegal is illegal, nothing more, nothing less. But Major League Baseball had since held, until 2004, that it didn't need to spell out in its agreement with the Players Union that steroids were not allowed. Did it need to? It shouldn't have to. But some people, obviously officials of MLB and at least one sportswriter, think that's a free pass.

In an article published March 27, 2005, Carl Slezak of the *Chicago Sun-Times* wrote: "Steroids were not a banned substance in baseball when McGwire played." This was in response to an argument that Mark McGwire, who has been accused, most notably by Jose Canseco, of using steroids, should be admitted into the Major League Baseball Hall of Fame. First ballot, he says.

The problem with Mr. Slezak's statement is that, despite Major League Baseball's lax stance on steroids up to 2005, the substances have been illegal in America since 1991. Federal law supersedes the MLB, the NFL, the NBA, even the U.S. Olympic Committee. Period. If Congress were to step up its backing of a ruling that covered all sports, its interest in the topic could be justified as something more than use of taxpayer money and newspaper fodder.

Why Do Such a Thing?

Because of an apparent hardship to find one set of hard and fast rules. The United States cannot afford to worry about other countries and their testing policies. The United States must, perhaps unfortunately, trust world antidoping associations with catching cheaters outside its borders. On a moral level, knowing that athletes representing America are clean, is a victory in itself.

Would It Be Healthier?

Yes and no. Athletes in professional sports would be less likely to use banned performance-enhancing substances from fear of prosecution, but those who buy, use, and distribute steroids via the black market would go about their business vastly unchanged.

How Would This Change Sports?

It would be the most profound change in athletics since the inception of the shot clock. In October 2005, a United Nations-led effort was being pressed for acceptance by Olympic-competing nations to accept the World Anti-Doping Agency code as a uniform drug testing standard in all sports. Even if passed, it must be ratified and accepted in each nation separately to be put into effect.

When Testing Works

For the people trying to keep drugs out of sports, the fight can often seem arduous and maybe, at some point, useless. But no doubt they take solace in the opportunities they do have to catch those who cheat. The USADA is in charge of drug testing, in and out of competition, for Olympic sports in America.

The following, a breakdown of USADA statistics for testing, is taken from usantidoping.org:

2001

	1st Quarter	2nd Quarter	3rd Quarter	4th Quarter	Total
Camp	86	144	68	37	335
In-Competition	841	1182	397	591	3011
OOC	156	295	432	499	1382
Totals	1083	1621	897	1127	4728

2002

	1st Quarter	2nd Quarter	3rd Quarter	4th Quarter	Total
Camp	51	160	216	54	481
In-Competition	506	843	1071	419	2839
OOC	660	572	572	573	2377
Totals	1217	1575	1859	1046	5697

2003

	1st Quarter	2nd Quarter	3rd Quarter	4th Quarter	Total
Camp	18	337	117	96	568
In-Competition	521	1441	554	381	2897
OOC	1289	589	551	901	3330
Totals	1828	2367	1222	1378	6795

2004

	1st Quarter	2nd Quarter	3rd Quarter	4th Quarter	Total
Camp	0	242	228	46	516
In-Competition	825	1271	758	329	3183
OOC	1041	1443	739	708	3931
Totals	1866	2956	1725	1083	7630

Nearly 3,000 more tests were performed domestically in 2004 as compared to 2001. But, are the additional tests doing more?

The following is a compilation of athletes who have tested positive and faced sanctions from USADA tests:

Athlete	Sport	Sanction	Substance	Release Date
Annette Hanson	Cycling	1-month suspension	ephedrine	12/18/2001
Jeff Laynes	Bobsled	2-year suspension	manipulation of forms	12/7/2001
Jeff Laynes	Track & Field	2-year suspension	stanzolol	12/7/2001
Greg Siem	Bobsled	2-year suspension	test refusal	11/9/2001
Michael Picotte	Swimming	4-year suspension	test refusal	11/6/2001
Antoinette Wilks	Track & Field	10-month suspension	methylphenidate	9/18/2001
Tony Dees	Track & Field	lifetime	nandrolone metabolites	9/17/2001
David Klaassent VanOorscho	Cycling	public warning	pseudoephedrine	9/17/2001
Adam Brozer	Karate	1-month suspension	pseudoephedrine	8/13/2001
William Finneran	Karate	1-month suspension	ephedrine	8/13/2001
Jose Guzman	Cycling	3-month suspension	ephedrine	8/9/2001
Bobby Smith	Track & Field	public warning	ephedrine	7/31/2001
John Kasper	Bobsled	2-year suspension	Dianabol	7/16/2001

Athlete	Sport	Sanction	Substance	Release Date
Tony Dees	Track & Field	2-year suspension	nandrolone metabolites	6/12/2001
Matt Bricker	Diving	2-month suspension	ephedrine	5/21/2001
Robert Howard	Track & Field	public warning	ephedrine	5/14/2001
Hazel Clark	Track & Field	public warning	pseudoephedrine	5/7/2001
Raelyn Jacobson	Fencing	1-year suspension	amphetamine	5/1/2001
Leon Settle	Track & Field	public warning	ephedrine	12/10/2002
Tipton Peterson	Wrestling	2-year suspension	testosterone, methandienone (Dianabol) and stanzolol	12/3/2002
Shawn Mandolesi	Softball	2-year suspension	19-norandrosterone and 19-noretiocholanolone	12/2/2002
Sebastian Bea	Rowing	2-year suspension	Missed test violation	11/19/2002
Kyoko Ina	Figure Skating	2-year suspension	test refusal	10/25/2002
Crystal Cox	Track & Field	public warning	ephedrine	10/16/2002
Joseph Miller	Cycling	3-month suspension	failure to appear for test	10/4/2002
Juan Pineda	Cycling	2-year suspension	19-norandrosterone and 19-noretiocholanolone	9/25/2002
Hannah Gray	Cycling	public warning	ephedrine	9/20/2002
Marcus Clavelle	Track & Field	2-year suspension	methandienone (Dianabol)	9/11/2002
Andrew Garcy	Weightlifting	2-year suspension	testosterone	9/6/2002
Duane Dickey	Cycling	1-year suspension	phentermine, boldenone, and nandrolone	8/30/2002
Tammy Thomas	Cycling	lifetime	norbolethone	8/30/2002
James Hamilton	Track & Field	public warning	pseudoephedrine	8/2/2002
Steve Siler	Swimming	2-month suspension	ephedrine	7/22/2002
Kirk O'Bee	Cycling	1-year suspension	testosterone	7/18/2002

Athlete	Sport	Sanction	Substance	Release Date
Albert Reed	Paralympics	2-month suspension	ephedrine	6/25/2002
Alex Wood	Fencing	3-month suspension	pseudoephedrine	6/24/2002
Luis Bordes	Track & Field	public warning	pseudoephedrine	6/14/2002
Brooke Blackwelder	Cycling	8-month suspension	19-norandrosterone	5/22/2002
Justin Gatlin	Track & Field	2-year suspension	amphetamine	5/14/2002
Scott Hennig	Track & Field	2-year suspension	methandienone (Dianabol)	5/3/2002
Barney Reed	Table Tennis	2-year suspension	19-norandrosterone	4/24/2002
Kelly Milligan	Skiing	3-month suspension	pseudoephedrine	4/8/2002
Jamie Mason	Weightlifting	6-month suspension	ephedrine	3/28/2002
Keri Byerts	Fencing	3-month suspension	pseudoephedrine	3/27/2002
Joyce Bates	Track & Field	public warning	ephedrine	3/15/2002
Desiree Owen	Track & Field	2-year suspension	androstendione	3/6/2002
Chip Minton	Bobsled	2-year suspension	testosterone	2/20/2002
Jake Jensen	Track & Field	2-year suspension	testosterone	1/28/2002
Pavle Jovanovic	Bobsled	2-year suspension	19-norandrostendione	1/27/2002
Dave Owens	Bobsled	2-year suspension	testosterone	1/25/2002
Joseph Pastorello	Boxing	18-month suspension	19-norandrosterone	1/22/2002
Gary Houseman	Cycling	1-year suspension	Tetrahydrocannabinol	12/19/2003
Rachel Walker	Track & Field	2-year suspension	methylphenidate	12/12/2003
Chase Shealy	Track & Field	2-year suspension	amphetamine	12/9/2003
Chuck Lear	Archery	public warning	metoprolol	12/5/2003
Damu Cherry	Track & Field	2-year suspension	19-norandrosterone	11/24/2003
Kathi Krause	Cycling	1-year suspension	tetrahydrocannabinol acid	11/22/2003
Kenny Pierce	Sailing	2-year suspension	test refusal	10/20/2003
Amber Neben	Cycling	6-month suspension	19-norandrosterone	10/6/2003

Athlete	Sport	Sanction	Substance	Release Date
Chesen Frey	Cycling	2-year suspension	testosterone	9/30/2003
Rob Sears	Cycling	2-year suspension	test refusal	9/4/2003
Hiram Cruz	Judo	2-year suspension	androstenedione	9/2/2003
Stephen Rehrmann	Swimming	public warning	pseuedoephedrine	8/11/2003
Frankie Caruso III	Boxing	2-year suspension	Furosemide	8/7/2003
Trent Blair	Paralympic Track	public warning	pseuedoephedrine	8/1/2003
Michael Gausman	Swimming	3-month suspension	Tetrahydrocannabinol	8/1/2003
Edris Gonzalez	Weightlifting	6-year suspension	testosterone	7/15/2003
Andrew Eggerth	Track & Field	2-year suspension	19-norandrosterone and testosterone	7/2/2003
Kicker Vencill	Swimming	2-year suspension	19-norandrosterone	6/24/2003
James Lester, Jr.	Boxing	public warning	ephedrine	6/17/2003
Kristen Lewis	Swimming	public warning	pseuedoephedrine	6/17/2003
Nancy . Swider-Peltz, Jr	Speedskating	public warning	pseuedoephedrine	4/4/2003
Scott Moninger	Cycling	1-year suspension	19-norandrosterone	4/3/2003
Chad Otterstrom	Snowboarding	2-year suspension	methylphenidate	4/2/2003
Richard Cohen	Judo	2-year suspension	Missed test violation	3/26/2003
Tara Zwink	Snowboarding	2-year suspension	11-nor-Tetrahydrocannabinol-9-Carboxylic Acid	3/18/2003
Sarah Baham	Swimming	4-year suspension	test refusal	1/29/2003
Emily Carlsten	Track & Field	2-year suspension	amphetamine	1/15/2003
Mickey Grimes	Track & Field	2-year suspension	Norandrosterone	12/31/2004
Dean Goad	Weightlifter	2-year period of ineligibility	elevated testosterone-epitestosterone (T/E) ratio	12/17/2004
Chelsea Redwood	Cycling	2-year period of ineligibility	phentermine	12/11/2004
Michelle Collins	Track & Field	4-Year Suspension	EPO, the testosterone/ epitestosterone cream, and THG	12/10/2004

Athlete	Sport	Sanction	Substance	Release Date
Eddy Hellebuyck	Track & Field	2-year suspension	r-EPO	12/9/2004
Tyrone Banks	Paralympic Powerlifting	2-year Period of Ineligibilty	Boldenone	11/30/2004
David Fuentes	Cycling	2-Year Suspension	oxymetholone	11/16/2004
Jerome Young	Track & Field	Lifetime Ban	Human Recombinant Erythropoietin	11/10/2004
Chris Del Bosco	Cycling	Public Warning	tetrahydrocannabinol	11/5/2004
Alvin Harrison	Track & Field	4-year suspension	anabolic steroids, insulin, erythropoietin (EPO), growth hormone and modafinil	10/19/2004
Phil Zajicek	Cycling	public warning	cathine (norpseudoephedrine)	10/13/2004
Doug Middleton	Softball	2-year suspension	androstenedione	10/12/2004
Rae Monzavous Edwards	Track & Field	public warning	tetrahydrocannabinol	10/6/2004
Joseph D'Antoni	Cycling	2-year suspension	recombinant human Erythropoietin (rEPO)	9/24/2004
John Capel	Track & Field	public warning	tetrahydrocannabinol	9/21/2004
Paul Hill	Paralympic Basketball	2-year suspension	19-norandrosterone and 19-noretiocholanolone	9/10/2004
Torri Edwards	Track & Field	2-year suspension	nikethamide	8/11/2004
Bernard Williams	Track & Field	public warning	tetrahydrocannabinol	8/9/2004
Calvin Harrison	Track & Field	2-year suspension	modafinil	8/2/2004
Regina Jacobs	Track & Field	4-year suspension	tetrahydrogestrinone (THG)	7/17/2004
Tim Rusan	Track & Field	public warning	tetrahydrocannabinol	7/9/2004
Anthony Basile	Skiing	1-year suspension	tetrahydrocannabinol acid	7/2/2004
Geneviève Jeanson	Cycling	public warning	failure to appear for test	6/14/2004
Robert Rausch	Weightlifting	2-year suspension	hydrochlorothiazide	6/11/2004
Kelli White	Track & Field	2-year suspension	erythropoietin (EPO), anabolic steroids, modafinil	5/19/2004

Athlete	Sport	Sanction	Substance	Release Date
Kevin Toth	Track & Field	2-year suspension	tetrahydrogestrinone (THG) and modafinil	5/4/2004
John McEwen	Track & Field	2-year suspension	tetrahydrogestrinone (THG) and modafinil	4/29/2004
Melissa Price	Track & Field	2-year suspension	tetrahydrogestrinone (THG)	4/29/2004
Johnny Vasquez, Jr.	Boxing	2-year suspension	test refusal	4/22/2004
Chryste Gaines	Track & Field	public warning	modafinil	4/20/2004
Sandra Glover	Track & Field	public warning	modafinil	4/20/2004
Christopher Phillips	Track & Field	public warning	modafinil	4/20/2004
Eric Thomas	Track & Field	public warning	modafinil	4/20/2004
Adham Sbeih	Cycling	2-year suspension	recombinant human Erythropoietin (rEPO)	3/25/2004
Lyndsay Devaney	Swimming	2-year suspension	test refusal	3/23/2004
Caitlin Thompson	Fencing	public warning	L-methamphetamine	3/12/2004
Mary Hofer	Synchronized Swimming	2-year suspension	test refusal	3/5/2004
Lance Frye	Weightlifting	3-month suspension	pseudoephedrine	2/6/2004
Mickey Grimes	Track & Field	public warning	ephedrine	1/13/2004
Terrmel Sledge	Baseball	2-year suspension	19-norandrosterone and 19-noretiocholanolone	1/13/2004
Thomas Turnbow	Baseball	2-year suspension	19-norandrosterone and 19-noretiocholanolone	1/5/2004

From 2000 to 2004 the number of athletes suspended rose more than 50 percent, while the increase in tests was a lower percentage. The problem with being able to say whether the testing is effective is that a number of athletes sanctioned in 2004 were involved in the BALCO proceedings. How many would have been caught without that historic battle?

And even though advances have been made, those inside the sporting world say it's still not enough.

During interviews for this book, one trainer of Olympic champions spoke only on the condition she would not be named. But her responses shed great light onto the problem American sports are facing. An excerpt:

Q *So when it comes to the United States bringing home more medals than any other country each Olympics, you think there's more to it than training?*

A Correct.

Q *Can you explain what that is?*

A Americans have better drugs.

Q *But the United States is a melting pot of elite athletes. They come from all over the world to train in America while there are plenty of other countries where steroids are legal. Why not go there?*

A In nations where drugs are legal they don't strive to make variants. Almost everything they have is tested for.

Q *And the United States is something of a leader in innovation for new drugs?*

A I think BALCO exemplified that fairly well, don't you? But it isn't just the drugs, of course. Getting them is easy, even in countries with difficult restrictions. Even in Canada it is possible to get anything, it's just a little more expensive.

Q *If it isn't the steroids, what else?*

A You have to remember, everything that increases performance isn't a steroid. But it isn't just the drugs, or steroids, but how they're administered. American trainers know what isn't tested for and how to get by it.

Q *Victor Conte said beating drug tests was as easy as taking candy from a baby. Do you agree?*

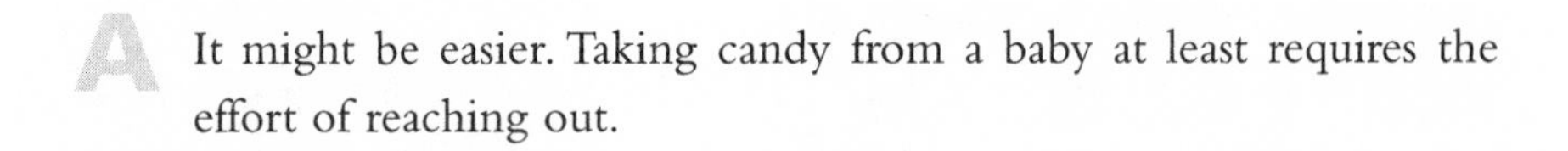

A It might be easier. Taking candy from a baby at least requires the effort of reaching out.

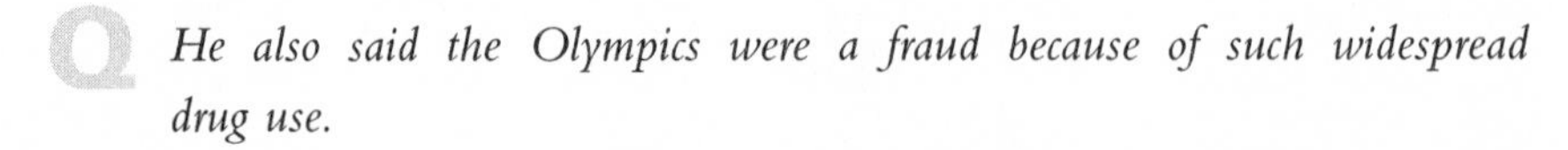

Q *He also said the Olympics were a fraud because of such widespread drug use.*

A It's such a shame, isn't it? The games are so tainted it is worth tears.

Steroids—Over the Border, Into the Minds

Anabolic steroids and other performance-enhancing drugs are given a lot of credit for many athletic feats that take place throughout the United States. On occasion there is speculation, especially among swimmers, that Chinese athletes are on some type of drug regimen. This is mostly because of the fact that many Chinese swimmers have been caught doping. Otherwise doping in sports is a generally low-key topic in most countries outside of America, and yet, the United States doesn't dominate every Olympic event. How valuable are steroids to an athlete's performance? Are they at all? Is it all strictly mental, in that players who are on performance-enhancing drugs just believe they have to be the best?

Obviously if performance-enhancing drugs didn't work, athletes wouldn't use them. Side effects aside, they wouldn't spend the money on them. One way to evaluate effectiveness is to examine the Olympic medal count of countries where steroids are either legal, or very easy to obtain. In certain European countries, for example, steroids are not legal but they are available at nearly every neighborhood pharmacy and sold without prescriptions.

Below is a comparison of the total number of Olympic medals of countries where steroids are accepted, unlike the United States, which is included for analysis purposes.

Country	1988	1992	1996	2000	2004
USA	94	108	101	97	103
China	28	54	50	59	63
Thailand	1	1	2	3	8
Indonesia	1	5	4	6	4
Turkey	2	6	6	4	10
Mexico	2	1	1	6	4

In 1990 the Anabolic Steroid Control Act was passed in the United States. While the U.S. Olympic Committee and the International Olympic Committee had already been testing athletes, it seems that the use of performance-enhancing drugs would surely have dropped between the 1988 Seoul Olympics and the 1992 Games in Barcelona. Yet, the United States remained second in medal count (behind the USSR and a Unified European team and increased its total by 14 in the 1992 games. In other countries where the drugs have been widely available, only China and Russia have made large strides in Olympic competition. Is it safe to say these countries have better drugs, and therefore can attribute their success to chemical dependency? Except for China, which has shown larger-scale problems with doping, there are too many factors to consider that would enable steroids to be linked to such great performances. The limited economy in Russia and Mexico, turmoil around the borders in countries like Turkey, and smaller populations for others are major factors.

If as some critics suggest, steroids are such an integral part of athletics, why haven't countries like China, with over four times the population of the United States, taken the top spot in the precious medal standings, at least up to this point in history?

Steroids are not miracle drugs. They can help reduce recovery time and increase muscle mass, but whether their benefits outweigh their consequences—not necessarily in health measures—is debatable by various professionals. Turning to two of the nation's most respected sport psychologists offers a different look into the psychology of a steroid user than most people get in their daily dose of steroid hysteria. And along with their profession, these psychologists offer what could be a new wave of performance enhancement, drug free.

Interview with sport psychologist Dr. Charlie Maher

Q *As athletes are continually looking to improve their performance, some choose to use performance-enhancing substances and anabolic steroids, albeit illegally. As one who has practiced sports psychology for decades, including work with three professional teams, do you personally believe sports psychology can be a perhaps more healthy alternative to steroids?*

A The use of empirically validated principles and procedures of sport psychology can help athletes enhance their performance. This is especially the case with respect to how athletes think about and deal with their results (self-evaluation) and how they maintain their minds in moment during competition (focus of attention). In essence, sport psychology can help athletes become more focused and mentally at ease with themselves, both as people and as performers, and these improved psychological states can help set conditions for improved performance of these athletes. As such, applications of sport psychology can help athletes to become stronger and more efficient mentally and emotionally. However, application of sport psychology principles and procedures cannot make for stronger bodies for athletes or help athletes physically recover quicker from workouts and competitions. So, if an athlete wants to help enhance his performance and he considers development of his mental game as something to be embraced and not feared, in this sense, sport psychology can be considered as a healthy alternative and indeed a more economical one than anabolic steroids and other performance-enhancing substances, although not in a one-to-one clinical trial type of comparison.

Q *In all of your years of working with athletes, have you practiced sport psychology with anabolic steroid users? If so, do they respond any differently to your program/methods than an individual not using juice?*

A I have worked with athletes who were using anabolic steroids. Currently, however, I have no anecdotal or other case-based experiential evidence indicating that steroid-using athletes react differently to the application of sport psychology methods and procedures than non-steroid-using athletes. The common denominator here for both of these groups is their motivation to perform well and to execute, especially in pressure situations; both groups want to perform well and win.

Q *Many steroid users prefer to "stack" their supplements, for example using half a gram of testosterone, 300 mg of Deca-Durabolin, and 6 IU of growth hormone, each week. Do you feel that those types of regimens interfere with the mental state of athletes? 'Roid rage is still a debatable concept; do you have any opinion, from a psychological point of view, on the realism of that topic?*

A From a psychological perspective, including from an anecdotal basis of judgment and from my knowledge of their stacking patterns as relayed in confidence to me by some athletes, I have observed—for the most part—not many emotional differences between athletes who have "stacked" anabolic steroids and those athletes who have used anabolic steroids and who have not stacked, in terms of behavioral and emotional side effects. I do remember one, though, who become more agitated when discussing competitive pressure and failure, and one other who become more distracted during discussions with me (e.g., less eye contact). The notion of 'roid rage, though, seems real and this condition/state requires further understanding and study.

Q *Given the reaction of steroids on an athlete's mental state, do you feel performance could be further enhanced by stacking steroids with a program to improve psychological performance during a game/meet?*

A Not really. Athletes who are involved in stacking of steroids do not seem to have enough time and commitment to devote to a performance-enhancement program that is based in psychological principles and procedures. I don't think that such athletes would follow through with the mental program in a consistent manner.

Q *Athletes who use anabolic steroids expect to be stronger, faster, and all-around better athletes. Obviously this isn't true; if one isn't at least a good athlete without steroids, one certainly won't be a pro with them. But those are the expectations; what could one expect to see as far as benefits if beginning a program of sport psychology?*

A A sport psychology program for an athlete is customized to his sport and to the competitive demands therein. Thus, a customized sport psychology program will be centered on one or more psychological goals the athlete wants to commit to and to work on, such as improving self-confidence, remaining focused during competition, maintaining composure during distracting game situations, or communicating better with the coaches. These psychological goals are linked to specific sports and methods. As such, athletes learn to make progress toward and attain these kind of goals through personal precompetitive and competitive routines and through other methods that are part of sport psychology (e.g., positive self-talk; visualization). The expectation from attaining these goals is that performance of the athlete will improve in specific competitive situations or areas.

Q *One of the main problems in sports is that when Major League Baseball players, for example, are found using steroids, impressionable young people often follow their lead. The hazards to developing individuals is obvious, especially with the potential to close growth plates. If one were to use anabolic steroids, there seems to be an unwritten rule it is best to wait until fully grown, perhaps mid-20's. Is there a limit or "prime" age to begin a program of sport psychology?*

A For the athlete, the most opportune ages when sport psychology can be meaningfully introduced directly and clinically to competitive youth athletes is when they have developed physically to the point where they have become fundamentally sound, where they have an understanding of their sport, a desire to be part of it, and where it is clear that they have natural talent for the sport. This is likely to be about the time that youth are at beginning high school ages. Before that time, sport psychology should be educative in nature, primarily focusing on parents and youth coaches and others who can influence young athletes.

Q *Since the explosion of steroid-positive tests, have any players confided in you that their performance is being affected without juice?*

A Since the time of increased testing, there has been one player who has expressed concern that his performance may have been affected due to not using anabolic steroids and related agents. Interestingly, though, this player has been motivated to better understand why he has become "psychologically addicted" (his words, not mine).

Q *Just from your professional observation, do players have a different mentality now that the truth about steroids in baseball is coming out?*

A Some players have become more vigilant in expressing in public what they think about the area. For instance, they are more apt to say that the time has come for stricter standards in public—the politically correct response—while still being concerned about who continues to use and who is still getting a competitive advantage.

Q *Are any players/teams you work with, in any of the Big Three sports, exhibiting any sort of nervous behavior now because pressure is on to clean up the games?*

A I would not call it nervousness, just that some players are being more vigilant in what they say and what they do, on site—clubhouse and locker room, et cetera.

12

Scandals

A History Lesson

In 2004–2005, Congress spent a great deal of taxpayer money to harass professional athletes and argue over the proper course of action in drug testing in sports, specifically Major League Baseball. What it seems had been forgotten is that they did this very same thing between 1988 and 1990. Media reports stated there was a rise in the use of anabolic steroids in amateur and professional sports, and supposedly in high school as well. The Anabolic Steroid Control Act was implemented, grouping derivatives of male hormones and other drugs in the same category as heroin and cocaine. The act seemed to be set up more to curb cheating in sports and less to keep children away from the drugs. Either way, it failed in the early 1990s and the latest round of hearings has done little, if nothing else, to do better. Regardless, it shouldn't have to come to this. The control act in the '90s should have been definitive or it shouldn't have been at all. Steroids are illegal says Congress, so why doesn't it fight for a player to be suspended for a certain number of games each time he is caught? Simply, Congress is ignoring its own laws. It's hypocritical and it sends the wrong message. Congress needs to, in this and any other endeavor, stick to its guns one way or another. It hasn't and it doesn't look like it will. Don't stop counting, though, tax dollars will continue to foot the bill for everything from airplane tickets to get each silent participant into the building to the coffee in the break room. It's one thing to pay for something that will solve a matter, it's another to throw money in the toilet. It's like trying to tear down a brick wall with bare hands, which, for many athletes who want something done about the steroid situation, isn't the first time they've felt like that.

During the 1970s and 1980s it is estimated that 10,000 or more athletes from East Germany were unknowingly given a regimen of anabolic steroids for years. Some recipients were as young as 11 years old. In total, over 1,000 people ranging from trainers to scientists knew what was going on and participated, under advisement from the government to keep quiet. The doping process was state-sponsored, highly secretive, and intended for world domination in athletics. The Cold War was on, the tensions were high around the world. Athletics, it seemed, were a way to be noticed as superior in a different facet of life, other than the military.

The suspicion of the German Democratic Republic (GDR) doping machine increased more and more from one Olympics to the next. In 1972 the GDR won a total of 66 Olympic medals, compared to the Federal Republic of Germany's (FRG) haul of 40. In 1976 the GDR brought home 90 Olympic medals compared to the FRG's total of 39. And in 1980, perhaps the biggest wash of the entire scandal, during an Olympics the United States had boycotted, the GDR won a tainted 126 medals. The medal counts descended from there, but the doping didn't stop. Two doctors were charged in 1997 with doping their nation's finest swimmers until as late as 1989. Most of them were teenagers, many now facing serious health problems.

While the program was carried over various sports, swimming was a particularly prime target because of the number of medals given out during each Olympiad. Swimming in East Germany, like many sports, had a place in state-sponsored institutions that were created simply to train athletes to the highest level. School was put behind sports, and everything was dictated for the athletes. Their meals were prepared for them and served at given times; their health care, education, sleep, training; and everything else was on a set schedule that was overseen by the best physicians, trainers, and scientists in the country. Unbeknownst to these athletes, many of whom were just children selected for training based on their parents' physicals characteristics, much of their diet was consumed along with small pink and blue pills, which in their case were large doses of anabolic steroids. Later on, injections of testosterone were given to both males and females.

The doping scandal was not only wide in scale and complex, but it was intelligent. The athletes, who were both the tools and perhaps the only innocents in the entire ordeal, all had to give urine samples at home before major competitions abroad. Any athlete who tested positive for steroids at home was given a reason to miss the event, while an athlete who could pass the drug tests went instead. This kept the pressure down. As apparent as the visual signs were, without scientific proof—a positive drug test—no one could say for certain that something was happening within East Germany.

When the Berlin Wall finally came down and the truth matched the suspicion, there was a backlash against everyone involved: the trainers and government officials who ordered and kept watch over the program, but especially the athletes. It wasn't until 2004 that the last East German swimming record was broken.

Into the 21st century, over three decades later, more and more information keeps coming to light about what really happened in the East German doping machine.

But what has been learned? What should have been learned?

The GDR doping regime was so sophisticated for its time because it was able to keep drugs in its athletes that could not be detected. They were virtually given a free pass to dope and compete with a chemical edge. They were able, despite obvious physical changes and performance changes, to continue unabated. They were, simply put, ahead of the drug testers.

Just like BALCO.

It took decades before a similar, large-scale scandal came to the forefront—perhaps, it was possible for athletes to use performance-enhancing drugs and not get caught. BALCO was the new GDR and proved yet again the same point: drug testing wasn't, and isn't, cutting it. It's underfunded at the least and perhaps less cared for. People would rather, and no one can blame them, put their money and tax dollars up for a new stadium or field over additional scientific research to ensure more cheaters are caught. Most people know that as soon as the drug testers catch on to one drug, there will likely be another that is undetectable. In that, too, lies the problem.

The cat and mouse game of cheaters trying to stay ahead of the drug testers is a recipe for disaster. It may not take more than a single alteration of a drug to keep it from being detected, but the question is what did that alteration do to the chemical composition of the drug and what changes will it induce in the human body?

The East German doping scandal produced a variety of health problems for many GDR athletes, in general those who were still growing at the time the drugs were administered. Abnormal hair growth, inability to conceive children, and tumors have all been reported by former GDR athletes. One female athlete, who won a European Championship title, went as far as changing her sex because she felt she was more man than woman after years of male hormone administration.

The point is that the drugs were new when the GDR used them, and more and more drugs are being developed by underground laboratories in order to stay ahead of the drug testing game. History already offers a potential outcome. It is up to the powers that be to decide what to do to avoid risking a repeat of the GDR drug scandal.

BALCO—The Next Big Thing

The Bay Area Laboratory Co-Operative, better known simply as BALCO, started when track coach Trevor Graham turned in a syringe containing THG, a drug that had previously been undetectable in drug tests, to the U.S. Anti-Doping Agency. The fallout would cause an earthquake in the sports world, and the globe is still shaking.

Kelli White was a shining star of American track and field—U.S. National Champion, International Association of Athletics Federations World Outdoor 100- and 200-meter champion—there was no doubt she would shine at the Athens Olympics. But in Paris at the 2003 World Championships, she tested positive for modafinil, was stripped of her medals, hit a downward spiral, and started talking. With that, American sports took a shot in the arm and learned more about itself and its problem with drugs than it had in one hundred years before.

After admitting to the use of THG, EPO, and modafinil, White ultimately received a two-year banishment from competition, ridicule from the media and fellow athletes, and disappointment from friends and family members. Her coach, Remi Korchemny, was among several people indicted along with the Bay Area Laboratory Co-Operative.

BALCO was supplying White, and many—perhaps still an unknown number—of other athletes with designer steroids. Comparing White with BALCO shows how two different entities respond to trouble.

Kelli White has since accepted her punishment and moved on to try to become a voice for tougher regulations in sports. *True Sport*, a publication written for and sent to all Olympians in the United States, released an interview with White in which she expressed remorse and sorrow for her actions. When asked how she felt winning in 2003 at the World Championships, knowing she was competing with illegal substances in her body, she responded, "I felt extremely bad and knew it wasn't right and wasn't fair to anyone. . . . It weighed heavily on my mind throughout the entire competition." And in sports where the slightest of mental abandonment can be the difference between first and last, this says one of two things: either Kelli White was simply the best mentally and physically and could have won without drugs, or, it's a testament to how good the drugs she was on really are.

Concluding her interview, White advocated the release of more information to athletes and said one benefit of that is to "remind athletes that there's more to life than sports and athletics." But with a recent survey out that asked athletes if they would take a pill guaranteeing them a gold medal but also death just a couple of years later, 75 percent said yes. When sports are so important and become an athlete's life work, side effects are hardly a deterrent.

And when a gold medal means everything, unscrupulous athletes have no problem financing a training regimen that could put them one step closer.

Victor Conte commented during an interview on the news program *20/20* in December 2004 about how easy it was to administer undetectable steroids to an athlete. At the same time, Conte was naming names even before Jose Canseco had his book, *Juiced*, published.

Conte called out Marion Jones, Tim Montgomery, Bill Romanowski, Dana Stubblefield, and Barrett Robbins among others, and added that he believed over half of all athletes take some sort of anabolic steroid. All the while, he praised what he had done. Of White's supplement regime he called it, "the most sophisticated in the history of the planet Earth."

Conte and his BALCO labs also provided steroids and human growth hormone to other athletes who have since admitted cheating, most notably Jason Giambi, who said he received the drugs from Greg Anderson, the personal trainer for Barry Bonds. While Anderson denied giving drugs to Bonds, Bonds himself admitted to using two different steroids in the 2003 season that came to him by Anderson. Supposedly, Anderson said the supplements were flaxseed oil and a cream for arthritis.

After the BALCO case broke, the rest of hell broke loose with it. Major League Baseball took the heat and with it, the government took its step forward. Some of the sport's biggest stars were put on show, more as a circus act than an actual congressional hearing. Sammy Sosa and Mark McGwire, the two big hitters of the original post-Maris home run race, both denied steroid use, though McGwire did so in lesser words. With that, he tarnished his reputation and more than likely, his Hall of Fame chances. McGwire claimed he didn't want to talk about the past, only the future. He didn't want to talk about whether he did or did not use steroids and simply said instead that steroids were bad. He quoted no facts, no dates, no names. If nothing else, he saved himself from charges of lying under oath, unlike his fellow professional Rafael Palmeiro. Palmeiro, during his denial of steroid use, pointed his finger and firmly denounced accusations of steroid use. In August of 2005, Palmeiro's urine wasn't as sure as he was that he hadn't used drugs, and it tested positive for stanozolol (Winstrol).

As for Victor Conte, he avoided trial by accepting a plea deal that had him admitting to just one count of money laundering and, perhaps most ironically, to just one count of illegally distributing steroids. Those charges were a far cry from the wrath that had seemed most certain to be dispensed. The government charade had fallen for unknown reasons, and Conte made off with a four-month prison stay in a minimum-security facility and equal time on house arrest following his big-house stay. The government apparently conceded that its case wasn't going to hold water, and spent more time and money putting away a minor criminal (at least on paper) like Conte than perhaps ever before. The case was a legal system bazaar that left a bad taste in the mouth of everyone on the prosecution side and was no doubt an ego-blistering fiasco for the Justice Department. Maybe worse for the sporting world—though better for his former clients—Conte's settlement did not require him to make a single statement for or against any athlete accused of steroid and other performance-enhancing drug use.

Except Marion Jones. In Conte's *20/20* interview with Martin Bashir, he openly spoke of Jones's drug use on his own accord. Jones later filed suit against Conte for, reportedly, $25 million. While Jones has since passed a lie detector test, it is worth mentioning that upon the first strike from Conte, Jones made a reference to BALCO as if she had had minimal contact and was only slightly educated about the company and its chief. Bodybuilding publication *FLEX* magazine pointed out in an article about BALCO that in 2001, it was Conte who pitched the piece the magazine would run that year on Jones and her training. *FLEX* writer Jim Schmaltz wrote, "At the time, Jones spoke glowingly of Conte and his sports supplements."

So what have we learned from this?

Obviously that someone is lying. A lot of people are probably lying, and no one can agree. We get more questions than answers that are more confused rather than being straightened out. Why are some sports fighting for tougher rules and others are resisting? Why are players' unions fighting tougher regulations?

But, the one thing that is known for sure, is that sports in America are tainted. If the drugs, steroids, and human growth hormone were all it took to become a champion, then other countries would be producing record-breaking performances time after time, but they're not. It takes an exceptional athlete to excel and perhaps drugs set them apart once they reach the top—which, under current rules, is a shame. The playing field needs to be level, with everyone having the same opportunities to win on their own accord.

An argument has been made that steroids should simply be legalized, that everyone should be able to use them and then the playing field would finally be truly equal, because no one would be cheating. Naturally that idea has been peppered with rebuttals, many of which are good reasons. But the one that stands out most is concern for athlete health. Critics say that legalizing steroid use in sports would simply mean more deaths on the field, on the track, or in the pool. Because, some people say, steroids cause cancer, uncontrollable bouts of rage, depression, and a slew of other horrific side effects. Is that the truth? In a word, no. One thing that would most certainly ruin the athletes, and not just the sports, is stupidity. And a free reign on steroid use in sports would do nothing more than put one athlete against another in a game of who can take the most drugs. And when steroid use crosses with stupidity, even pro-steroid athletes and physicians agree: bad things happen.

The Government Attack on Freedom—A Scandal in Itself

The United States government has put little to no effort toward banning tobacco, a well-known killer of people of all ages, including direct users of cigarettes and even those who are simply around them. But since the BALCO sports scandal, everyone from senators in the highest ranks to mayors of small towns have been up in arms over sports supplements on the market.

Is it a plot to keep America medicated on expensive prescription drugs? Maybe, that theory most certainly isn't new. But what seems more likely is something that is far more innocent, yet immensely more dangerous: keep the American public ignorant. The same government that is cracking down on steroids now is the same government that allowed their sale from the 1960s into the 1980s without having any direct information on the actual medical purposes for the drugs. The government knew steroids were effective because they were being consumed in large doses by weight lifters and other athletes, and at the time that was apparently enough. Dianabol, for example, was sold for 23 years before being pulled in 1983 by the FDA for failing to supposedly do what the labels said it would. That is still 11 years after the FDA required all companies producing the drugs to add "WARNING: Anabolic Steroids do not enhance athletic performance" to their labels. Where did that assumption come from? The exact individual who decided that would prove beneficial in curbing use is unknown, but whoever it was started the plethora of lies over the next several decades in reference to steroids. Of course anabolic steroids can increase athletic performance, it's why they are so popular in athletics today. Even the same drugs such as Dianabol and Anadrol that were blasted by the government as ineffective for athletic performance in the 1970s, are still some of the most popular steroids today. History tells the truth a whole lot better than the U.S. government. And steroids were only the beginning of the misinformation dispensed by the government, the media, motivated politicians, and other advocates for regulation of the supplement industry.

Creatine, the most commonly and widely available sports supplement to date, is naturally found in meat and is produced in the body by amino acids. This organic acid, found in muscle tissue, supports a variety of functions and powers muscle contractions throughout the entire body. Creatine has been shown to help induce increases in muscle mass and has been theorized to also increase anaerobic and aerobic endurance. Reportedly discovered as early as 1835, creatine has long been used for performance enhancement. Only since the year 2000 has creatine been brought into the redundant argument against steroids. The problem? Creatine is not a steroid. It's not even close to a steroid, but because of its benefits to athletes, or people in general for that matter, it has been under fire. In 2005, creatine was shown in studies to increase healthy brain function. Here's a suggestion: maybe some of the same uneducated people speaking out against creatine, would benefit from some reference material—not media-produced, but scientific studies. Creatine, of course, was only the beginning.

Ephedra too has been attacked, and subsequently banned, by politicians who had a lack of understanding. It has been said about any number of things that, "The truth will set you free," but unfortunately it won't. The American Medical Association didn't want steroids banned in the early 1990s when they became controlled substances, and the same sort of thing was seen a decade later when the majority of health-based businesses fought against banning ephedra. Another loss because politicians, and subsequently the media, have made a hysterical mess out of nothing. Can ephedra be dangerous? Yes. So can drinking too much water. Can creatine be dangerous? Even at large doses, this hasn't been proven yet.

The biggest problem with receiving a fair shake from lawmakers is that they carelessly bundled supplements like creatine with controlled substances like steroids. Whether steroids should be illegal is irrelevant, as many people, even supporters, have accepted the fact that they are and simply moved on, but it is absolutely unfair to the public to try to restrict the use of a naturally occurring supplement that has proven to be beneficial with few to no side effects. If politicians want to get serious about defending public health, the battle needs to be immediately redirected to alcohol, tobacco, and other street drugs. They can still hold on to their belief, if they choose to be so ignorant, that supplements like creatine are a danger to the public, but like the adage goes: if your boat starts sinking, you plug the biggest holes first.

Congress should fight to promote more regulation in the supplement industry by testing for quality and purity, not by banning substances that when made properly can vastly improve the health of consumers. This, more than the restriction of access, is needed. As an example, in January 2003, elite U.S. swimmer Kicker Vencill tested positive for 19-norandrostenediol and was subsequently banned from his sport for two years. Vencill swore his innocence in the face of ridicule, and said he would take whatever measures necessary to clear his name. And he did. Vencill hired a lawyer and eventually sued the makers of a multivitamin he had been taking, Super Complete, by the supplement maker Ultimate Nutrition. After his positive test, Vencill had the supplements in his cabinet tested. Super Complete turned out to be the culprit behind his violation. The vitamin was contaminated with not just one, but three different steroid precursors.

After a trial by jury, Vencill was awarded nearly $600,000 just weeks before his suspension ended. He then returned to the pool, but because of the ban he was removed from the 2003 Pan-American team he had qualified for, and his opportunity at qualifying for the 2004 Olympic team was dashed.

But with the precedent set by this case and perhaps the lessons learned from it, does this mean anything to the rest of the athletes who have tested positive by cross-contamination? Under current rules by drug testing federations, no. And in reality, it shouldn't, because as the United States Anti-Doping Agency makes clear, athletes are responsible for anything they put into their bodies. Period. But, what this and other cases should do is present cause for tighter regulations on the supplement industry. Most important for consumer safety, but also for athletes like Vencill, who aren't alone in this type of misfortune.

NFL running back Mike Cloud and bobsledder Pavle Jovanovic both filed suit against popular supplement maker MuscleTech of Canada. The athletes reportedly submitted test results that showed MuscleTech's most-promoted whey protein powder, Nitro-Tech, was contaminated with precursors of the steroid nandrolone. In a fitting response as an attempt to save face, MuscleTech filed countersuits against the athletes.

Long-Term Studies

One of the main arguments against the use of anabolic steroids is the familiar phrase "There are no long-term studies." Which, in simple terms is untrue. In fact, anabolic steroids, whether for good or bad, have undergone some of the best long-term studies of any drug: personal response. It's one thing for a drug company to test a substance on lab animals and deem it safe or unsafe, and it's another to have real human responses to a drug. Anabolic steroids, in comparison, have far fewer side effects than many newer drugs. This is comparing 50 years of steroid feedback to just a few years on new drugs that have been pulled from the market and/or caused large class-action lawsuits.

The defense by politicians and the media for bashing anabolic steroids—that the long-term effects are simply unknown—is unfounded and ridiculous. The National Institute on Drug Abuse released a research report covering anabolic steroids in which it admits in the opening line: "Since the 1950s, some athletes have been taking anabolic steroids to build muscle and boost their athletic performance. Increasingly, other segments of the population also have been taking these compounds." Meaning for roughly 50 years people have been taking anabolic steroids for one reason or another. Where is the epidemic of deaths? We know from history that many of the East German athletes are suffering or have suffered irreversible side effects and death because of their steroid abuse. That, though, is different in two main ways: the majority of those athletes suffering are women, a group that, in the minds of even the biggest proponents of steroid use, should not use steroids or only use them in very low doses. And, many of the drugs were completely untested and used in immensely large doses. They did not simply use steroids, they abused them.

The HBO *Real Sports with Bryant Gumbel* episode covering steroids showed one older male discussing his decades of steroid use and his claim to have had zero irreversible side effects. Of his friends, he said none of them have had side effects that were seriously life threatening or irreversible either. If "average Joe" responses aren't enough, the greatest bodybuilders of all time are still alive and well, and for those who have passed away, none of their deaths have been related to anabolic steroid use. This is at the least very surprising because, generally, professional bodybuilders use steroids more along the lines of "abuse." Arnold Schwarzenegger, whose steroid use has probably been used most against him in the political realm, is alive and Schwarzenegger did have heart surgery, but this was a congenital issue, not steroid related.

So if competent, healthy humans can report decades' worth of steroid use, why is it still said that there are no long-term studies? What constitutes long term? Governor Schwarzenegger was born in 1947 and used steroids beginning in his teenage years, and yet he remains in good health as he nears 60. Some steroid users have reported good health after decades of drug use into their 70s. The average life expectancy in the United States for men is about 75 years. Getting within five years of the average length of life after having used steroids for whatever amount of time, seems to be a long term study in itself.

And other studies *have* come out showing effects labeled "long term."

According to a report from Northeastern University, steroid use can effectively change long-term behavior and aggression levels. The study found that in adolescents, steroid use can permanently alter the ability of the brain to produce serotonin. This study confirms what those who have studied the topic routinely say: developing humans should not use steroids. On April 5, 2005, an MSNBC report on steroid use in adolescents stated, "In a small 1991 study at the University of Michigan, 84 percent of participants reported some kind of withdrawal effects from steroids." Other well-known, and legal, substances that are known to cause withdrawal symptoms are caffeine, tobacco, and alcohol.

Also in its research report on anabolic steroids, NIDA wrote: "Studies show that, over time, anabolic steroids can indeed take a heavy toll on a person's health. The abuse of oral or injectable steroids is associated with higher risks for heart attacks and strokes, and the abuse of most oral steroids is associated with increased risk for liver problems. Steroid abusers who share needles or use nonsterile techniques when they inject steroids are at risk for contracting dangerous infections, such as HIV/AIDS, hepatitis B and C, and bacterial endocarditis." NIDA kindly pointed out, again, that there are severe side effects associated with *abuse*.

The facts are out there, and politicians, the media, and those in the general public who stand behind the excuse "We don't know what will happen" need to reevaluate their positions. There's enough information out there that if someone is going to speak out for or against steroids, that person should be well read on the subject. This isn't to say everybody should be for or against steroids, but if anyone wants to take a stance, there is more than enough information to enable him to make a call. And because of this knowledge, the government should be *forced* to make a decision. Anabolic steroids are illegal because of their supposed detrimental effects and the lack of long-term studies. Both of these reasons are bogus, and were bogus even when the Anabolic Control Act of 1990 was put into place. If the government wants to keep steroids illegal, it should demand that manufacturers of steroids prove beyond a doubt that they are harmful to healthy adults when used responsibly. And while they are doing that, they should ban cigarette smoking. Because, of course, a government should never be so blatantly hypocritical.

Good Side of Gear

The media says steroids are bad. Steroids can kill you. Steroids can do this, that, and a whole lot of other things. Certainly there isn't a good side to something so vicious, is there? Given the track record of the American media, it's hard to believe anything that doesn't come with live footage. Steroids fall into the realm of overhyped, exaggerated fishing stories.

Steroids have a host of benefits for the average citizen of a major, industrialized country. Unfortunately, most of these uses are nonexistent or severely limited because of the negative image steroids present. A large source of unease is that sports, mere games to many people, and cheating within them, has caused this negative image to increase and prevent advancement on steroid use.

Steroids are often given to men after testicular cancer forces the removal of one or both of the testes. They are generally given in a low dose at set intervals for the life of the patient. In a sense, this is a long-term study in itself, which, as of yet, has not produced any side effects. The dose is often criticized as not large enough to bring about the kinds of health issues that athletes face, except that another medical purpose uses much larger quantities of steroids. Transsexuals, in this case women who want to become men, are given large doses of anabolic drugs to induce male characteristics.

Anabolic steroids are also given to adolescent males with pituitary disruptions. When given at the proper stage, the drugs help them develop their fully intended male-gender features.

A huge breakthrough related medically to steroids could be the creation of a male contraceptive one day. Because of the complexity of a woman's menstrual cycle, it is theorized that a male version could be much safer in comparison, though again, because of the current image of the drugs, research has been limited.

The facts are out there. Steroids are safe and effective for a variety of people with needs. Not just people who want to gain more muscle or burn more fat, but people who need them medically. The media and government attacks on the drugs from just one facet of their use is preventing many people with *needs* from getting help with relatively inexpensive sources of treatment.

The Other Side of Science

There are varied opinions on the positives and negatives of anabolic steroid use in society. The media, as hard as they might try, cannot change scientific fact that has proven that steroids, when used in moderate doses, are not life threatening; not harmful in short- or long-term periods of use; and the side effects that are known, such as testicle shrinkage, are temporary. It is simply a game of politics in which each side plays up the pros and cons for its own benefit. The media says steroids are bad, hazardous, and will kill the users after bouts of use. Living, breathing, healthy athletes point to themselves as proof that steroids do no harm if used responsibly. They offer up their healthy vials of blood as evidence, their low heart rates, and exceptional athletic ability as fact. But are physiological changes the only thing that should be considered in the argument on steroids?

Because of the illegal status anabolic steroids currently have in the United States, Canada, and several other countries, the most frightening result of the steroid debate is that it may be teaching youth to cheat. Regardless of whether steroids will kill a healthy man, when children grow up hearing that their role models and favorite players on professional sports teams are using, and at points abusing, steroids they may be inclined to do so themselves. Action by attraction. Mimicking whom they want to be like. Children with top-level aspirations grow up thinking that if they can swing a bat like Barry Bonds, they could play Major League Baseball. They think if they can jump as high as Lebron James that they could play in the NBA. Maybe if they could replicate the swimming stroke of Michael Phelps they too could win Olympic gold medals. Maybe if they could hold a cadence on a bicycle like Tyler Hamilton, they could be on the winning team in a future Tour de France. But there is always more to the makeup of a professional than his trademark swing, dunk, or stroke. Bonds has been mired in steroid controversy, admitting steroid use while denying he knew what the drugs really were. Hamilton has been banned from cycling after testing positive for EPO, only keeping his Olympic gold medal because of a mishap in the handling of his samples from Athens.

Dozens of athletes over the years have spoken out that their status as a role model was not asked for, simply laid upon them because they excelled in their game. They shouldn't have to watch everything they do, they say, because some young person idolizes them. And that's perfectly true. No one should be expected to be a better person than he is. But should children be told whom they can and cannot look up to? Try telling an amateur cyclist he can't look up to Tyler Hamilton, but he can look up to Lance Armstrong. Armstrong, who retired after winning seven Tour de France titles, has been accused countless times of drug use. Is that any better? What if the argument is posed that Hamilton, a proven drug user, was a vital part of several races Armstrong went on to win? Children look up to winners, and saying that maybe, possibly, Armstrong may have taken second once or twice without a drugged-up Tyler Hamilton isn't going to iron out the wrinkles of a child's inspiration. To many of them, steroids are an afterthought. The point is, a winner is a winner. Hamilton, still in possession of Olympic gold, is a winner, even if he is a cheater.

A large part of the equation is that many steroid users don't get caught until they have amassed a fortune and unequalled fame. They get caught, their true fans still support them—such as Rafael Palmeiro, who under oath swore he never used steroids and subsequently tested positive—and they take the slap on the wrist and move on. Maybe they stop using the juice, or maybe they just go on a different drug that isn't tested for. Some athletes may not use drugs until they are already a professional and just looking for an edge. So many kids would sell every toy they own, every possession they have, in exchange for the opportunity to play one single game on a real, professional baseball diamond. With the desire running so high, who really cares if steroids are what gets you there? The social conscious needs to be more concise, more streamlined. Acknowledging the realities of steroids is needed, because throughout the sea of lies, deceit, and misinformation, children will continually blow it off, grab their equipment, and go out and play, always chasing the dream of being the best and making it big.

After the September 11 terrorist attacks, the footage of the planes hitting the towers was removed from television screens, supposedly, because it caused people to be afraid, to hate, to think a variety of things. No doubt children who watch the news with their parents were a large factor in this decision. The topic is different, but the fact remains: children watch. And when all they hear about steroids and other performance-enhancing drugs is that they coincide with professional sports, they'll get a variety of ideas from that, too.

Paying for the Truth

When it comes to the truth on matters of health, or maybe more accurately the matter of life and death, answers should be straightforward. If someone knows the answer to something that could affect your quality of life, he should say so. If he doesn't, he shouldn't try to answer. Or, better yet, he could do some research to find the correct and proper information if he still wanted to be able to offer the data. Unfortunately, when it comes to the media and the use of performance-enhancing drugs, lies and misinformation are most often the only things someone can get for the price of oxygen.

Some information on anabolic steroids and other drugs is true. When a reporter says that steroid use can stunt the growth of an adolescent, that is a fact. Anabolic drugs can signal growth plates to close, forever halting a child's vertical development. Other reports are laughable, such as when a *Seattle Times* reporter, in a May 31, 2005, article, included "Steroids can make you less attractive," as one reason to stay away from steroids. Aesthetics are obviously something that is personal, so can this really be included as a negative side effect? Male pattern baldness can happen, but some people say bald is beautiful. Some acne can occur, which women may not find overly appealing, but don't they typically appreciate muscles? Could it balance out? It's not worth scientific evaluation, but in an argument against gear, this reason doesn't hold water.

Beyond what is true and what is laughable lies the absurd and unfounded. Also included in the list: "Steroids can put you on the bench for the whole season," claiming that the ligaments and tendons of the body can't handle the extra muscle. A poll conducted on the bodybuilding forums of IronMagazineForums.com found that the majority of users after a first cycle of steroids gained between 20 and 30 pounds. Nowhere was there, or has there been, reports of tendon or ligament damage because of this immense weight gain in a short period. Yes, it is possible for ligaments to be torn if a steroid user is performing weighted exercise repetitions with a load that is above his general capability, because steroid-induced muscle growth does occur at a faster rate than ligaments and tendons can keep up with. Most intelligent users can easily avoid this, sometimes there are accidents, but to make such a blanket statement is ridiculous.

In fact, having a larger-than-normal amount of muscle has been known to save lives. In the case of professional bodybuilder Michal Kindred, it protected him from death and helped him make one the of most remarkable comebacks in sports history. Kindred was involved in a motorcycle accident, which resulted in his back being broken in three separate places. The doctors told him that the only thing that saved his life was his muscle. From that point on though, doctors said Kindred would never walk again, let alone lift weights. As the years passed, Kindred not only regained his mobility, but once again pursued bodybuilding. His return to life climaxed when he received his IFBB pro card, certifying his status as one of the elite in his sport.

Even good journalists fall into a bias trap at times. This reporter also included another wide-open statement with: "Steroids can make you look like the opposite sex." This too depends on interpretation. Can steroids turn a man into a woman or a woman into a man? No. Can they provide the features? Yes, some. Again, it comes down to an inappropriate blanket statement. Some women do grow excess body hair while using steroids, generally, though, in areas they already shave. The reporter wrote that women can have disruptions in their menstrual cycles, which is also true, and he wrote that men can experience shrinkage of the testicles and impotence because of steroid use, which is also true. But no matter how frequent or infrequent the changes in a woman's menstrual cycle may be, and no matter how small the increase or large the decrease in a male's testicle size, these have no bearing on sexuality. Women will not grow testicles; men will not start having menstrual cycles. Why, then, include these effects in an article on steroid use and why not mention that these problems are, 99 percent of the time, remedied when a user ends the steroid cycle?

Number six on this specific list of anti-steroid arguments is "Steroids cause liver damage." In a word: wrong. To be precise, which should be the rule when something like this is stated in a widely read publication, or in any publication for that matter, *oral* steroids *can* cause liver damage. Most steroids are injected and cause no functional changes in liver function. Oral steroids, which are 17 alpha-alkylated so that they can prevent themselves from being broken down in the liver, do cause the liver to work harder. So does alcohol. These drugs can be hepatotoxic, but again, blanket statements reveal ignorance and spread ludicrous allegations that do nothing to inform the public. For example, there has been no real increase in hepatic angiosarcoma since the 1970s, and yet steroid use has supposedly boomed. If there was a correlation, the numbers of cases of the disease and of steroid consumption would follow each other appropriately.

Misinformation such as the above is literally passed around every single day, thousands of times an hour, maybe even per minute, around the world. In gyms it's common to hear a teenager lifting heavy with bad form as he tells his buddies about the latest risk of steroids. Listen closely, and it's the same thing the reporter on CNN, Fox, or any other cable or local news station just said from behind the sports desk. If it was true it would be wonderful that the media was providing this information and that it could travel so fast and inform the needing-to-know public about health risks, but when it's overhyped, overblown, and blatantly wrong, it's sad and an injustice to the viewers who don't know any better, and a slap in the face to those who do.

If reporters and journalists dug into performance-enhancing drug use the same way they go after the latest story for the news at five, a lot of drugs may not even be illegal. One can only wonder why steroids get a bad rep for their supposed side effects, and yet tobacco and alcohol in North America take in enough revenue to outmatch that of most other countries combined. The tequila alone coming out of Mexico each year makes the country more money than most small countries make with all of their agricultural outlets. That same tequila also pushes some people into depression, into abuse, into driving cars that they end up using, albeit unintentionally, as murder weapons. Yet, alcohol is defended because it's regulated. Why aren't steroids? If steroids were legal only for people age 21 and over, not only would it be easier to understand them and prevent useless, factless reporting, but it would make it easier to keep steroids out of sports and, maybe, out of the hands of children. It's all about education, something the subject of anabolic steroids lacks.

Few media outlets are willing to take the risk of telling the truth, using research, about steroids. Of the many fitness magazines out there, many of which use professional bodybuilders to sell products and yet downplay steroids (the same drugs these individuals are using), there is one that stands out from the pack. *Muscular Development* magazine is a monthly publication with professional athletes and physicians on staff to study, research, and report on steroids and other drugs. Not every article is pro-steroids, not every article is against them. Generally the magazine, like this book, prints the facts and lets the reader decide. The only problem is that *Muscular Development* is a bodybuilding magazine, which has a limited audience. Steroids of course are far more widespread than in gyms, so the capacity to disseminate correct information is lacking, and thus losing, the battle against misinformation on television. Fact: no magazine, no matter how truthful in its writings, will ever reach more people than a television news program. And, because of this, lies abound. What would happen if a company would actually step up to the plate? For a long time it seemed like a dream, not just from steroid users, but from everyday people, and even many journalists, who just wanted the facts, good and bad, to get out there.

Enter HBO. *Real Sports with Bryant Gumbel* took the first significant step toward a mass-media outreach on the facts of steroids. In his specialized segment on steroids, Gumbel leads by saying, "As frequently evidenced by officials nationwide, Americans, when drugs are concerned, rarely choose logic when they can opt for hysteria. Case in point, the recent hoopla over steroids."

Furthermore, Americans don't necessarily jump to conclusions but are instead fed with hysteria. When the media pushes hysteria over logic, there is no going back. Gumbel's point is clearly made, and he continues by saying, "In light of the media excess, the public pronouncements and the wailing in Washington, one would assume that the scientific evidence establishing the health risks of steroids is overwhelming." He pauses for a moment, probably giving most viewers the opportunity to nod their heads. He continues, "But it's not. On the contrary, when it comes to steroid use among adult males, the evidence reveals virtually no fire despite all the smoke."

Before the program switches to the HBO feature on steroids, Gumbel leaves the viewer with, "The science of steroids, or the absence of it, suggests some conclusions that few people want to hear."

Not to defend steroids, or make an appeal against them, HBO and Gumbel use one very, very powerful fact in their presentation: evidence. They don't focus on the fact that steroids may have caused Mark McGwire to hit so many home runs, and that steroids helped Barry Bonds hit even more. They focus on the health risks of steroid use among grown, sensible, intelligent adults—the same people left to decide whether or not they should drink and drive or smoke around children.

Real Sports followed John Romano, senior editor and columnist of *Muscular Development*, as he used steroids on camera and gave his opinion. Romano, in a close-up shot, asked a very good question, "Where are the bodies?" The HBO correspondent, too, admitted that he could not find one credible scientific study that linked steroids to death. The average gym rat didn't say this, but a reporter with a career in the balance went out on a limb to break away from the pack. But he didn't stop there, he showed the evidence. Of a stack of scientific studies, even the one that gave its subjects the highest doses of testosterone, which the show said was printed in the *New England Journal of Medicine*, reported no side effects other than acne and breast tenderness. In another study, the show highlighted and brought closer to the screen a government report that stated "the incidents of life-threatening effects appear to be low."

The show and the list go on and on about the lack of evidence of steroid detriments. Interviewed are physicians and athletes who are active and living examples of responsible steroid use in adult males, interviewed as well is Dr. Gary Wadler who is completely against steroids. On either side, the *Real Sports* segment was a shining example of how steroids should be presented by the media. Simple, thorough, truthful. A clear-cut premise, a well-thought-out production, and agreement on both sides about what is and is not known about anabolic steroids. The media, however, tends to either not want the truth to be known, or does not in many cases want to take the time to do any sort of research.

What is perhaps most disconcerting is that the media is not wasting time with what it is presenting, but that what it is presenting is wrong. If every news station would only report fact-based information when it comes to anabolic steroids and focus on the real issue—what steroids do to sports—more progress would certainly be made. It all revolves around the media and it always has.

Also as mentioned in the HBO report, in 1988 Ben Johnson broke the world record in the 100-meter sprint, beating America's best in Carl Lewis. Johnson tested positive and the sporting world nearly rioted. Four years later, Lyle Alzado died, and prior to his passing, blamed steroids for his condition. Whether intentional or not, this opened yet another way for the media to blame steroids. Thus, as with the congressional hearings in 2004 and 2005, the government collaborated in the early 1990s and, against even the DEA's wishes, passed the Anabolic Control Act, forever, as it has since seemed, inducing hysteria against steroids. Slowly, this trend can be reversed with responsible, intelligent, researched reporting.

Once the truth about steroids has been told, in a consistent manner, the hysteria will die by its own hand. The steroid controversy can only be played with smoke and mirrors so long before the cover is blown. After people are presented with a fair and balanced review, they can make their own judgment on whether using these drugs is something they want to do. The media can then focus on how to keep drugs out of sports, providing a level playing field, which, it so likely seems, is the toughest battle to fight. Because despite how it seems, steroids aren't the only factor that keeps the Olympic flame from shining as bright as it could, or keeps the record books of Major League Baseball from looking at least slightly tarnished. Bribes, equipment, judging, a host of things are keeping sports from being contested evenly, but even so there could never be the same type of bias that steroids receive in the media.

While it may be unfortunate that it takes a top-tier cable channel to come forward, it's a step in the right direction. No one argues that steroids dilute the enjoyment of sports for some people. A lot of athletes feel discouraged knowing that they are competing against athletes using illegal drugs; others, perhaps those using them, feel they are leveling the playing field. A big debate on the changes that have occurred in the sporting world is developing, and that debate may live on for many years to come. But the fact remains that all sports, Olympic or professional, remain sports—games. People shouldn't have to fight through a maze to know whether something will harm them or their families. One day, with concerted effort toward the truth, people won't have to pay just to get the facts.

Romano writes a monthly opinion piece for *Muscular Development*. He is a steroid advocate who keeps up with media happenings about steroids and often responds to them in his own forum. The following excerpt from one of his columns is particularly relevant to the often misguided media presence revolving around steroids.

The Way I Look at It—
The Romano Factor—The Ham Story
by John Romano

Reprint courtesy of *Muscular Development* magazine (www.MuscularDevelopment.com) Vol. 42, no. 6 (June 2005)

The following instances upon which I will comment all have a common thread. This commonality is part and parcel of the whole gross misunderstanding being propagated by the media, as well as those in charge, and can be summed up quite well by the following anecdote.

Zig Ziglar is a famous and accomplished motivational speaker and sales trainer. I used to listen to his tapes and follow his lectures quite closely during the late '80s when sales was my chosen career path. One of Ziglar's anecdotes in particular holds much truth as it relates to the whole mess in which we find sports mired today. So, I'm going to go ahead and share it with you in the hopes of setting the stage for the rest of what you are about to read.

As the story goes, one Easter Sunday, Zig noticed the women in his kitchen preparing to bake a ham. Upon readying the ham for the oven, mother summarily hacked off the hock end of the ham before she put it in the pan to bake. Noticing this, the young daughter asked her mother why she took the end off the ham.

"Because that's what you're supposed to do," replied mother.

"But, why?" asked the daughter.

"Because that's how you do it."

"But why?" insisted the daughter.

"Because I always cut the end off the ham before I bake it."

"But *why*?" pressed the daughter.

"Because I've always done it that way," replied mother. "That's the way my mother taught me."

"Okay, but what's the *reason* you cut the end off the ham?" the daughter asked again.

"Because you just do."

Well, the daughter wasn't satisfied. She went into the living room and asked her grandmother. The grandmother replied, "Because you always cut the end off the ham before you cook it."

"Yes, but why?" asked the granddaughter.

"Because you just do," replied granny.

"I understand, granny, but what's the *reason* you cut it off?"

"Because that's the way you cook a ham," replied granny.

"But why?" insisted the granddaughter.

"I just always have. That's how my mother used to do it."

So, the granddaughter got on the phone and called the nursing home and spoke to her great-grandmother.

"Great granny, why do you always cut the end off the ham before you bake it?"

"Well, that's just the way I've always done it, dear."

"Yes, but *why*?"

"Well," great grandmother replied, "I've always had to do it because a whole ham wouldn't fit into my pan."

I think this is a good example of the hysteria-driven reasoning associated with steroids these days. The knee-jerk reaction to steroids by members of the media and supposed "experts" is that steroids are bad. (These are not doctors, clinicians and scientists who specialize in the field, but coaches, team owners, the U.S. Surgeon General and just about every news anchor and talk show host). Without exception, they all say steroids are bad, steroids are dangerous, steroids will kill you, rot your liver, give you cancer, etc. Why?

Because they do.

But why?

Because they are bad for you.

But, why?

Because they're dangerous . . .

Unfortunately, those who disseminate such hogwash do so because they are grossly uninformed, educated by media-driven hysteria propagated by professional alarmists with an agenda that rests on the latest national best-selling crusade to save our children. Not once has a member of the mainstream media, a government official PR, a representative from any congressman's office *ever* contacted us and asked us to recommend a round table of steroid experts to genuinely debate the issue on the scientific facts. Instead, it's just, "Shut up, Alice, and follow the rabbit into the hole."

This is, apparently, the mindset our government is adhering to when debating the steroid issue: Steroids are bad just because they are; elite athletes use them to be better athletes; our nation's young aspiring athletes see this behavior as not only acceptable, but also admirable; these kids then use steroids with no education or guidance whatsoever; some of these kids get themselves into trouble; outrage spreads like wildfire. Hence, we must do *something*. Unfortunately, that something is totally wrong, from every perspective except one—the Mad Hatter's.

Let's take a look at just how far the government is willing to shove its head up our asses.

The much anticipated congressional hearing on steroids came and went. I watched the whole 11-plus hours' worth and can pretty much tell you that while quite a bit was spoken, little was said—particularly by those it was hoped would speak volumes. The process was arduous and uncomfortable for both the politicians asking the questions and for the players avoiding them. Anyone who thought this controversial hearing by the House Government Reform Committee would accept baseball's plan to rid the sport of illegal performance-enhancing substances was sorely disappointed.

The Government Reform Committee, formerly the Government Operations Committee, came about to restore limited government. Supposedly, the committee has broad jurisdiction to hunt around for oversight, but not to inform the rest of us about whatever the committee thinks we ought to be told. In perhaps as vivid an example of real-life irony as we're ever likely to see on live TV, the committee contrived to inform America, especially our precious youth, that dangerous and illegal drugs are dangerous and illegal. To prove that, they subpoenaed a bunch of baseball players and league suits to hopefully describe the extent to which these dangerous and illegal drugs pervade baseball.

Unfortunately, much of the hearing was either tearful denial, tear-jerking testimonial of bereaved parents or staunch proclamations by players geared toward doing everything in their power to rid baseball of drugs. When the players took the stand, the hearing became a forum to scold the players, not just for allegedly taking substances that are unsafe, but for doing something immoral. Then, of course, to give the ousted players a chance to scold Canseco for telling the world what they did. Those who use performance-enhancing substances were called cheaters, cowards and bad examples for the nation's children.

Of particular interest was the exchange between Mark McGwire and several congressmen. Sitting calmly after his emotional opening statement, McGwire, who retired after the 2001 season, refused a request by Representative Elijah Cummings, Democrat from Maryland, to give a clear answer about whether he had used steroids.

"Are you taking the Fifth?" Mr. Cummings asked.

McGwire responded, "I'm not here to discuss the past, I'm here to be positive about this subject."

Representative William Clay, Democrat from Missouri, said: "Mr. McGwire, we are both fathers of young children. Both my son and daughter love sports and they look up to stars like you. Can we look at those children with a straight face and tell them great players like you play the game with honesty and integrity?" Mr. McGwire replied, "Like I said earlier, I'm not going to go into the past and talk about my past." Yet Mr. McGwire offered to be a spokesman against steroids. "My message is steroids are bad, don't do them," he said.

When Representative Patrick McHenry, Republican of North Carolina, asked how he knew they were bad, Mr. McGwire replied, "I've accepted my attorneys' advice not to comment on this issue."

McGwire deflected other questions that could bear on his 70 home-run season in 1998. That year he set the single-season record, which has since been eclipsed by Barry Bonds, who hit 73 homers in 2001. Bonds was conspicuously missing from the hearing.

Earlier in the day, Senator Jim Bunning, Republican of Kentucky and a Hall of Fame pitcher, testified that he thought players who used steroids should have their records wiped from the book. Mr. McHenry asked the baseball players if using steroids was cheating.

"That's not for me to determine," McGwire replied.

McHenry pressed him. "For you, is it cheating? Yes or no?"

McGwire repeated, "That's not for me to determine."

Curt Schilling said, "Yes."

Rafael Palmeiro said, "I think it is."

Sosa and Canseco each said, "I think so."

I don't know why, but it sure looked like it was McGwire who took the hardest beating. I'm sure at the end of the day all he wanted to do was go home to his hot-ass wife, bury himself in her willing arms and cry himself to sleep.

It was unfortunate that the interrogation of Commissioner Bud Selig, union chief Don Fehr (arguably the real culprits in the plot) and the other suits didn't begin until early evening, when just about everyone was tired and full. They should have gone on first, as this was the most revealing and spirited session of the day.

THE WAY I SEE IT . . .

The entire event was a farce. First of all, Representative Henry Waxman says the committee must investigate because baseball's leaders will not do an investigation. But Baseball, threatened by Senator John McCain, investigated the problem and then reopened and revised its collective bargaining agreement to insinuate more rigorous testing and more severe penalties for steroid infractions. That should have been the end of it. But, no, they had to drag poor Mark McGwire out of retirement and beat the shit out of him.

Stanley Brand, attorney for those the committee had subpoenaed, says the House rule granting the committee's jurisdiction provides no indication that the committee is empowered to review a collective bargaining agreement between private parties. Not even the National Labor Relations Board, he says, evaluates "the substantive merit of collective bargaining agreements." But it sure sounds good on the PR machine, especially when our impressionable kids are tossed into the fray. Grabbing onto that proverbial golden goose of politics, Texas Republican Joe Barton, who chairs the Energy and Commerce Committee, warned all sports everywhere, "If you don't clean it up, we're going to clean it up for you."

In the days leading up to the hearings, the politicians kept harping on how this was about health issues and the children, but at the day's end there was no substance in any message for kids. Representatives Tom Davis and Henry Waxman, chairman and ranking member, respectively, of the House Government Reform Committee, had aspired to catch themselves at least one witch during the hunt, but came home with not even a frog. I imagine in their minds though, the day was a success. Remember, we all know steroids are dangerous!

THE ATHLETES' PLEDGE

As far as the players go, their impassioned pledge to do all they could to rid baseball of drugs during the congressional hearing eerily echoed the sentiments of another high-profile elite athlete, now turned governor. While not a party to the hearing, former bodybuilder, action star, and current governor of California, Arnold Schwarzenegger downplayed his use of anabolic steroids during an interview with George Stephanopoulos on "This Week," stating they were not controlled substances at the time and he received medical supervision. However, during the recent Arnold Classic, he called for an end to steroids in bodybuilding, saying that we need to do more to get rid of them because steroids are dangerous. He called our sport "bodybuilding, not body destruction."

Whether it was by Arnold's cue or just coincidence, all players who testified pledged to do everything in their power to spread the message that steroids are bad so don't do them. McGwire even said he would instruct his foundation to take action.

THE WAY I SEE IT . . .

You know, that's all good. I don't know a single steroid-using athlete who would state that for all the good those drugs have done them, they are good for kids. Resoundingly, we all agree kids should *not* use steroids. That said, the education regarding their dangers is patently insufficient, egregiously false or over exaggerated and horrifically inaccurate.

I find it reprehensible that any sports celebrity who gained fame, wealth and notoriety by using steroids would decry their dangers when all is said and done and then tell us—not just kids, but everyone—that they are dangerous and we should not use them. There is absolutely no good reason why responsible adults, not playing on a sports team that forbids their use, should not be entitled to exercise their freedom and use performance-enhancing drugs that are scientifically proven to be safe when used properly under medical supervision for a variety of cosmetic and life-enhancing reasons.

The fire and brimstone speeches against steroids need to have a better scientific basis or else they are going to be viewed just like anything else you tell kids to stay away from just because you said so. Remember, it took a child to challenge the hacking off of the end of the ham.

The research is prolific that scare tactics don't work on kids. Routinely, they are smarter than we give them credit for. They know how to get to the truth. When you have guys the likes of Sean Hannity from Fox News' "Hannity and Combs" saying something as ludicrous as "Lyle Alzado died from steroids," we are eventually going to have a problem.

When Jose Canseco was on Bill Maher's show, he was pressed about the dangers of steroids. Unfortunately, Canseco must have been tired or just not on Maher's page, but Maher challenged Canseco when Jose said he believed steroids were good for him. Maher disagreed, saying steroids are dangerous. Canseco insisted that for him, they were not. Maher finally ended the squabble by saying something like, "Fine, they will rot your liver, but you think they're good for you," and he dismissed the issue and moved on.

Rot your liver?! This, from a guy who could drink the entire Sixth Fleet under the table? I wish Jose had challenged him on that! I guess in Maher's mind steroids are more dangerous than alcohol.

That's the problem, folks. Celebrities, news anchors, political pundits, bereaved parents, coaches, team owners and politicians are spreading erroneous information that steroids are the most dangerous drugs on earth from a pulpit of high visibility and authority. How do they know? They don't. For some reason, all these supposed authorities say steroids are dangerous, but they don't know how or why. In other words, it's Easter, Gracie, hack the end off the ham!

13

China—East Germany Repeated?

The East German doping machine was a scandal that most people in sports would rather forget than relive, but pretending it never happened only provides comfort until a scandal of equal or greater proportion hits again.

China is by far the biggest threat to a clean sports world, and history backs that statement. More Chinese athletes have tested positive than those of any other country around the globe. If cheating in sports by way of drugs was represented by a pie-shaped diagram, the rest of the world would be only a small slice compared with China's share. Sports in China are more than games, they are status symbols for the entire nation. As hosts of the 2008 Olympic games, China has its hopes set very high on a strong performance.

In July of 2005 reports emerged from various news sources such as NBC, that China and Russia have "teamed up" to dethrone the United States as reigning overall Olympic champion in total medal count and gold medal count. China has specifically zeroed in on track and field and swimming, because of the high volume of medals awarded in these categories. China wants to take these sports by storm because America is strong in both, and if the Chinese not only win the event, but take medals that the United States would have normally had on its tally, it would be a double victory.

The problem for China is that, especially in swimming, the country doesn't have exceptional talent, and it most certainly doesn't have a clean record. A string of positive tests over more than two decades attests to this profoundly. China claimed in 2005 to be sharing resources and training techniques with Russia, another nation with a less than stellar Olympic record of cleanliness in its athletes. And adding suspicion is the fact that after the last partnership China held for training techniques, which was with East Germany in the mid-1980s, their performances, and positive tests, exploded.

China wants to focus on swimming, and the world should focus on it as well. China has long been accused of cheating and, after claims of innocence, has many times had to eat its words. Its history shows a lack of talent in the pool, consistency in performance, and a large number of positive tests. Economic development, and its effects on human development, may be a cause of China's deficit. It may also be the reason the country has turned so often to drugs.

In 1984 at the Los Angeles Olympics, not one Chinese swimmer made it to an Olympic final. Not only did the Chinese not medal, but they were not even in contention for a medal, every representative having been eliminated in the preliminaries. This wasn't a new experience as this predated the rise-and-fall pattern China would later follow; this was normal. The country was not known for producing exceptional swimmers.

Training athletes for peak competition at the elite level is a very long process that involves training techniques; coaching advances; and stronger, better, more developed athletes. Some countries take decades to advance a program in order to place one or two athletes in an Olympic final. China somehow bypassed this unwritten rule. After the 1984 games, a coach from the East German doping system spent upward of a year in China, lecturing on "advanced techniques." What techniques exactly were discussed remain unknown, but the coach was well versed in drug use. In the end, the results were monumental in the swimming pool. In 1988, four short years later, China placed 10 swimmers in finals and captured three silvers and a bronze. No doubt, it was a more than suspicious jump for a country in a single Olympiad. No other country had ever, nor has any country since, made such a jump. The critics said China was doped to the gills but Chinese officials swore otherwise. It wouldn't be long before their feet were inserted into their own gaping jaws.

In 1990 at the Chinese National Championships, China publicly announced that three athletes were caught for doping violations. Politically this was a good move for the country, publicly it was very bad. The motivation behind this was grand, however. Because of the jump China had made between 1984 and 1988, it was continually being scrutinized on what was going on at its state-sponsored training facilities. With the next Olympics only two years away, the pressure was building. These positive tests were announced and the public cried foul, using it as proof that the program was littered with doping. China went on the defensive saying that these positive results were proof that it was combating the problem. The probability is that it was likely a cover-up for a much more intricate program. The Chinese were able to learn much from the East Germans, especially after classified documents came to light after the unification with West Germany. Whereas the East Germans would simply leave athletes at home who would have tested positive, China and every other country was fully aware of what was going on. As a way to improve its public image against drugs in sports, China likely took steps of its own to try to stem the onslaught of accusations. With the Olympics getting closer, and knowing how its athletes were swimming two years out, it was only a matter of time before a breakthrough performance won a gold medal, and with it, a great deal of trips from drug testers to Chinese training facilities.

And, sure enough, in 1992 there was more of the same: more positive tests, more amazing performances. Two more Chinese athletes tested positive in 1992 for illegal substances. While at the Olympics that year China not only increased the number of athletes who placed in finals, but it captured four Olympic gold medals. In eight years the country moved from having no athletes in medal contention, let alone in a respectable position with the expectation to medal, but to four gold medals, the highest prizes in the sport. A country had never risen to such prominence so quickly except, of course, the East Germans. By this time the atmosphere was becoming eerily reminiscent.

What is also important to note is that these improvements were coming almost strictly from the women's side of the field. Thus, if doping allegations proved true—as many test results already had—these gains would make perfectly good sense. Strength is derived from testosterone, the male hormone. Women naturally have a much, much lower amount of testosterone in their bodies and it takes much less exogenous hormone to induce performance-enhancing benefits. Men are faster in the water because of their sheer size and power, not necessarily because of grace of stroke. Giving male hormones to Chinese women would add a great deal of power and explosiveness to a gender that generally lacked those attributes. As a result? Faster swimming. Specifically, four gold medals.

After China's 1992 showing in Barcelona, Chinese officials continued to claim their athletes won on talent alone, fending off continued doping allegations. Then in 1993 the Chinese swimmers lacked the same sort of pop they had shown in the previous two Olympics. A sign of lying low?

In swimming, big meets generally occur at two-year intervals. The 1992 Olympics in Spain were followed by the Atlanta games in 1996. In between, in 1994, the World Championships took place in Rome. It was also in these two-year intervals that China seemed to somehow bring about amazing performances again, which it lacked in prior years, and it also seemed to sacrifice athletes to positive drug tests.

By July, two months before the big event in Rome, four more Chinese athletes tested positive. China's performance at the World Championships seemed to confirm it and, again, it had that East German flare. Chinese women won 12 of 16 events. China said their training was just superior. If that was so, why were two more Chinese athletes caught and suspended within one month after Rome? And, why then, were China's male swimmers stuck in an abysmal trench they seemingly had no way out of? In a country of one billion people, with such advanced training techniques, why could not one male be a standout in the same sport its women were currently dominating? It appeared easy enough to explain to the educated viewer: female hormones are easier to manipulate. A main problem for men who take exogenous testosterone is the potential side effect of gynecomastia. Women already have large amounts of estrogen and the feminizing effects go unnoticed, because they belong. This effect for men requires surgery for removal. Women who experience increased hair growth just need a razor.

Before the Asian Games that year, five more Chinese athletes tested positive, and it has been reported as many as 10 more were on the border of failing the testosterone-epitestosterone test. Thanks to a new test for dihydrotestosterone (DHT), eleven Chinese athletes failed the drug test at the Asian Games. Was this their drug of choice prior to the new test? Possibly. Unfortunately, no retroactive tests were conducted.

And then, as history would show, China slowly fell out of the spotlight after 1994. As far away as 2006, Jingye Le's 100-meter freestyle time of 54.01 still stood as a World Championship record, which she made in 1994's Rome games, as does He Cihong's 1:00.16 in the 100-meter backstroke and 2:07.40 in the 200-meter backstroke.

With no major competition in 1995, China stayed close at home. The country also has exhibited a pattern of sending incomplete teams to meets or not having others travel at certain times. This too was a learned technique from East Germany. At the end of 1995, just one year before the Atlanta Olympics, only 10 Chinese swimmers were ranked in the top 25 for long course meters events. In 1988 China had placed this number of swimmers in Olympic finals, and had supposedly created such wonderful advanced training techniques since then. What happened? A common theory is that, much again like East Germany, China keeps its athletes out of the public eye during off years so that they can more easily avoid drug tests.

By this point in swimming history, just over a decade since the last Olympics where China won zero swimming medals, nearly half of all positive drug tests were from Chinese swimmers. Drug testing abilities were climbing, and China somehow wasn't keeping up with its own athletes—neither catching them nor keeping them above the bar—and their performances in 1996 only added fuel to the steroid fire. Only this time, it was because of their lack of talent. The upward path of Chinese swimming was discontinued in Atlanta with China winning only one gold medal. And then 1997 produced both a rebound and renewed public outrage.

In 1997 Chinese swimmers set world records and swam 10 times that were faster than the gold-medal-winning performances in Atlanta. One record, set by Wu Yanyan in the 200-meter individual medley, still stands in 2006, still nearly a second faster than the next fastest swimmer who holds the American record. On a particularly interesting note, Wu was later fined and banned from her sport in 2000 for four years after failing a drug test. Wu swam her world record time, however, in Shanghai, China. If the governing body of Chinese sports was aware of cheating in China's swimming program, it would have been easy to cover up any positive drug test within its own country. FINA ignorantly defended these performances, despite the fact that Chinese athletes had a tendency to swim well within their own country, and would sometimes swim far off those times outside of it. But, whether Wu was doping at the time or not, in just the following year, China made its biggest mistake offering a peek into its tight-lipped world of drug use.

At the 1998 World Championships in Perth, Australia, the games were touted to be another spectacle of modern swimming, with a multitude of broken records. The Chinese team specifically, following a big year in 1997, was hoping for a great showing. What this showing was fueled by, at least partially, was soon to be discovered. A customs agent searching the bags of swimmer Yuan Yuan found vials of enough human growth hormone inside a thermos packed with ice to supply the entire Chinese squad for the duration of the World Championships. The rest of the team's bags were for some reason not searched. *AsiaWeek* magazine reported that the coach said he was the one trying to bring the growth hormone, Somatropin, into the country for a physician friend of his. The problem was that an Australian doctor can acquire Somatropin, and that the drugs were found in a swimmer's bag, not the coach's luggage. Growth hormone is also illegal to import into Australia, which a physician in the country would surely know. To further put holes in the coach's story, a mixing solution was also found with the growth hormone, which the drug would be useless without—except of course to a physician who would certainly have plenty already.

Accusations that this was certainly proof of a state-sponsored drug program flew around. China responded with allegations of its own saying that it was the swimmers themselves who decided to bring the drugs and they were doing so on their own accord. At first this conflicted with the coach's story, but it also conflicts with sheer economics. A supply of somatropin for a year costs tens of thousands of dollars, which is far more than the yearly income of about $1,000 that the average citizen in China makes. This is without going into the financial lives of the athletes who make much less. Even the supply found in the luggage would have cost hundreds if not thousands of dollars, which is most certainly out of the reach of any Chinese athlete. In its reporting, *AsiaWeek* also quoted "a former State Sports Commission insider" who claimed that two decades before, the East Germans assisted China in setting up an elaborate doping program, which, the insider said, was still going strong to date, and that the program involved extensive research into how long before a competition an athlete would have to desist the drug use in order to prevent positive test results.

In the end, the Chinese swimmer caught with the drugs was given a four-year ban, and the coach a 15-year ban. Four swimmers tested positive in those games. Another important piece of the puzzle is that no swimmer tested positive for growth hormone, so that the four who did receive sanctions did so because of other drugs. Chinese athletes who had used or did use growth hormone were essentially given a free pass because to date an accurate test to find growth hormone cheaters has not been developed. The drugs found in 1998, as well as the inability to test for them, fuels concern that this has been and is continually being used as a source for Chinese performance enhancement.

The 2000 Sydney Olympics came and went with a ravaged Chinese team showing up to compete. Before the games even began team officials were saying the odds of winning a gold medal were essentially nonexistent. They were right. Not one Chinese woman medaled, coming close only once with a fourth-place finish in the 200-meter breaststroke.

Having lost the bid for the Sydney games, China was looking to win the opportunity to showcase its country for the 2008 Olympics, which prompted the idea that it was cracking down on cheating. As China did crack down, its performance level significantly dropped. And, sure enough, China was given the right to host the world's biggest sporting event in 2008. But first, there was Athens to contend with. China represented itself much better than just four years earlier, but was still well off its prime. Luo Xuejuan won gold for China in Athens in the 100-meter breaststroke, and China's 4x200-meter freestyle relay took silver.

The sports world would love to believe that China has cleaned up its act, but with the 2005 initiative to take down the domination of the United States, its affiliation with Russia, and the ever-present atmosphere reminiscent of East Germany, it's a tough pill to swallow. Also in 2005, a doctor who was a large part of the East German doping machine took a post in China to work with its national teams. If what the *AsiaWeek* insider said was true, and the East German-introduced doping setup is indeed alive and well, the doctor has found a nice place to call home.

As proof enough the doping hasn't stopped in China, in June of 2005 its entire Hubei weight lifting team was banned from China's National Games after six athletes were found using banned substances. The athletes who tested positive were banned for two years, the coach banned for life, and the team as a whole banned from international competition for a year. Also banned from the games prior to the start of competition were three track and field athletes. Long jumper Wang Lina, relay member Niu Nana, and 400-meter athlete Sun Hongfeng all tested positive for 19-norandrosterone. Zeng Liqing, a cyclist, was banned for the use of EPO. It wasn't just the athletes being doped; Xu Xianyu was banned for two years after her horse tested positive for an illegal substance. The horse was banned from competition for one year.

Still on the defensive, Chinese sporting officials claim they are serious about drug testing and that during the National Games they performed between 110 and 200 drug tests per day. The event ran for 11 days, so drug tests totaled anywhere from just over 1,200 tests up to 2,200. The problem? Tens of thousands of athletes were competing at the games.

And yet, with its history and potential future, the biggest worry about China may not be its likely preference for undetectable drugs that can beat the system. China has linked sports to politics, and both sports and politics to pride. Its athletes have a mind-set that winning on a field, a court, or in a pool means national success. A gold medalist is treated like a national hero, whereas a loser—someone who doesn't medal—is treated like a plague. Chinese athletes then will take whatever pill they're handed, allow whatever needle to be injected in them, and think it is OK.

With the impending advent of gene doping, China could be at the forefront of modifying the body far beyond human capabilities, and far beyond the scope of drug tests. If the past has any chance of repeating itself, China could be a much more intricate, and dangerous, version of the despicable East German doping scandal. This one though, may never be able to be stopped.

A Missing Generation

Craig Lord is a sportswriter for the *Times* in London and has long covered athletics and, specifically, the sport of swimming. In 1998, Lord, a long-time antidoping campaigner, broke the story that

Michelle Smith, the Irish swimmer who won three gold medals at the Atlanta Olympic games, faced suspension for tampering with a drug testing sample. He writes about what the future may hold for the next generation of China's "Golden Flowers."

Beyond the well-researched world of so-called designer steroids, insulin growth factor, growth hormone, EPO and other means of cheating that make their way on to the list of banned substances in sport, a far more worrying world is dominating debate among some of the world's leading scientific minds and the sporting bureaucrats they serve: gene therapy.

In the words of Professor Arne Ljungqvist, Sweden's best-known anti-doping expert based at the Karolinska Institutet and chairman of the World Anti-Doping Agency's Health, Medical and Research Committee: "This is a disturbing trend because not only is gene doping in sport wrong, it can also be extremely dangerous."

Gene therapy research has reached a critical phase. Already practiced on humans as part of strictly controlled experiments, gene therapy promises to become a widely available form of treatment for injury and disease. However, advances in the science of gene therapy have a darker side: gene doping—the unscrupulous use of genetic modification of athletes to enhance sports performances.

WADA held its first gene doping symposium in New York's Banbury Centre in March 2002. In December 2005, some of the world's leading gene researchers gathered alongside WADA and the upper echelons of the International Olympic Committee, including its president Jacques Rogge, for a follow-up symposium on the status of research in the field of gene-doping detection.

"Gene doping represents a serious threat to the integrity of sport and the health of athletes," said Richard Pound, a former swimmer and chairman of WADA, an organization that has already devoted significant resources and attention to finding ways of detecting gene doping.

It will not be easy, though there is one significant difference between the old world of steroids and the new world of gene therapy in terms of hunters and hunted: whereas the poachers were often miles ahead of the gamekeepers in years gone by, this time around anti-doping scientists are working closely alongside genetic scientists with the aim of ensuring that, as new therapeutic methods are being developed, anti-doping scientists will find new ways to detect gene doping.

Theodore Friedmann, an American professor, one of the world's leading gene researchers and chairman of WADA's Gene Doping Panel, said: "Gene doping will in all likelihood soon be with us, and I would not be surprised if the first tentative steps had already been taken."

He is not alone. Indeed the first finger has already been pointed—at China by the head of the American Swimming Coaches Association and member of the Coaches Commission of FINA, the international governing body for swimming.

The picture painted by John Leonard, a long-time US swimming coach and anti-doping campaigner, is as horrifying as it is simple. It is a fact, confirmed by China's national team coaches, that 100 of China's most talented junior swimmers were gathered together for a test day in Beijing in late 2001 after the capital won the right to stage the 2008 games.

Of the 100, 50 were chosen to remain with the national team in Beijing under the "care and feeding" of national team coaches. They travelled to international competition and are well known to rivals and anti-doping agents, though many never made it beyond China's borders despite having clocked the fastest domestic times in their respective events by 2004. Obvious candidates for the Olympic Games that year did not show up in Athens.

The 50 children who did not remain in Beijing take a very different route. Leonard's theory, backed by testimony of sources within China, the identities of whom cannot be revealed, is as follows: the 50 leave the capital in late 2001 and are not seen or heard of again until six months or so before China welcomes the world for the games in 2008, when those among the missing children who have survived and prospered reappear as the fastest shoal in the world, untested, both in international waters and by anti-doping agencies. They have spent the past seven years in a faraway pool in a distant province in the clutches of one Zhou Ming, former head coach of China who was banned for life. While some of the children emerge fit to be champions, others have fallen victim to this genetic experiment in which they have been the guinea pigs.

Some background is helpful at this stage: in 1994, Zhou, as China head coach, led a group of women swimmers, known as the Golden Flowers, to 13 out of 16 world titles in Rome. As suspected, the blossoming talent had been crossed with an anabolic steroid for competitive hardiness and a month after Rome, as a plane carrying the China team for the Asian Games touched down in Hiroshima, drug testers, sent by the incisive mind of one of the world's leading pathologists, the late Professor Malcolm Cameron, from Britain, waited to pounce. Eleven athletes, among them seven swimmers, two of those world champions and Zhou's personal charges, tested positive for steroids.

More scandal followed in January 1998, when Yuan Yuan, a woman breaststroke world medallist, was stopped by customs officials at Sydney airport as she headed to Perth for the world championships. A dozen tubes of human growth hormone were unearthed in her kit bag (enough to supply the entire team), while five teammates tested positive for diuretics in the days that followed and China headed home in shame.

Almost 40 Chinese swimmers and coaches were suspended for doping offences during the 1990s, about half of the entire tally of positives in the history of the sport, discounting those discovered but never reported beyond East Germany by the official International Olympic Committee laboratory at Kreischa, 30 miles south of Leipzig.

It is against that background that Leonard believes what others find unbelievable: that China is hosting a rogue program that has started to dabble in gene doping.

"Some of you might ask, 'what became of the other 50?' I asked that question also," says Leonard of the 50 children said to have gone missing. "No one will say, or no one connected with Chinese swimming will say. No Chinese coach with whom I have spoken thinks that China just 'ignored' the other 50 elite age-group athletes. They just don't know—or won't say—where they are."

His contacts believe that a rogue program is training and manipulating "talented youngsters in some remote area of China, unknown, perhaps, even to Chinese Swimming authorities and coaches." That program uses "a variety of sophisticated doping methods and perhaps the brave new world of genetic enhancement," according to Leonard.

Some go further. Rumours abound among coaches and swimmers that the world has already witnessed, unwittingly, genetically enhanced athletes. Two case examples have been cited: two Chinese boys improved rapidly over 1,500 meters freestyle in 2001 and 2002, rising during that period from beyond the world's best 200 to places among the top 30 fastest. In 2003 both "disappeared" from the ranking lists, meaning that they did not compete, neither in China—officially—nor in international waters. Instead, China sent Xin Tong to Athens. He finished 33rd out of 34 swimmers in a time about a minute slower than the best times of the two rapid improvers.

The belief is that one of those boys had mitochondria (energy producing cells) genetically enhanced but is now suffering serious health problems as a consequence, according to sources within the community of world-leading swimming coaches.

Two boys fitted the bill in terms of rapid improvement in performance: Chen Yu and Li Zhang. In 2005, Li Zhang reemerged to establish Asian records over 200, 400 and 1,500 meters freestyle, coming within a fingernail of joining the elite sub-15-minute club over the longest distance when he won the Asian Games title in Macau in November. Chen has not been heard of since 2002.

A source close to Chinese swimming, said: "What Leonard is saying is not entirely a fantasy. There is a vast youth program in all sports in China. You are talking about hundreds of thousands of children. To hide 50, if they are being hidden, would not be difficult, though I suspect that hide is the wrong word. They are just out of contact."

Communication with China remains difficult. When the issue of the "missing" children was raised, calls and e-mails to the Chinese Swimming Federation went unanswered. The source said: "How could they? They probably don't know what you're talking about. In which case how are they able to say they are cleaning up the drug problems of the 1990s. You can't test invisible swimmers."

Among key concerns of anti-doping agencies is that it may not be possible to test at all when it comes to gene doping and the first sign of trouble may be serious ill-health or the death of an athlete.

"Sportspeople are taking immense risks when they add new genetic material into their bodies. Already there have been at least two deaths during experiments conducted to treat the sick. Two people have, for example, developed leukemia," said Professor Friedmann. "The seriously ill can take such a risk perhaps, but for young, healthy sportsmen and women, it is completely unacceptable."

One of Sweden's leading sports scientists said it was difficult to provide explanations in layman's terms. "The closest you can get to explaining just how dangerous this can be is to imagine that you introduce a gene that makes a bald man grow hair again. All good and well, but many genes are known to work with other genes. They do not function in isolation, so the effect of the manipulation may be that the bald man does indeed grow hair again but he may also find that his kidneys collapse or that he develops cancerous growths. It is a hugely complex world full of dangers."

One challenge that anti-doping experts are trying to tackle is the fact that gene therapy methods will be relatively simple to use once they are made available through the advanced work carried out by pharmaceutical companies and others driven to exploit the market in this new world of gene therapy. All that may be needed is a standard laboratory. The genes attractive to sport are well defined: those that stimulate tissue growth and boost strength, and those that increase stamina by stimulating the production of red blood cells.

Certainly, there is big money to be made in the gene market. The European Union has just invested £100 million in a DNA project designed to experiment on mice, which share 99 percent of human genes, to find genetic therapies for humans.

The symposiums in New York and Stockholm have been held behind closed doors, with the media allowed access only to press conferences at which questions are fielded and some information is provided. The finer details of how anti-doping agencies hope to combat the threat of gene manipulation are being kept out of the public arena, for fear that the knowledge could be of value to rogue scientists and doctors who hope to gain from creating lucrative sporting monsters of the future.

Magnetic resonance imaging technology may be of great use. Scientists are already working on techniques that allow them to watch genes working in "real time." The purpose of the research is to provide a vital tool for identifying new drug targets, or monitoring the function of therapeutic genes. It might also have applications in the anti-doping field.

Ultimately, anti-doping agencies might even suggest methods that will be resisted by human-rights watchers the world over: each of us may have a unique genetic fingerprint, which could be taken and recorded at birth. Changes to that fingerprint might be taken as evidence of manipulation.

14

Gene Doping

Ever since the invention of the motion picture to record human events, there have always been individuals who seemed to somehow, in some way, defy nature. Someone, or some people, who didn't seem quite like everyone else—not quite completely human, in a sense—have always been around. Overly large, Greek-god, theatrical-sized muscles have progressed from the world's first strongman, Eugen Sandow (born Friederich Wilhelm Mueller, who was the model for the Mr. Olympia bodybuilding contest trophy), to every professional bodybuilder since then including, of course, the first 10 men who have been called the world's best bodybuilders: Larry Scott, Sergio Oliva, Arnold Schwarzenegger, Franco Colombu, Frank Zane, Chris Dickerson, Samir Bannout, Lee Haney, Dorian Yates, and Ronnie Coleman.

But muscles aren't the only things that have entranced audiences, especially in a sporting arena. Not necessarily heavily built, sprinters have enjoyed a great deal of the spotlight for their 100-meter endeavors. The distance is arguably the most popular, most watched, most anticipated event of any Olympics. Famous sprinters often become household names after achieving a world record or an Olympic medal: Ben Johnson, Marion Jones, Justin Gatlin.

Football, baseball, and basketball too have all seen players who defy physical laws. Great quarterbacks like John Elway, Joe Montana, Dan

Marino, Peyton Manning. Great hitters like Babe Ruth, Roger Maris, Mickey Mantle, Joe DiMaggio, McGwire, Bonds, the list goes on and on. Basketball dominators like Wilt Chamberlain, Larry Bird, Michael Jordan, Yao Ming, Shaq. Height, talent, speed—unthinkable prowess in all of those features and more. All of these athletes are similar in that they seemingly were bred to be the best in their chosen sport.

Is it evolution? Or is it technology? As sad as it seems, there's another, albeit hidden, commonality in the histories of our greatest athletes.

Of the above-named sprinters, Ben Johnson has been sanctioned for using banned substances. Marion Jones has also been accused by individuals, such as Victor Conte, who says he personally witnessed Jones inject herself with illegal drugs.

Of the bodybuilders, the best of the best from before even Arnold's day were taking physique and performance-enhancing drugs. Arnold himself in his day, as well as every professional today uses anabolic steroids including a mixture of other drugs for every purpose from strength gain to potent fat burning: growth hormone, clenbuterol, Cytomel—some use all of them, some don't. While the drugs bodybuilders consume aren't necessarily the same, they have the same purpose. Could Larry Scott have been bigger than the eight-time Mr. Olympia, Lee Haney, if the same level of steroid advances had been available during his time? Maybe. Genetics play a huge role in how big muscles can grow, even with massive amounts of steroids. Muscle shape is also genetically predetermined. Because aesthetics—proportion and symmetry—are a judged part of bodybuilding contests, not everyone has the genetic capacity to be a Mr. Olympia contestant.

But what if you could change your genetic code?

Naturally there's more to a performance than someone's bodily makeup, but at the Olympic Games the competitors are all on the same field, in the same pool, or on the same court.

At high altitude in Mexico City, Jim Hines set the world record in the 100-meter sprint with 9.95. That record, made at the only major meet in such thin air, lasted 11 years. Tommie Smith's 200-meter record also stood for 11. In the 400-meters, Lee Evans ran 43.86, which remained the global standard for an unprecedented 29 years. Bob Beamon flew through the air in Mexico to land a long jump of 8.90 meters, a top mark for 23 years.

Now what if these athletes had been on drugs? Maybe Hines would have run a 9.90, a 9.85, or a 9.79, the same mark that Ben Johnson captured many years later during his time on illegal drugs. Hines could have set a record that might have lasted 30 years or more. Now what if, even as far back as 1968, in baggy track uniforms and before Nike track shoes, Hines had been genetically altered to react faster, to maintain his muscular endurance longer, kick harder, push from the ground more efficiently? He could have run a nine flat, maybe even an eight flat. It seems unbelievable for a normal human, but it's not out of the realm of science. And it could happen sooner than anyone would like to think.

Mice, the unfortunate little critters that seem to catch the brunt of research in all forms, have already been genetically altered to learn more easily. That alone, if it were possible to be applied to a human, could help an athlete improve beyond what is seen as "reality" now. If an athlete could listen to everything a coach says and actually apply it, there's no telling exactly how well one could perform. But it doesn't end there. Mice have also been altered to grow larger skeletons (which could translate to height in humans), produce more red blood cells (improve oxygen circulation), and grow more muscle (run faster, hit harder, etc.).

Keep in mind, many of these genetic advancements are a result of the completion of the Human Genome Project and intended for the diagnosis, prevention, and cure of diseases. Of course, though, when there's money to be made, it doesn't take long before someone is willing to try anything—even the manipulation of his own body—to get it.

Tomorrow's Creation

Imagine that one day, world records won't be something that athletes work hard to break. Instead, picture records simply as measures of mechanical advantage and technological advances. The idea that athletes could someday have their genetic makeup altered for increased athletic performance used to seem so far-fetched, but it's not. It's possible, and it's here. And it could be the undoing of professional sports, or the dawn of a new era.

To understand gene doping, what it is, how it is done, and what it can really do, one must understand how the body is made up and how it functions. Most important, one must understand what these things called genes really are, and why they are so vital to life and the athletic ability of the world's athletes.

What Are Genes?

A "gene" is described by the American Heritage Dictionary as a "hereditary unit consisting of a sequence of DNA that occupies a specific location on a chromosome and determines a particular characteristic in an organism. Genes undergo mutation when their DNA sequence changes."

Genes are essentially the blueprint for a human life. Genes, which combine to ultimately form someone's "genetic code" or more simply his "genetics," are what determine physical structure. Height, eye color, the number of fast-twitch and slow-twitch muscle fibers, those things are all determined by a person's genetic makeup. Some people are genetically predisposed to attributes that ultimately offer the ability to be a better athlete than someone else in a given sport. Many professional basketball players, for instance, are extremely tall, which is an obvious benefit. Sprint track athletes and sprint swimmers are usually genetically gifted with more fast-twitch muscle fibers. Professional bodybuilders are another example of people with genetic extremes. They're able to grow larger muscles than the average human.

In the world of sports, many people are under the assumption that if they took steroids or other performance-enhancing drugs, they too could be Olympic champions or professional athletes. However, genetics have a great deal to do with a successful career in sports. Professional bodybuilders, for example, are the exact opposite of the old saying "Champions are made, not born." It is common in gyms around the nation for an extremely muscular individual to walk by a group of people, and for someone from that group to whisper, "If I was on steroids, I could be that big." Generally, this is completely untrue. An individual whose genetics predispose him to 15- or 16-inch biceps would, conceivably, never be able to produce the musculature necessary to be a professional, competitive bodybuilder, no matter how many drugs he abused. There is a natural limit to the amount of muscle the human body can carry, and this limit varies from person to person. There is also a limit to the amount of muscle that steroids and other drugs can assist someone in putting on. And with that, different people respond differently to steroids, with some people seeing much greater gains than others. This, again, is determined by genetics.

As history has shown, not every basketball player or football player has to be extremely tall, and not every track athlete has to be born with great speed. These are simply advantages to the individual and are passed down through a person's parents. It is possible, and even likely, that a child whose both parents possess a given trait—such as height—will also receive the trait. Professional NBA center Yao Ming's parents were allegedly chosen in a genetic experiment. His mother, Fang Fendi, a basketball star in China, was six feet three inches tall. Yao's father, Yao Zhiyuan, has been reported to be as tall as six feet ten inches. When Yao was born he was nearly two feet long and is now seven feet five inches tall.

What Is Gene Doping?

Gene doping is a by-product of what was to be called "gene therapy." The World Anti-Doping Agency defines gene doping as "the non-therapeutic use of cells, genes, genetic elements, or of the modulation of gene expression, having the capacity to improve athletic performance."

Gene doping is set to be the next step in athletic advancement and, as of now, the next step in cheating. Gene doping could quite possibly, and easily, put steroids out to pasture. Steroids are intended to be caught. Steroids are excreted and are able to be tested for, assuming testing agencies know what to look for. Genetic alterations, which are the ultimate goal of athletes who would choose to pursue gene doping techniques, are as of yet indistinguishable, and no test has been developed to deter them.

The mind-set of people who have or will pursue gene doping is potentially more severe than that of steroid users. Steroid users are quite generally aware of what they are doing, of the side effects that may occur, and of the fact that many of the benefits they gain while on the drugs are only temporary. The athlete who has or will pursue gene doping is essentially unhappy with who he is and his God-given talents. By introducing genes into a healthy body, he is knowingly changing his genetic makeup and therefore, who he really is. Their minds and thoughts may remain the same, but with changes in physical characteristics at the genetic level, the people themselves experience true change.

Gene doping is the name of the act any individual undertakes that alters his genes with the intent to compete in an athletic competition. This is different and should not be confused with those who may, one day under physician supervision, use genetic therapy to enhance specific characteristics. Worldwide, people enhance themselves physically with the use of cosmetic surgeries and drugs such as steroids, which are legal in many countries. Should genetic therapy reach a level in which it can offer these same benefits with minimal risk and zero harm to others, the procedure, like steroids, should be legal for sound-minded adults to undertake. This does not include athletes. Like politicians who accept that their backgrounds will be exposed during an election year, athletes must understand they are on a larger stage. What is one thing for an average citizen is not the same for them. Caffeine used to be on the banned-substance list for elite-level Olympic athletes. It is these things, like genetic therapy, that athletes must understand are not available to them while they are competing on the world stage, and they must not, in an effort to keep a sport fair, pursue them in unethical manners. For those who do, it is not genetic therapy, it is gene doping.

How Is Gene Doping Done?

Gene doping can be carried out in a variety of methods. The most simple device of introducing gene therapy into a human body is through a virus. A virus is created with the modified gene and injected into the body.

The following list of viruses used to transport genes is from http://www.fda.gov:

- **Retroviruses**—A class of viruses that can create double-stranded DNA copies of their RNA genomes. These copies of its genome can be integrated into the chromosomes of host cells. Human immunodeficiency virus (HIV) is a retrovirus.
- **Adenoviruses**—A class of viruses with double-stranded DNA genomes that cause respiratory, intestinal, and eye infections in humans. The virus that causes the common cold is an adenovirus.

- **Adeno-associated viruses**—A class of small, single-stranded DNA viruses that can insert their genetic material at a specific site on chromosome 19.
- **Herpes simplex viruses**—A class of double-stranded DNA viruses that infect a particular cell type, neurons. Herpes simplex virus type 1 is a common human pathogen that causes cold sores.

Another method is the introduction of the gene as naked, double-stranded DNA and injecting it directly into muscle.

What Are the Possible Side Effects of Gene Doping?

The side effects, at least the potential side effects, are largely unknown at this point. The majority of gene-therapy-related incidents have been on individuals who had a need for the therapy, not on individuals of above-average health like athletes. What can be determined at this point is that gene therapy, even successful treatments, are not without risks. Death has been attributed to gene thearpy experiments.

The first tragedy that occurred with the experimentation of gene therapy happened with a case of ornithine transcarbamylase (OTC) deficiency. An 18-year-old male who had OTC was injected with a gene that was intended to improve his condition. Within hours after the treatment, the patient developed a high fever and the ammonia levels in his blood rose to dangerous levels. His blood began to clot and his liver hemorrhaged. Soon after, the patient passed away as a result of the attempt. And this case wasn't the only one that started out with high hopes and eventually experienced a downfall.

Researchers and physicians have "successfully" used gene therapy and transfer to treat children with severe combined immunodeficiency disorder (SCID). This disease, more commonly known as "Bubble Boy syndrome," affects the proper function of the immune system. Treating SCID was one of the first major breakthroughs using gene therapy. The potential risks were unknown, but later it was discovered that some of the patients with SCID who were treated with the therapy developed leukemia. Doctors at Necker Hospital in Paris acknowledged publicly that it was the gene therapy that triggered the response. According to Dr. Theodore Friedmann of the University of California-San Diego, "The bubble boy issue for example shows that there are many surprises lurking around the next corner, and we can't predict what will go wrong. I predict if you alter muscle function in one way, the body will give in others to maintain a balance of homeostasis."

And while striving for that balance, an athlete who wants to gene dope could experience far worse side effects. An individual with SCID already has an off balance in a negative order, which the gene therapy attempts to resolve. A healthy athlete who has been "normal" for decades. may experience detriments beyond the scope of current predictions.

Average athletes carry out their doping with steroids in their own home, a gym, or a trainer's office. Some have expensive physicians on their payroll, but most can't afford that. This leaves them or their colleagues to effectively cheat on their own. Steroid administration is fairly straightforward, and essentially so is gene doping. But as Dr. Friedmann points out, "It's easy to do and quite easy to do very badly. It's extremely difficult to do it well in a clinically valid and justifiable way." As an example he adds, "There are about 700 clinical studies that have been carried out around the world and you can count on three fingers the number that have really been found effective. It's extremely hard to do these things well. The concepts are easy on paper but in a study is very, very, very difficult. It's easy to imagine doing it badly, it's difficult to imagine many people who could do it well technically and ethically."

And even if it can be done?

According to Friedmann, "It's an enormous amount of work to put a gene into a human and make sure it does something you intend it to do and not a million other things. And you don't know what those million other things could be. It's not possible to know all of the side effects, and that's why it's still called research in the therapeutic area. You don't know what will happen and it needs careful research. You don't know what the side effects will be and, honestly, I think it's good that there will be some side effects. You want to not be surprised by them and you don't want to harm people."

A large point of misunderstanding is that introducing something into the body is almost always going to cause some sort of unbalanced reaction.

The body is naturally predisposed to attack anything that is introduced through an exogenous source. The use of steroids weakens the immune system as the steroid makes its way through the blood; when an entire gene is introduced, the change in the immune system (unless the gene specifically targets the immune system) is unknown.

The FDA also points out the potential in gene therapy for the virus that the gene is attached to to become active once inside the patient and cause disease of its own.

What Is the Potential of Gene Doping?

The benefits of gene doping are as much left up to cheating athletes as to researchers. Researchers will continue to examine ethical uses for gene therapy, therefore continually increasing the potential for safe administration. If and when these abilities trickle down to cheating athletes, it will be their call on how far they are willing to risk taking it. Some athletes take more steroids than others, some athletes will no doubt try to push the gene limit further.

At first one can assume athletes will try only to increase their abilities through artificial means enough to gain the "edge." Usually a second or, in some sports, a tenth of one second is the necessary advantage needed to win. But over time, one can assume with athletes repeatedly trying to one-up each other, that the limits will be pushed far past extremes. Roger Bannister proved to the world that the notion of a "four-minute mile" being beyond human capability was nonsense. But could gene doping usher in the era of the three-minute mile?

"It's possible," according to Dr. Friedmann. "It may be possible to engineer a quasi-human kind of creature to run a three-minute mile. It's conceivable that with increases in enough muscle function and oxygenation that there may be a possibility of that kind of achievement."

The majority of tests are currently carried out on mice and other animals and lab creatures. "Schwarzenegger Mice," as they have been dubbed, have been created in lab tests using gene therapy. The mice have seen an increase of as much as 30 percent in muscle mass. But it's important to caution against assuming that will always happen, says Dr. Friedmann. "Mice are not human and humans are not mice, so you can't be absolutely sure. A lot of gene therapy studies that are successful in mice don't work nearly as well in humans. But, still, the mouse and other animal studies are in many areas, prerequisites to understand the biology."

Outside sports, genetic therapy can be an enhancement in many ways, which in and of itself brings about debate. While there are many obvious diseases that gene therapy can be used to cure, such as Parkinson's and potentially Huntington's, there are others in which the differential is not so clear. As Dr. Friedmann poses the question, "There's a terribly fuzzy area between what is a clear disease and what is enhancement; height and cognition and memory and strength and for instance, muscle weakness that comes normal as result of aging—is that a disease or not?"

And therefore, should genetic therapy be used as an essential fountain of youth, if possible? If aging is combated, there would be a host of problems because of the overpopulation conundrum that would certainly ensue. But in the realm of benefits for gene therapy, stopping or slowing break down because of aging is essentially possible. Knowing that gene therapy can cure sickle-cell anemia, should it be used to enhance the same features in healthy humans that it fixes in diseased ones?

Understanding the Capabilities—Example: Myostatin

When seeking to grasp the concept of genetic therapy capability, most educated scientists, as illustrated in the previous interviews with leading experts, will say that increased oxygen capacity and improved usage of oxygen are the most relevant factors in increasing athletic performance. On the contrary, many athletes and trainers who have only a slight grasp of gene therapy will point to the increased capability of the body when the myostatin gene is modified. In this case, modification of myostatin refers to blocking or deleting the gene more so than modifying it.

While myostatin offers the best insight to the benefits of gene therapy, it also has a dark side that any unscrupulous athlete looking for an advantage had better be aware of before trying to undergo any treatment.

Myostatin (formerly known as growth and differentiation factor 8) regulates muscle tissue growth in the human body. For example, higher concentrations of myostatin in an individual, or animal, may cause the body to have less muscle mass. The myostatin protein is produced in muscle cells and circulates throughout the body via the blood. On contact with muscles, the protein alters muscle tissue and can slow or halt the development of muscle. This, then, could easily lead one to believe that the removal of the gene would lead to amazing increases in muscle mass. In reality, it offers as much in results as it does in promise. Scientists found and labeled myostatin in 1997. The removal of the gene was then tested on mice, in which the results were amazing. The mice on average grew to carry two to three times the muscle mass that unmodified mice carried. The removal of the myostatin gene proved to truly be a boost in the capabilities of muscle growth. Research has also shown that the Belgian Blue cattle family have a defective myostatin gene, which has been credited as the reason for their much-increased supply of muscle.

So the upside, naturally, is to use this knowledge and treatment to assist individuals who have diseases that challenge muscle function. Muscular dystrophy has already been targeted as a disability that may possibly be treated with myostatin alterations. The downside, unfortunately, is that the depletion of muscle stem cells could worsen the disease over time. There is no proof the benefits or alterations will be permanent without side effects. There are individuals, specifically a German boy diagnosed in 2004, who have been found to have defective genes that have allowed for increased muscularity and function, but because the genes have not been completely removed they are, at least for now, relatively healthy. Long-term effects on their bodies cannot be predicted, and only time will tell for a true-to-life study. The promising science is coming in the form of myostatin blockers rather than simple elimination.

The main detrimental side effect, which receives little press in the world of athletes who want to gain access to this science, is the potential harm to the heart. While appearing in the muscles, myostatin is also expressed in cardiac muscle and adipose tissue. The absence of myostatin results in extremely low body fat levels, as shown in Belgian Blue cattle, which could, if to a degree too severe, be harmful for humans. The harm to cardiac function is of most concern. The heart as we know is a muscle, and the lack of myostatin would have the same effect as for other muscles in the body. An enlarged heart, whether caused by the use of growth hormone, steroids, high blood pressure, or the lack of myostatin, has been shown to increase the risk for heart failure, heart attack, and stroke.

For athletes looking into the alteration of myostatin, they must consider what benefit a temporary athletic improvement would be, even on the grandest scale, if they were disabled or otherwise too ill or, worse yet, deceased, and unable to enjoy the accompanying fame.

Currently on the market, myostatin blockers are being sold, though these supplements have no research behind them to offer any proof they actually do as the labels say.

How Can Gene Doping Be Stopped?

In a perfect world athletes would use their own morals and ethics in an approach to sports and cheating would not be an issue. Unfortunately, the world is far from perfect and there are agencies out there with intent to stop the sanctity of sports from being completely tarnished. Dr. Friedmann, for example, works with both the World Anti-Doping Agency and the United States Anti-Doping Agency as an advisor on the new frontier of genetic alterations. He predicts tests will be available to catch gene doping because of signature changes that will be left in the body. He explains, "The concepts of these new approaches that are being examined in research programs show that an endogenous gene will have many effects on many tissues. A foreign gene in an unusual place, in doses the body may or may not be used to, will cause other changes that will be kind of a signature." He likens this to the now standard test for EPO. These signatures, according to Dr. Friedmann, will be able to be obtained via blood, saliva, or urine.

Research to prevent gene doping is currently being adequately funded, according to Dr. Friedmann, and he believes that should gene doping appear in the 2008 Olympic Games in Beijing, that some form of test for the process will be ready.

Some proponents of genetic therapy use in sports say it's evolution and that it should be allowed. The notion naturally is not shared by all, whether it can be stopped and even if it cannot. "You can't stop murder and yet there are laws and agencies who speak against it and who chase murderers and put them in jail," said Dr. Friedmann. "I think if there is a concept that real sport involves following rules and doesn't involve cheating there will be a role for WADA and USADA. Sport is changing, it's a moving target. It depends on what you are trying to protect. Are you trying to protect the concept of fair and open competition and excelling and effort and achieving impossible goals through work rather than chemistry? It may be 50 years from now that the romantic view of sports is deader than it is now, but I don't know. I like that it represents a noble effort."

Dr. Garry Nolan of Stanford University is a leading expert in gene therapy. He is associate professor of microbiology and immunology. In the following interview, he uses his expertise to answer several frequently asked questions about the future of gene doping in athletics, and express his belief the 2008 Olympics will be free of genetic modification.

Q *To begin, when you received your bachelor's degree in genetics from Cornell University in 1983, did you ever think then that one day healthy, elite-level athletes may want to take advantage of your field of study for their own personal gain in the Olympics and professional sports?*

A I wouldn't say specifically that I envisioned it, but I was in my younger days an avid reader of sci-fi where ideas of personal enhancement through genetic engineering, either mental or physical, were often discussed in the context of modifying social behavior. It was just fiction, but the objective of enhancement through that approach didn't appeal to me. However, what it speaks to is that it's clear people will always look at whatever is available to them in their immediate environment as to how it might benefit them. The majority of people will say "How can I legally benefit? How far can I go?" Then there are the rogue elements that want to push it and see how far beyond ethical boundaries they can go.

Q *It seems like every time steroids get to the forefront of news, new legislation passes. The Anabolic Control Act of 1990 set in after Ben Johnson's doped world record. Steve Bechler died with a bottle of Ripped Fuel in his locker, and his death was blamed on ephedrine, which was subsequently banned. Mark McGwire was found with androstenedione and soon prohormones and other steroid precursors were banned. Steroids are back and the supplement* *industry is under attack now. The DEA and AMA didn't want steroids banned, and various physicians have said since then that because of such rulings, research on the drugs for legitimate purposes has suffered. Do you fear with the potential of gene doping entering the sporting world that moral uses by the advancement of gene therapy could be hindered?*

A

I think it will make people ask the question about boundaries for cosmetic enhancement. People change themselves, sometimes considerably, for personal gain such as modeling, so one might ask "Why is it different here?" Why is it accepted to enhance one form of excellence, physical beauty, for a commercial setting, and physical strength is not? Personally, I think attempts to change physical ability in sports is wrong, it's a broken social contract. We understand the game in modeling is doing whatever is necessary to be "beautiful" to the camera, but certainly in the sports world there is an agreement as to the means by which you achieve excellence. If anything it will make us carefully define "what is medical" versus what is cosmetic.

Importantly, I think what science can achieve for people as medicine—as opposed to enhancement of athletic physical prowess—can certainly withstand open scrutiny, and we should value the discussion. No one will say "No, we shouldn't talk about this in the open." We know parents attempt to get human growth hormone for their children, we know people use it when they get older for physical enhancement in ways that are medically and ethically responsible. Interestingly, these people, they aren't competing in the Olympics, but they are competing in other things and maybe at lower levels of sports? There's a groundswell of information in a cloudy area of what's happening with drugs being used in nonpro sports. If you are better in the tennis club than others because you use enhancing drugs, does that make you a "cheater?" People think pro sports are more sacred; why is the emphasis on them? It's a broader question than whether or not sports will limit advancement of enhancement practices that are perhaps considered elective.

Do you think gene therapy will eventually replace steroids?

A I don't think it will replace steroids any time soon because steroids are too easy, and the results are all around you immediately if you ever bother to look around at a gym. We can find supposed steroid enhancing agents in health food stores, to supposedly boost testosterone levels and the like; whether they work or not I don't know, I've read a lot of things that say they don't, but still, claims convince people. Also, I think the controversy around genetically modified foods has raised the consciousness of people in realizing that genes are a whole new class of agents—something you better think twice about before you mess with them. I think there's enough of a "negative vibe" around genes that people will want to leave it in the hands of experts. As scientists we need to push the safety aspects of what we do, acknowledge the dangers, and do it in a way that makes people really think twice before they use them inappropriately. That doesn't mean people won't eventually take advantage of gene therapy on a limited basis in sports. Certainly anyone sufficiently trained could literally take a stab at it and inject . . . DNA into a muscle that expresses some genes that "might" enhance, but at present the worst-case result could be "no effect," cancer, or the need to actually take that piece of the muscle out, whether it be due to inflammation or other unexpected changes. It's all about the level of control you have when you put it into the body and knowing the real effect of what putting that protein into the wrong place could do to human physiology. It has taken billions of years to get us where we are today, we can't think just because we have some knowledge now that we have the tools to do this properly for personal enhancement.

Q *Based on current research, what do you believe the possibilities are in realistic terms as far as using gene therapy on athletes for performance enhancement? Sure, we've seen "Schwarzenegger Mice" but is it really, at least at this point, probable for healthy humans to benefit from it?*

A Yes. I think it's possible to assume that people might have tried to take advantage of it. Personally, I think they would be taking a huge risk. One way to look at it is, though, that when it comes to human behavior and an available resource if something *can* happen, history says it often finds a way to happen.

Q *If an athlete were to be genetically modified, what, if any, proof would remain? From a drug testing standpoint, would it be at all possible to tell a genetically modified athlete from a "natural" athlete?*

A You might if you start first with the list of what the proteins/hormones are that you're looking for; you would have a hard time distinguishing the hormone because it's a small molecule and there is no way to tell where it came from, and for all intents and purposes, for most tests it's the same molecule. But for a protein produced from a cell that you've engineered to produce something like EPO or HGH, there are signatures that might be attached to the proteins as they are secreted from the cell: a normal protein made from its normal site of production maintains a certain signature and we can know what that signature is, and we can develop tests to see when that protein is made and whether or not it has a different signature. The limits on such testing are whether you can fashion a suitably sensitive test.

Q *Is there any way to tell at this point what kind of side effects may occur in a healthy human who undergoes gene therapy?*

A I imagine if it goes overboard there are known things that can occur to certain physiologic states, maybe some change in the body, but that all depends on what the gene therapy is. I would say it's tough to create a blanket test. One thing I know is the body is enormously resilient to physiological change. Assuming such rogue athletes know what they're doing they'll keep it within bounds. But I just don't think yet there is sufficient knowledge to do this properly. There are a lot of mights and maybes and ifs. Just because it might not exist now doesn't mean I don't think it's possible. I just don't think it's going to be a widespread problem any time soon. I think it's a bogeyman right now, frankly.

Yes, there might be a person who might feel desperate enough to do this; I think the best of the athletes are sufficiently well watched these days that they would want to be really careful. Someone who is going to do this needs to know it is not necessarily detection-proof.

Q *Assuming this sort of gene therapy can be done, relatively free of detrimental side effects, what kind of performance enhancements could we expect to see? Is this something that could put the capability of a mile runner into the low three minutes? Faster?*

A At this point what I would say is, based on my own knowledge of what we can do grossly, I think better oxygen usage, and whatever more oxygen can do for an athlete, is certainly possible. Certainly muscle strength through HGH and steroids helps, but for gene therapy, we just don't know enough at this point to modify fast muscles versus slow muscle groups to come up with something sufficiently subtle. We just don't know enough about the science yet. That doesn't mean we won't or there's a specific limit to what it can or could eventually do, but we go by what the science has told us to this point.

Q *Based on your expertise in the field, what do you believe the odds are that there will be genetically modified athletes in 2008 at the Beijing Olympic Games, and will testing be ready to stop it?*

A I would say the chances for a genetically modified athlete to be just about zero at this point. I think there will be adequate testing and knowledge of the known drugs like EPO and HGH and hormones. Frankly, why engineer yourself and take those risks when you can inject the materials? The chances for being detected are not diminished by engineering if we are talking about EPO or HGH. Any more "subtle" engineering of specific muscle groups or enhancements takes an unusual level of knowledge and ability that frankly does not exist. Again, people watch too many Hollywood and "Frankenfood"-inspired stories. Athletes would really be taking a big risk for themselves, from cancer to local growths to very profound changes to their physiological structure. That said, I will never underestimate the ability of people to purposely be stupid, so people might end up disfiguring themselves in an attempt for such engineering.

As well, I think the difference between steroids and gene therapy is that there's almost a common acceptance of steroids in the locker room community; there's been enough trial and error at this point that people think they can get away with it. I don't think there will be locker room discussion about injecting oneself with a gene. Can you imagine how fast a rumor of that would fly—there would be little ability to keep something like that hush-hush. Ethics and truth will, in the long run, win out. Even if there is a "one off" athlete who manages to do this in a way that enhances their capability, I don't think it will be anything that will destroy the sport. It will be noticed and found out and it will never be anything that will be prevalent.

The broader question is really, what do we do with the knowledge we are collecting? Circling back to the beginning—a day will come, no time soon—where we will begin to understand how some gene signatures provide better capabilities than others. When will we as a society start to use that information and how will we use it? Books and essays ad nauseam have been written on those subjects, and this issue with athletes is really just one facet of that very complex issue.

Author Acknowledgments and Thanks To

Don Anderson, my grandfather, for the faith and encouragement, then and still today.

Dr. Charlie Maher, who offered up a rare look inside the mind of a professional athlete, provided with perfection.

Dr. David Hansen, for the enthusiasm.

Dr. Robert Olivardia, for the time on several occasions to share knowledge.

Dr. Roland Carlstedt, whose calendar is as busy as the most occupied of us all, but who still came through with scholarly material to support the notion that the mind is still more powerful than any drug.

Dr. Theodore Friedmann, for the knowledge and positive outlook on sports.

Gary Hall Jr., for the optimism and interview.

Garry Nolan, PhD, for the insight into the future of medicine and sports.

Gregg Valentino, for laughs and jokes, but most of all for honesty and truth.

Ian McLeod, for the research assistance.

Jay Bates, for teaching me and helping me find my sense of voice.

Matt Nader, my training partner, for helping carry the weight in times of need even when the muscles give out. G.F.I.D.

Megan, my wife, first editor, and best friend, for the ability to keep me grounded and calm through good times and bad, for the aid, inspiration, and love.

My family: My parents Tom and Janice Tani, my brother Michael Jendrick, and my Grandmother Christena Warwick, for the constant encouragement and support through anxiety, deadlines, and headaches. Your faith in me was invaluable to this book as it is to my life.

Muscular Development magazine, Steve Blechman, John Romano, Gregg Valentino, and the rest of the crew; the insight and integrity of your publication is a light in the dark world of misunderstanding and misreporting.

Rick Collins, Esq., who continues to keep himself up to date and available for those in need, whether for legal purposes or for the enlightenment of the public.

Tom McCarthy, my editor, for the humor and patience. And many thanks as well to all of his team at Lyons who worked on this project and helped prepare it for the world to read.

Werner Reiterer, for coming to the truth and having the courage to write about it.

Index

C

D

N

O

E

F

G

X

Y

Z